Also by Matthew Kelly

Resisting Happiness

The Rhythm of Life

The Seven Levels of Intimacy

The Dream Manager

Rediscover Jesus

Off Balance

The Culture Solution

Building Better Families

Book of Courage

A Call to Joy

Mustard Seeds

The Long View

Why Am I Here?

and others . . .

blue sparrow

✥ ✥ ✥

THE RHYTHM OF LIFE

LIVING EVERY DAY WITH PASSION AND PURPOSE

MATTHEW KELLY

BLUE SPARROW BOOKS
North Palm Beach, Florida

Published by Blue Sparrow Books.

ISBN (Hard Cover): 978-1-942611-37-0
ISBN (Soft Cover): 978-1-942611-40-0
ISBN (Audiobook): 978-1-942611-41-7
ISBN (Ebook): 978-1-942611-26-4

Book design by Jan Pisciotta

For more information, visit:
www.matthewkelly.com

THIRD EDITION

10   9   8   7   6   5   4   3

Printed in the United States of America

About the Author

Matthew Kelly has dedicated his life to helping people and organizations become the-best-version-of-themselves. Born in Sydney, Australia, he began speaking and writing in his late teens while he was attending business school. Since that time, millions of people have attended his presentations in more than fifty countries.

Today Kelly is an internationally acclaimed speaker, author, and business consultant. His books have been published in more than twenty-five languages, have appeared on the *New York Times*, *Wall Street Journal*, and *USA Today* bestseller lists, and have sold more than thirty million copies.

He is the founder and owner of Floyd Consulting, a corporate consulting firm that specializes in increasing employee engagement. Floyd serves businesses of all sizes with its coaching, training, consulting, and keynote speaking services.

At a time when traditional publishing is in transition and turmoil, Kelly is also passionate about giving other authors a chance to pursue their dreams. He accomplishes this as the founder and CEO of the Eucalyptus Media Group.

His personal interests include golf, live music, literature, spirituality, investing, travel, and spending time with his family and friends.

CONTENTS

DO NOT LET YOUR LIFE BE LIKE A SHOOTING STAR,

WHICH LIGHTS UP THE SKY FOR ONLY A BRIEF MOMENT.

LET YOUR LIFE BE LIKE THE SUN,

WHICH ALWAYS BURNS BRIGHTLY IN THE HEAVENS,

BRINGING LIGHT AND WARMTH TO ALL THOSE ON EARTH.

LET *YOUR* LIGHT SHINE!

PART ONE

WHAT
DO YOU WANT
FROM LIFE?

EVERYTHING IS A CHOICE

Everything is a choice.

This is life's greatest truth and its hardest lesson. It is a great truth because it reminds us of our power. Not power over others, but the often untapped power to be ourselves and to live the life we have imagined.

It is a hard lesson, because it causes us to realize that we have chosen the life we are living right now. It is perhaps frightening for us to think that we have chosen to live our life exactly as it is today. Frightening because we may not like what we find when we look at our lives today. But it is also liberating, because we can now begin to choose what we will find when we look at our life in the tomorrows that lie unlived before us.

What will you see when you look at your life ten years from now? What will you choose?

Life is choices.

You have chosen to live this day. You have chosen to read this book. You have chosen to live in a certain city. You have chosen to believe certain ideas. You have chosen the people you call friends.

You choose the food you eat, the clothes you wear, and the thoughts you think. You choose to be calm or restless, you choose to feel appreciative or ungrateful.

Love is a choice. Anger is a choice. Fear is a choice. Courage is a choice.

You choose.

Sometimes we choose the-best-version-of-ourselves, and sometimes we choose a-second-rate-version-of-ourselves.

Everything is a choice, and our choices echo throughout our lives . . . and into history . . . and on and on into eternity.

Most people never fully accept this truth. They spend their lives arguing for their weaknesses, complaining about their lot in life, or blaming other people for their weaknesses and their lot in life.

You may argue that you are forced to live in a certain city or drive a certain car, but it is not true. And if it is, it is true only temporarily and because of a choice you have made in the past.

We choose, and in doing so, we design our lives.

Some may say that we do not choose our circumstances. You'd be surprised. We have much more power over the circumstances of our lives than most men and women would ever admit. And even if circumstances are thrust upon us, we choose how we respond to those circumstances.

Others may argue that they did not choose the country they were born in or the parents they were born to. How do we know we didn't choose these things? We are all endowed with free will. Did we not have this free will before we were born? Perhaps one day we will realize that we have chosen much more than we have even imagined.

I hope that day is today.

For the day we accept that we have chosen to choose our choices is the day we cast off the shackles of victimhood and are set free to pursue the lives we were born to live.

Learn to master the moment of decision and you will live a life uncommon.

Do You Really Know
What You Want?

Several years ago I found myself standing before a class of high school seniors in Cape May, on the Jersey shore, in the United States. I had been invited to speak to them about life beyond high school graduation, but I found myself more interested in what they might have to say than in what their teachers thought they needed to hear.

I began by asking them how long it would be until they graduated. In a burst of excitement and energy, they replied in unison, "Eleven days."

What I really wanted was to enter into the unbounded territories of the hopes and dreams these young men and women held about their future. There were eighty-four students before me that morning, representatives of the future. I was curious. I wanted to know what they yearned for. I wanted to be invited into their hearts and minds.

I invited myself by asking, "What do you want from life?"

For a few moments there was silence. Then, as they realized that my question was not rhetorical, a young man called out, "I want to be rich." I asked him why he wanted to be rich. "So I can do whatever I want," was his reply. I asked him how much was enough. "A million dollars," he said, and I remember wondering how many people think that a million dollars will change their lives.

Then I raised the question again.

A young woman said she wanted to be a doctor. I asked her why. "So that I can help people, relieve suffering, and make a lot of money," she replied. I wished her well and hoped she would be able to keep her reasons in that order as the years passed.

I asked the question again: "What else do you want from life?"

A young man toward the back called out, "I want a beautiful wife." His friends giggled, and I asked him if he had been successful in locating one yet. He said that he hadn't, and I sympathized with him, explaining that I had not, either.

Then I asked him if he knew what he was looking for in a woman. He said he did. So I explained that the best way to attract that kind of person was to become that kind of person.

I asked the question again: "What else do you want from life?"

This time a young man with a firm and confident voice said, "The president. I want to be the president of the United States of America."

I then proceeded to ask him how he intended to achieve this goal. He unfolded for me and his fellow students a plan that included undergraduate studies in international business and political science, followed by law school, local political campaign involvement, a number of summer internships on Capitol Hill, a time in the United States Army, and an array of community service.

It was clear that this dream had not entered his head during this brainstorming session that I had forced upon these high school seniors. His wasn't a pipe dream or the vain dreaming we do while we sleep; rather, it was the dreaming that we do in the daylight hours, which gives birth to purposeful living and forms our future. Perhaps one day he will become the first African American president of the United States of America!

I wished him well in his endeavors. The mood had changed. The young minds before me had been dragged deeper into this session of dream making by the realization that one of their peers had already spent a lot of time thinking about this very question. So I asked it again: "What else do you want from life?"

"Happiness—I want to be happy," a young man said.

"How will you find or achieve this happiness?" I asked. He - didn't know. I asked him if he could describe it, but he couldn't. I assured him that his desire for happiness was natural and normal and that we would talk about it later in our discussion—but that comes a little later in this book.

Again I posed the question: "What do you want from life?"

A young woman said, "A man to share my life with." I asked her, as I had asked the young man earlier, if she had succeeded in locating one. She wasn't shy, and she volleyed by saying, "How will I know when I find him? How will I know he is the one?"

"Wait for the man who makes you want to be a better person, a man who inspires you because he is always striving to better himself.

"It's not about how he looks, or how he looks at you. Not that these things are not considerations. It's not about gifts. All too often gifts are only excuses and apologies for not giving the only true gift—ourselves. When you are wondering if he really is the one for you, consider this one idea: You deserve to be cherished. Cherished! Not just loved. Cherished!"

We held eye contact for a moment or two, her eyes began to well with tears, and I knew she understood.

Now, the room was filled with a profound silence as I asked the question again: "What else do you want from life?"

After a few moments of that silence a crowd exudes when it is almost exhausted of input, a young lady said, "I want to travel."

I encouraged her to travel as early in her adult life as possible, explaining that "travel opens our minds to different cultures, philosophies, and worldviews. Travel opens our hearts to the people of foreign lands and their different traditions and creeds. Travel dissolves the stains of prejudice that infect our hearts and societies.

Money spent on travel is money well spent on an education that you will never receive from a book or in a classroom."

Now, I asked the question one more time: "What do you want from life?" But the crowd was quiet, and exhausted, and still.

I was surprised. I was disappointed. I felt an ache within me.

In less than twenty minutes, eighty-four high school seniors had become exhausted of their hopes, dreams, plans, and ambitions for the future. If that was not completely true, then whatever they had failed to share was either not worth sharing or they lacked the confidence to share it. Seven students had been able to summarize the dreams of all eighty-four. Was I still in the land of infinite dreams and opportunities? I wondered.

If I had asked them to tell me what was wrong with the education system, our discussion might have lasted for hours. If I had asked them about their favorite sporting highlight, or television sitcom, the discussion might have lasted all day. Have we become more interested in spectator sports and television sitcoms than in our own future?

It constantly amazes me that men and women wander the earth marveling at the highest mountains, the deepest oceans, the whitest sands, the most exotic islands, the most intriguing birds of the air and fish of the sea—and all the time never stop to marvel at themselves and realize their infinite potential as human beings.

∽ ∽ ∽

More people have access to education today than ever before. But I cannot help but feel that the modern educational experience is not preparing us adequately to attend the rich banquet of life. Certainly the young people of today have mastered the use of technology and are capable of solving complex scientific and mathematical problems, but who and what do these serve if they cannot think for themselves? If they have no understanding of the meaning and purpose of their own lives? If they do not know who they are as individuals?

That impromptu question—"What do you want from life?"—has become a regular part of my dialogue with friends, colleagues, loved ones, and strangers on planes. I ask it as a tool to help me to understand others, and I ask it to further understand myself.

For the most part, the answers people tend to give are vague and general, not at all thought out. Most people seem surprised by the question. I have been accused of being too deep on a number of occasions, and only very rarely does someone say, "I want these things . . . , for these reasons . . . , and this is how I intend to achieve them. . . ." Without exception, these are the people who are living life passionately and enthusiastically. They very rarely complain, they don't talk negatively about others, and you never hear them refer to happiness as some future event linked to retirement, marriage, a promotion, or some unexpected windfall of money.

So, what do they have that most people don't? They know what they want. Do you know what you want?

Most people can tell you exactly what they don't want, but very few have the same clarity about what they do want.

If you don't know what you want from life, everything will appear either as an obstacle or as a burden. But one of the great lessons of history is that the whole world gets out of the way for people who know what they want or where they are going. Be assured, if you don't know where you are going, you are lost.

Do not say, "I am too old."

Don't say, "I'm too young."

Tiger Woods was three years old when he shot 48 for nine holes on his hometown golf course in Cypress, California.

Julie Andrews was eight years old when she mastered an astounding four-octave singing range.

Mozart was eight years old when he wrote his first symphony.

Charles Dickens was twelve years old when he quit school to work in a factory, pasting labels on bottles of shoe polish, because his father had been imprisoned for debt.

Anne Frank was thirteen years old when she began her diary.

Ralph Waldo Emerson was fourteen years old when he enrolled at Harvard.

Paul McCartney was fifteen years old when John Lennon invited him to join a band.

Bill Gates was nineteen years old when he cofounded Microsoft.

Plato was twenty years old when he became a student of Socrates.

Joe DiMaggio was twenty-six years old when he hit safely in fifty-six consecutive games.

Henry David Thoreau was twenty-seven years old when he moved to the shore of Walden Pond, built a house, planted a garden, and began a two-year experiment in simplicity and self-reliance.

Ralph Lauren was twenty-nine years old when he created Polo.

William Shakespeare was thirty-one years old when he wrote *Romeo and Juliet.*

Bill Gates was thirty-one years old when he became a billionaire.

Thomas Jefferson was thirty-three years old when he wrote the Declaration of Independence.

Coco Chanel was thirty-eight years old when she introduced her perfume Chanel No. 5.

Mother Teresa was forty years old when she founded the Missionaries of Charity.

Jack Nicklaus was forty-six years old when he shot 65 in the final round, and 30 on the back nine, to win the Masters.

Henry Ford was fifty years old when he started his first manufacturing assembly line.

Ray Kroc was a fifty-two-year-old milkshake machine salesman when he bought out Mac and Dick McDonald and officially started McDonald's.

Pablo Picasso was fifty-five years old when he painted *Guernica*.

Dom Pérignon was sixty years old when he first produced champagne.

Oscar Hammerstein II was sixty-four years old when he wrote the lyrics for *The Sound of Music*.

Winston Churchill was sixty-five years old when he became - Britain's prime minister.

Nelson Mandela was seventy-one years old when he was released from a South African prison. Four years later he was elected president of South Africa.

Michelangelo was seventy-two years old when he designed the dome of St. Peter's Basilica in Rome.

Auguste Rodin was seventy-six years old when he finally married Rose Beuret, whom he met when he was twenty-three.

Benjamin Franklin was seventy-nine years old when he invented bifocal eyeglasses.

Frank Lloyd Wright was ninety-one years old when he completed his work on the Guggenheim Museum.

Dimitrion Yordanidis was ninety-eight years old when he ran a marathon in seven hours and thirty-three minutes, in Athens, Greece.

Ichijirou Araya was one hundred years old when he climbed Mount Fuji.

Whether you are sixteen or sixty, the rest of your life is ahead of you. You cannot change one moment of your past, but you can change your whole future. Now is your time.

ᔪ ᔪ ᔪ

What do you want from life? What are your dreams?

Think about it. Stop reading. Ponder it. Write your answers down. Make a list.

Put this book aside now—and before you read on, spend five minutes or five hours answering the question for yourself. What do you want from life?

Maybe you have already thought long and hard about this question but have never written it down. On the other hand, if you have never taken time to seriously address the question, don't pretend that you have. Take the time. Think it over. Write it down.

There are no right or wrong answers. Write quickly. Don't think too much. Don't analyze or edit yourself as you make your list. Write everything down, even the ones you feel are foolish. Your answers don't have to be definitive. They will change over time. That's okay. In fact, some of them will probably change by the time you finish this book. But it is still important to write them down now. It will help you as you read through the rest of this book and as you venture through the rest of your life. So write your list, and when you are done, date it.

Start a new notebook. I have what I like to call my dream-book. It's a regular journal with blank pages, and I fill those pages with my hopes and dreams and words and ideas that inspire me.

Each day in my quiet time, I flick through the pages of my dream-book and I see things I had written three, four, five years ago, things that seemed impossible at the time. Today they seem insignificant, because I have grown, achieved those dreams, and moved on. I now also realize that other things I thought I wanted are not as important to me as I imagined they were.

Even if you write your list now, put it away and don't look at it for a year. When you do take that list out one year from now, you will be amazed by the self-revelation it will afford you.

Stop reading. Put the book down. What you are about to write on that paper is infinitely more important than anything else I have to say in this book.

THE HAPPINESS PARADOX

Whatever you wrote on your list, chances are those are the things, places, people, and experiences that you believe will make you happy. You may object, saying that you have written some of the things on your list because you know that by doing them, you will make someone else happy. But by making them happy, you will also share in that happiness. Even if you wrote on your list that you wanted world peace and to feed the starving people of Africa and wrote those things for completely altruistic reasons . . . their attainment will also bring you great happiness.

The things you put on your list represent happiness to you.

Everybody wants to be happy. You want to be happy, and I want to be happy. The human person has a natural thirst for happiness, and we do the things we do because we believe they will make us happy.

From time to time, people do stupid things. We may look at them and scratch our heads. We may wonder, "Why would anybody ever do something so stupid?" or, "Don't they know that is going to make them miserable?" But be assured, the reason people do stupid things is because they mistakenly believe those stupid things will make them happy.

People do not wake up in the morning and ask themselves, "How can I make myself miserable today?"

The human heart is on a quest for happiness. We give this happiness different names and masks, and we live our lives in search of it.

This is the great modern paradox: We know the things that make us happy; we just don't do them.

⁓ ⁓ ⁓

There are four aspects to the human person: physical, emotional, intellectual, and spiritual.

Physically, when you exercise regularly, sleep regularly, eat the right sorts of foods, and balance your diet, how do you feel? You feel fantastic. You feel more fully alive. You're healthier, happier, and you have a richer, more abundant experience of life.

Emotionally, when you give focus and priority to your relationships, what happens? You switch the focus off yourself and onto others. As you do, your *ability to love* increases . . . and as your *ability to love* increases, your *ability to be loved* increases. You become more aware of yourself, develop a more balanced view of life, and experience a deeper sense of fulfillment. You're healthier. - You're happier.

Intellectually, when you take ten or fifteen minutes a day to read a good book, what happens? Your vision of yourself expands; your vision of the world expands. You become more focused, more alert, and more vibrant. Clarity replaces confusion. You feel more fully alive, and you are happier.

Finally, spiritually, when you take a few moments each day to step into the classroom of silence and reconnect with yourself and with your God, what happens? The gentle voice within grows stronger, and you develop a deeper sense of peace, purpose, and direction. You're healthier, you're happier, and you have a richer experience of life.

Physically, emotionally, intellectually, and spiritually, we know the things that infuse our lives with passion and enthusiasm. We know the things that make us happy. *We just don't do them.*

It doesn't make sense, does it?

On the one hand, we all want to be happy. On the other hand, we all know the things that make us happy. But we don't do those things. Why? Simple. We are too busy. Too busy doing what? Too busy trying to be happy.

This is the paradox of happiness that has bewitched our age.

Too Busy Doing What?

⊂══╪══⊃

Physically—we don't exercise regularly because we're too busy. We don't eat the right types of food, because they take too long to prepare, it's too easy to go through the drive-through, and we're too busy.

We don't sleep regularly, because there are still only twenty-four hours in a day. We feel as though our lives have a momentum of their own, that they would go on with or without us. Our list of the things we have to do just gets longer and longer. We never feel that we get caught up; we just get more and more behind every day. Seriously, when was the last time you sat down, took a deep breath, and said to yourself, "I'm caught up now!" So we rush around late at night doing fifty-five little things before we go to bed and robbing ourselves of the precious sleep that rebuilds and rejuvenates us. Why? We are too busy.

Emotionally—most of us know that the happiest people on the planet are those who are focused in their personal relationships. Relationships thrive under one condition: carefree timelessness. Do we gift our relationships with carefree timelessness? Of course we don't. We shove them into ten minutes here and fifteen minutes there. We give them the worst time, when we are most tired and least emotionally available. Why? We are too busy.

Intellectually—we don't even take those ten or fifteen minutes each day to read good books that challenge us to change, to grow, and to become the-best-version-of-ourselves. Why? We don't have time. We are too busy.

Spiritually—most people very rarely step into the classroom of silence to reconnect with themselves and their God. Why? We are afraid of what we might discover about ourselves and about our lives. We are afraid we might be challenged to change. And we are too busy.

∽ ∽ ∽

It begs the question, doesn't it? What are we all too busy doing?

For the most part, we are too busy doing just about everything, that means just about nothing, to just about nobody, just about anywhere . . . and will mean even less to anyone a hundred years from now!

QUIET DESPERATION

A hundred and fifty years ago, Henry David Thoreau left Concord, Massachusetts, because he believed it had become too noisy, too distracting, and too busy. He went off to Walden Pond to reconnect with himself and with nature. It took him only seven pages in his writings and reflections to conclude, "Most men lead lives of quiet desperation."

During my short life, I have had the privilege of traveling in more than fifty countries, and I have seen nothing to make me believe that Thoreau would change his mind today. Most people are not thriving; most people are just surviving, just getting by, just hanging on. It is, in fact, a rare and pleasant surprise to find someone who is truly thriving.

A friend recently drew my attention to a *Time* magazine article devoted to the question "Why is everything getting better?" The - article's author used economics as his sole measure and reason for life getting better. His only examination of our lives was economic. We are richer. We have more disposable income. We have more choices at the grocery store. We have more in our retirement accounts. We have more cars, and we can turn them in to the leasing agent every three years and get new ones.

Is everything getting better? It's a good question, but one that needs to be assessed a little more seriously than solely from the perspective of the economic index of happiness.

Allow me to offer just a few brief thoughts for your consideration.

We prescribe more medication for depression in America today than for any other illness.

The suicide rate among teens and young adults has increased by 5,000 percent in the last fifty years. If the massive increases in suicide among the younger generations of any civilization are not a sign that all is not well, nothing is.

Finally, it is becoming more and more apparent that suicide is directly proportional to wealth. What does that mean? Studies reveal that the more money you have, the more likely you are to take your own life. Peter Kreeft captured the alarming reality in a recent article of his own: "The richer you are, the richer your family is, and the richer your country is, the more likely it is that you will find life so good that you will choose to blow your brains out." Economics is clearly not a good measure of happiness.

Yes, we have more material possessions than ever before, but to directly conclude that "life is getting better" simply because of economic prosperity requires a naïveté and narrow-mindedness of monumental proportions.

If you scratch just below the surface of the economic success of our age, there are some very disturbing signs. In an age of unprecedented prosperity, there are millions who feel that something is missing in their lives.

What's the problem? What is missing? What is it that we need that we don't have? How do we get it?

A number of trends are emerging in our modern culture that are telltale signs that all is not well in the hearts and minds of the people. Depression and suicide rates nearing epidemic levels are certainly among them. But another emerging trend worthy of our consideration is our modern inability to sustain relationships.

More than one in every two marriages ends in divorce or separation. We are all familiar with the statistic, but have we stopped to seriously consider why? Have you noticed that fewer and fewer people are getting married? It is a fact that is masked by the enormous number of people getting remarried. Are you noticing more and more young people despairing about their partner's inability, hesitancy, or unwillingness to commit to marriage?

On top of all this, consider that the average man or woman is now likely to change jobs five times more frequently than his or her working grandparents. Is it just that the corporate world has changed? Or does it also say something about us?

Finally, on the simplest, most practical, everyday level, consider how many people make resolutions to diet, exercise, or just spend more time with their families and fail completely. Our inability to live the resolutions we make is another indicator. Indicator of what?

There is a crisis of commitment in our society. People seem unwilling to make commitments or, once made, unable to fulfill them. But where is the connection between the "crisis of commitment" and the suicide, depression, and quiet desperation of our age?

As great as this crisis of commitment may seem, it is secondary to a more fundamental problem. Most people sincerely want to fulfill their commitments. People don't get married to get divorced. People don't fail to keep resolutions because they want to fail. The crisis of commitment is the result of a far more serious crisis of purpose.

A great purposelessness has descended upon modern civilizations. People at large have lost any sense of the meaning and purpose of life; and without an understanding of our own purpose, there can be no true commitment. Whether that commitment is to marriage, family, study, work, God, relationships, or the simple resolutions of our lives, it will be almost impossible to fulfill without a clear and practical understanding of our purpose. Commitment and purpose go hand in hand.

Commitment is the logical and natural response that follows from an understanding of our purpose.

Everything in our lives is either pursued or rejected according to whether or not it will help us, and others, fulfill what we perceive as our purpose.

Someone who makes money his goal in life accepts or rejects everything according to whether or not it will help him achieve that goal.

Someone who makes pleasure the goal of her life accepts or rejects everything according to whether or not it will help her achieve her goal.

In the absence of a genuine understanding of the meaning and purpose of our lives, we substitute it with shallow and superficial meaning. The human person cannot live without meaning and purpose.

☙ ☙ ☙

Why is depression so dramatically on the rise? I cannot imagine anything more depressing than not having any sense of the meaning and purpose of your own life.

Why do so many young people immerse themselves in video games, alcohol, promiscuous sex, deafeningly loud music, and drugs? Is it possible that they use these things to distract themselves from the frightening reality of facing a life without meaning and purpose? Or is it that they use these things in a vain and futile attempt to fill the void of meaninglessness within them?

Why do so many people get so caught up in their work that they don't have time for anything else, even the people they love? Is it perhaps that achievement in their work is the only thing that gives them even the vaguest sense of purpose in their lives? Or that because they consciously, or subconsciously, believe that their work is their purpose, they completely commit to that purpose and refuse to let anything come between them and the fulfillment of what they have erroneously perceived as their purpose?

I am amazed how many women seek my advice in regard to a

husband who has no time for or interest in anything but his work. The problem is that he doesn't see his wife and children in relation to his purpose. He perceives his purpose as success and achievement in his work. The only place his wife and children have in this scheme is that the financial fruits of his work allow him to provide for his family.

Why are people having fewer and fewer children? Too often in our modern culture, children are perceived as "nice to have" if - you've got the time and the money and are prepared to suspend, or maybe even sacrifice, your career. Young couples today perceive the blessing of children not in relation to their true purpose, but rather in relation to their "quasi purpose" of financial independence.

For the most part, people today perceive their purpose in relation to success in the workplace and financial independence. The result is what we witness before us in our world today and what we too often allow ourselves to be a part of—a panicked frenzy of people rushing around, working too much, working too hard, working too often, in order to splash money around the global economy, by paying the mortgage on the house that they really - can't afford; wearing the clothes that are inordinately overpriced because they have some designer label on them; driving the car that in thirty-six months they will surrender to the leasing agent for another new one; giving less and less time to the people they love and care about; neglecting their real and legitimate needs; trying to ignore the quiet dissatisfaction that they sense deep within themselves; and distracting themselves with every manner of noise, pleasure, and entertainment from the fact that a great meaninglessness has descended upon their lives.

There must be more to life.

THE FIVE QUESTIONS

For thousands of years, men and women of every age, race, and culture have sought to understand the meaning of life. The people of our own time are no different.

Throughout history, scientists and philosophers, theologians and artists, politicians and social activists, monks and sages, and men and women from all walks of life have discussed and debated many questions in the quest to discover the meaning of life. And while their discussions have been many and varied, to my mind all of humanity's searching for knowledge and answers can be arranged under five headings, each of them a question.

These are the five questions that humanity has been asking consciously and subconsciously ever since human life first existed.

Although we may be unable to articulate them, you and I are constantly asking these questions. Whether we are aware of it or not, our whole existence is a searching to answer these five questions. We seek the answers to these questions directly and indirectly every day of our lives. And how we answer these questions determines the shape, form, and direction that our lives take on.

These are the five questions that humanity longs to answer:

1. Who am I?
2. Where did I come from?
3. What am I here for?
4. How do I do it?
5. Where am I going?

All religious texts are centered upon and seek to illumine the five questions—including the sacred writings of Israel, the Christian scriptures, and the Bhagavad Gita. The five questions also form the major themes in the writings of Confucius and Lao-tzu, Homer and Euripides, Sophocles and Shakespeare, Plato and Aristotle, Dostoyevsky and Aldous Huxley, Ernest Hemingway, C. S. Lewis, and Henry David Thoreau. They are the questions that testify to humanity's age-old search for the meaning and purpose of life. They are the questions that hungry hearts place at the center of their lives.

The second question, "Where did I come from?" introduces us to the ideas of creation and life. Within the fifth question, "Where am I going?," we become intimate with the realities of time, death, and eternity. Most religious traditions answer the second and the last question with "God," but the ideas that these questions unveil are complex. And though now is not the time, and this particular book is not the place, the second and the fifth questions deserve serious study and thought in their own right.

Questions three and four, "What am I here for?" and "How do I do it?," give birth to the mysteries of love, joy, misery, happiness, suffering, fulfillment, discontent, and, especially, the never ceasing struggle we witness and experience between good and evil. We live our everyday lives in the realms of questions three and four. And owing to their practical implications, we usually become fascinated and preoccupied with these questions. But in order to answer these questions, "What am I here for?" and "How do I do it?," it is imperative that we give serious thought and reflection to question one: "Who am I?"

Philosophically, this may all be very sound. Practically, however, the process of answering these five questions and conforming our lives to the answers we find is very difficult.

Each of us seeks to answer these questions in our own way. Experience is an excellent, though sometimes brutal, teacher. Yet at the same time, it is only the ignorance of youth that believes experience is the only teacher. As we grow wiser, we realize that life is too short to learn all of its lessons from personal experience, and we discover that other people, places, and times are all too willing to pass on the hard-earned wisdom of their experiences.

But where should we begin?

It has been my experience that nothing changes a person's life more than the discovery of one solitary truth: There is meaning and purpose to life. More specifically: There is a meaning and purpose to your life.

THE MEANING OF LIFE

◦━✦━◦

Our modern culture proclaims with all its force: What you *do* and what you *have* are the most important things. This is a lie. It is a deception that has led whole generations down the well-trodden path toward lives of quiet desperation. But it is a lie that is reinforced with such regularity that we have grown to believe it, at least subconsciously, and have shaped our lives around it.

Two of the most common tools of social judgment are the assessment of what make and model of car you drive and the question "What do you *do*?"

The whole focus of our culture is on *doing* and *having*. I get on the plane, and nine out of ten times, the person next to me will ask me, "What do you *do*?" We ask young children, "What are you going to *do* when you grow up?" and seniors in high school, "What are you going to *do* in college?" and college graduates, "What are you going to *do* now that you have finished your studies?" We live in a task-oriented culture. But this task-oriented approach completely ignores our need to connect the activities of our daily lives with our essential purpose.

Doing and having are natural, normal, and necessary aspects of our daily lives; the challenge is to do and have in accord with our essential purpose.

In this task-oriented culture, one of the real dangers is to slip into an episodic mode of living. What I mean is, the happenings of our day-to-day lives can become episodic, one after another, like the episodes of a soap opera. In a soap opera, there is always something happening, but nothing ever really happens. In every episode there is drama—activity takes place, words are muttered, but nothing really happens. People abusing one another, people using one another, people talking about one another, people plotting and scheming, but nothing meaningful ever happens. Their lives are filled with superficialities, and they are constantly restless and miserable. There is no theme, no thread—just another entertaining episode.

When the days and weeks of our lives become like this, we grow depressed, disillusioned, and miserably unhappy. The reason is that without a clear sense of the purpose and meaning of our lives, the emptiness is overwhelming. We try to fill the void with pleasure and possessions, but the emptiness is unaffected by such trivialities. There are moments of pleasure, but they are brief in a long succession of twenty-four-hour days.

∽ ∽ ∽

Pablo Picasso was walking down the street in Paris one day when a woman recognized and approached him. After introducing herself and praising his work, she asked him if he would consider drawing her portrait and offered to pay him for the piece.

Picasso agreed and sat the woman down there and then on the side of the street, brought out a sketchbook and pencil, and began to draw the woman. A small crowd of spectators gathered very quickly, but in only a handful of minutes Picasso had finished the drawing. As he handed it to the woman, he said, "That will be five thousand francs." Surprised at the price, the woman objected, saying, "But Mr. Picasso, it took you only a few minutes." Picasso smiled and replied, "No, my dear woman, you are mistaken, it took me a whole lifetime."

∽ ∽ ∽

The individual experiences of our lives cannot be separated from the whole. Life is not a series of separate episodes. All of life's experiences thus far have played a part in the person you are right now. The common reaction to this statement is to recall some negative or abusive event in our past and use it as an excuse for the person we are today. Such adoption of victimhood is one of the most destructive spirits at work in the human psyche in these modern times.

Victimhood denies the great truth that life is choices.

The point I am really trying to make here is that we are not a composite of everything that has ever happened to us, but rather what happens in our lives is almost always a result of those things we habitually think and those things we habitually do. Life is the fruit of discipline, or lack of it. We are our habits. For example, you cannot separate Tiger Woods's phenomenal performance and record-crushing victory at the 1997 Masters from the twenty years of his life prior to that event. His practice sessions fifteen years earlier at the age of six were as much a part of that Masters victory as his final approach shot to the eighteenth green.

Every disciplined effort has its own multiple reward.

$\wp \quad \wp \quad \wp$

Artistically and professionally, Pablo Picasso had a profound understanding of the value of compounding effort and experience. His professional life had theme and thread, direction and purpose—and was held together as one whole. His personal life lacked that wisdom. From lover to lover he passed, from wife to wife, from friend to friend—always moving on, eventually deserting even those who loved him. In the end, he abandoned all those who were close to him. Picasso's personal life was plagued by this episodic quality we have just discussed. He was unable or unwilling to apply the truth he had discovered professionally to the other areas of his life.

Life is the gathering of truth. Any truth we discover must not be allowed to remain isolated in one area of our lives, and certainly must not be allowed to remain merely in our minds. Rather, any truth life reveals to us must filter into every aspect of our lives, like blood to the cells of the body. Life is one. Truth should be lived.

What we *do* in the span of our lives may bring us financial rewards, status, fame, power, and unimaginable possessions, but lasting happiness and fulfillment are not the by-products of *doing* and *having*.

The *truth* is a startling contrast to the present culture's credo.

Who you *become* is infinitely more important than what you *do* or what you *have*.

The meaning and purpose of life is for you to become the-best-version-of-yourself.

I am often amused at how scared some people are to wonder, or ask, what God might want for them or from them. They imagine that God might want them to become a missionary in some obscure, poverty-stricken country or that God might want them to become a monk . . . or a nun . . . or that God always wants them to do the one thing they don't want to do.

What is God's dream for you? Do you ever wonder? Let me tell you.

God wants you to become the-best-version-of-yourself.

God doesn't want to control you, or stifle you, or manipulate you, or force you to do anything you don't want to do. Quite the opposite, in fact. God will let you do whatever you want to do, whenever you want to do it, with whomever you want to do it, and as often as you want to do it. When was the last time God stopped you from doing anything?

But if we can find the courage within our sometimes timid hearts to turn to God and ask, "God, what is your dream for me and my life?" God will whisper in reply, "Be all you can be. Become the-best-version-of-yourself."

Our essential purpose is to become the-best-version-of-ourselves.

Once we discover it and place this purpose at the center of our lives, everything begins to makes sense. Until we discover our essential purpose, nothing makes sense, and we wander around aimlessly, slowly being numbed into lives of quiet desperation.

It is the quest to improve ourselves, to be all we are capable of being, to test our limits, and to grow steadily toward the-best-version-of-ourselves that brings meaning to our lives.

If we return for a moment to our earlier discussion of happiness, we also discover that our yearning for happiness is intimately linked to our essential purpose. In each of the four areas—physical, emotional, intellectual, and spiritual—we discussed certain activities that bring us happiness. Why do we get a deep sense of fulfillment and happiness from those activities? Because they help us fulfill our essential purpose. The activities that help us become the-best-version-of-ourselves also fill our lives with sustainable happiness.

There is purpose and meaning to life. You were born to become the-best-version-of yourself. In the words of Robert Louis Stevenson, "To be what we are, and to become what we are capable of becoming, is the only end of life." In part 3 of this book, we will discuss how you place this truth at the center of your life by using it as a compass in your decision making.

Embrace this one solitary truth—you were born to become the-best-version-of-yourself—and it will change your life more than anything you have ever learned.

Seven Dreams

For many years I have been practicing the exercise we did together a little earlier—the "What do you want from life?" exercise. The first several times I made my own list, all I wanted was more of the things of the world. Then I discovered my essential purpose, and everything changed.

I started asking myself, "Which of the things on my list are going to help me become the-best-version-of-myself?" The good news was that I did have some things on my list that were going to help me become the-best-version-of-myself. I also had a lot of things that were indifferent to my essential purpose. The bad news was that I had some things on my list that were directly or indirectly going to cause me, or encourage me, to become a-lesser-version-of-myself. I began assessing the things on my list in relation to my essential purpose.

Like so many people, I have often believed that if I could change my surroundings—things, places, and people—then I would be happier. Discovering my essential purpose has caused me to realize that happiness is an inside-out job. All too often, what is going on around us is only a reflection of what is going on within us.

In my own life, I have become intimately aware of this truth in a number of ways. One example is my home. I am a fairly tidy person, but I have noticed that when I am confused on the inside, I stop tidying up around the house. I leave things lying around, and before long the place is a mess. I have also noticed that once the confusion within is solved, the question answered, or the issue resolved, almost immediately I start tidying up my house, office, and car.

When I am focused on becoming the-best-version-of-myself, I am deeply happy. It is the pursuit of our essential purpose alone that satisfies.

When you know you are striving to become the-best-version-of-yourself, that alone is enough to sustain you in happiness. When you don't have that, all the pleasure and possessions you can summon from the world cannot sustain happiness in the depths of your heart.

We spend our lives in the service of our desires. Sometimes those desires are good and their pursuit is to our benefit. At other times our desires are selfish and self-destructive. If there is purpose and meaning to our lives, then the highest levels of living must be linked to discovering that meaning and fulfilling that purpose. It stands to reason, then, that there should be a relationship between the purpose and meaning of life and our dreams.

Earlier, I asked you to stop and consider what you wanted from life and to write those things down. As you progress through this book, I would like you to remain open to revising and changing, adding and eliminating, some of what you had previously written.

My own dream list is constantly being revised. My dream-book is filled with pages and pages of dreams . . . everything from countries I'd like to visit, books I'd like to write, and the qualities I'd like my soul-mate to have, to living by the beach, driving a sweet little convertible, cycling down Haleakala at sunrise, and virtues I'd like to develop in my own character. And while many of these are exciting to pursue, I have done the exercise enough times to know that the most important dreams in my dream-book are the ones that help me become the-best-version-of-myself.

So, even though I am constantly dreaming new dreams, I have learned to dream with my essential purpose at the center of my life. With that in mind, I have developed seven core dreams that help me stay focused on my essential purpose.

These are my dreams. I believe that the pursuit of these dreams will lead us to peace, happiness, success, satisfaction, service, wholeness, and holiness.

They are my dreams, but they are also my dreams for you.

THE FIRST DREAM

I have a dream for you . . .
that you have complete control over your mental and physical faculties and that you are slave neither to food, nor drink, nor any other substance. I dream that you will be free, that you will have freedom in the truest sense of the word—the strength of character to do what is right in each situation.

THE SECOND DREAM

I have a dream for you . . .
that you are able to discern the people, activities, and possessions that are most important to you. And that you are able to give each of them their time and place according to their appropriate priority.

THE THIRD DREAM

I have a dream for you . . .
that you have the courage, determination, firmness, and persistence to perform the tasks that you choose, decide, and resolve to perform. That you perform them with a commitment to excellence and attention to detail.

THE FOURTH DREAM

I have a dream for you . . .
that you discover a unique talent that leads you to dedicate the professional aspect of your life to some work you can be passionate about. I dream that you may enjoy the rare privilege

of spending your days in meaningful work. That you serve your neighbor, your family, and your community in this occupation and that by it, you are able to provide for your temporal needs.

THE FIFTH DREAM

I have a dream for you . . .
that you grow in wealth in every sense of the word,
that you are never in need, and that whatever your wealth is,
you share it with all you can.

THE SIXTH DREAM

I have a dream for you . . .
that you find true love. Someone you can cherish. Someone who makes you want to be a better person. A soul-mate who can challenge you and love you. A companion who can walk with you, know you, share your joy, perceive your pain and heartache, and comfort you in your disappointments.

THE SEVENTH DREAM

I have a dream for you . . .
that you discover a deep and abiding interior peace.
The peace that comes from knowing that who you are,
where you are, and what you do is essentially good and
makes sense; that you are contributing to the happiness of
others; and that you are progressing toward becoming
the-best-version-of-yourself.

A NEW PERSPECTIVE

$\sim$

At different times in our lives, we all need a new perspective.

In the late 1960s, there was a young man who had a dream of becoming a famous musician. He knew exactly what he wanted, so he left high school and began to play his music wherever people would listen. But as a high school dropout and with little experience, he found it difficult to get work as a musician.

Before too long he found himself playing in small, dirty clubs and bars. Sharing his gift with a handful of drunks night after night became a discouraging habit. This was not his dream. He had dreamed of playing to sellout shows across America and around the world. He had dreamed of seeing his name in lights, of walking down the street and being stopped for autographs, of having his albums in every music store. He even dreamed one day he would play to a packed baseball stadium—an absurd thought in the late 1960s.

He had stumbled upon difficult times. Financially he was broke, professionally he was failing, and his only joy in life was the support of his girlfriend. They had so little money that they would sleep in Laundromats to save the expense of a hotel. But one day she got sick of being constantly on the road. This gypsy lifestyle was not her dream, either. She had dreamed of being married to a famous musician but was unaware of the hard work it takes to get to the top. It was not the life she had imagined, so she left him.

With his only joy in life gone, he decided to commit suicide. That night the young musician made a halfhearted attempt to end his life by drinking a bottle of furniture polish and a bottle of vodka. The next day, very sick, he checked himself into a mental institution.

Less than three weeks later, he checked himself out. He was a new man. He was refreshed, enthusiastic, and excited about life. He was cured. They had not given him any medication, nor was it anything the doctors or nurses had said to him. The other patients had cured him.

They reminded him of how fortunate and gifted he was, and they had shown him how much more life could be. He was given a new perspective on life.

That day, that same young man left the mental institution absolutely resolved to pursue his dream of becoming a famed musician. He was determined to travel and work and do whatever was necessary to achieve his dream.

Three years later, he wrote a song called "Piano Man," and today almost every person on the planet has heard of Billy Joel. And yes, on June 22 and 23 in 1990, Billy Joel played to sellout crowds of ninety thousand people at Yankee Stadium.

We all need a startling new perspective at least once in our lives. Billy Joel's experience in the mental institution gave him that new perspective. It is my hope that this book will give you that new perspective, too.

∽ ∽ ∽

I have always had a real passion for music, and I have always enjoyed Billy Joel's music. On a number of occasions I have had the opportunity to see him perform live and have never found that experience to be anything less than inspiring. It is rare to find musical genius mixed with such poetic thoughtfulness.

My favorite lyric of his is from a song entitled "Scenes from an Italian Restaurant." The song tells the story of Brenda and Eddie, two high school students who were the envy of all their peers. They were that popular couple, the king and queen of the prom, the couple who looked and seemed perfect together. The verse describes Brenda and Eddie driving around with the car top down and the radio on, hanging out at the diner, at the top of their world. Then Billy Joel drops in my favorite line, which says so much about adolescence. With it he also defines the major barrier that prevents most of us from achieving greater things in, and with, our lives. He writes, "We never knew we could want more than that out of life . . ."

There is more.

In all of our lives there is a great danger in believing that who we are, where we are, and what we have is all that there is.

There is more. Do you know what it is like to walk through the streets of Paris in the pouring rain without a worry in the world, enjoying every last drop of rain that falls on your face? Do you know what it is like to see *The Nutcracker* performed at the Sydney Opera House and sit so close that you can see the beads of sweat on the dancers' foreheads?

Do you know what it is like to dance with no music on a beach on the island of Crete with someone you love more than you ever imagined you could love? Do you know what it is like to feel so guided that it is as though God has His very hand on your shoulder and is whispering in your ear? Do you know what it is like to stand in the Sistine Chapel and look up in awe at Michelangelo's greatest work, listening to those around you speak in fifteen different languages, breathing more deeply than you ever have, and smelling the musty air of one of the most renowned places of worship and artistic treasures in the world? Do you know . . . there is more?

You cannot live without dreams. Dreams foster hope, and hope is one of the forces by which men and women live.

To dream is the easiest thing in the world. There are no limitations to dreaming. But as we grow we experience pain, failure, criticism, and disappointment, and we gradually limit our dreams.

We seek to live in the comfort zone. There is no such thing. It is much more difficult to try to live in a comfort zone than it is to follow our dreams, because the comfort zone is only an illusion, but our dreams are real. Will you spend the rest of your life chasing an illusion or following your dreams?

I will never forget a question I once heard Robert Schuller pose in an interview with Larry King. They were discussing the effects of the fear of failure on our decision-making process, and Schuller offered this question as a guide: "What would you attempt if you knew you could not fail?"

Do not be afraid to dream. Perhaps your fear is of failure. There is no shame in trying to attempt mighty things and failing. The shame is in failing to attempt those things. Michelangelo, the great Renaissance artist and poet, knew the value, power, and need for dreams when he wrote, "The greater danger for most of us is not that our aim is too high and we miss it, but that it is too low and we reach it."

Our dreams are a self-revelation.

Tell me what your dreams are and I will tell you what type of person you are. Define your dreams clearly and precisely and you will know for yourself what type of person you are. If you do not like what you discover, remember, you created your dreams, and in so doing, you formed the person you are today. If you don't like who you are and the life you are living, it may seem like bad news to hear that you have created the person you are today and the life you are living. The good news is, you can re-create your dreams and become a new creation.

Don't let the hustle and bustle of life drag you down. Don't allow the day-to-day drudgery of life distract you from your essential purpose—becoming the-best-version-of-yourself! Take time to dream. Imagine what you are capable of, and live that life.

Let us live every day in the counsel of Thoreau: "Go confidently in the direction of your dreams! Live the life you've imagined."

LIVE PASSIONATELY

❦

When I was twelve years old, I used to sing in the school choir, and often we would sing at funerals. Whether or not I knew the person who had died, funerals have always had a deep impact on my life. Every time I go to a funeral, or hear that someone I know has died, I always become more determined not to waste my life, not to take life for granted.

Every now and then I like to take a walk in a cemetery. Each tombstone tells a story. Some of the people were laid to rest last year, others a hundred years ago. Some of them lived for ninety-five years, others for twenty-five years. But I can hear all of them calling out to me in unison, sharing with me a message: "Life is short. Do not waste your life. Live life passionately."

Somewhere deep within you there is a desire to dedicate yourself to becoming the-best-version-of-yourself. I hope you feel that desire stirring within you. Foster that desire. Nurture that desire. Adopt habits that help you rekindle that desire. Otherwise your life is in danger of becoming an utter waste.

You will become like a candle in the wind, a victim of circumstance, and every time the wind stops blowing you will wish you had placed your essential purpose at the center of your life. But the winds of life will blow once more, changing direction and distracting you again from what is really important. You will get caught up in the episodic cycle of the modern world, and your life will bear no signs of continuity or consistency. You will achieve things, no doubt, and you will have things, but you will be restless and anxious. The sense that there must be more will haunt you continually, the feeling that something is missing will linger on the edge of everything you do. And many years from now, in the dim light of your distant memory, you will remember the dreams you ignored and abandoned. You will feel a pain that cannot be eased or consoled. Regret over things done can be eased over time. Regret over things left unsaid and undone is inconsolable.

Now is your time. You have one life, and it is short. Use it powerfully. Celebrate it as a precious gift. Don't allow fear to paralyze you. As Goethe wrote, "Be bold and mighty forces will come to your aid."

ᴄ⁄ᴏ ᴄ⁄ᴏ ᴄ⁄ᴏ

Itzhak Perlman is one of the finest violinists alive today. Several years ago, Perlman agreed to attend a charity reception after one of his concerts in Vienna. Tickets for the champagne reception were sold for the equivalent of five hundred American dollars per guest.

At the reception, while the guests mingled, Itzhak Perlman stood in a roped-off area flanked by security guards. One by one the guests were led into the roped-off area and introduced to Perlman. As one man entered the roped-off area, he stretched out his hand, shook hands with the violinist, and said, "Mr. Perlman, you were phenomenal tonight. Absolutely amazing." Perlman smiled and thanked the man graciously for the compliment. The man continued, "All my life I have had a great love of the violin, and I have heard every great living violinist, but I have never heard anyone play the violin as brilliantly as you did tonight." Perlman smiled again but said nothing, and the man continued, "You know, Mr. Perlman, I would give my whole life to be able to play the violin like you did tonight."

Perlman smiled once more and said, "I have."

That is the difference. While some of us are sitting around letting the sand in the hourglass of life empty, thinking, I would give my whole life to be able to do that, or, I hope that happens to me one day, people like Itzhak Perlman are getting the job done. They are giving their whole lives to the magnificent and meaningful pursuit of their dreams.

I have noticed that all men and women have dreams. I have noticed that some people achieve their dreams, and for others they seem always out of reach. Why is this? Does God have favorites? I don't think so. The reason is that some people dream and wait for their dreams to come true. Theirs is a vain type of dreaming. They look at others, whom they consider fortunate or lucky, and they think, I hope that happens to me one day! Other people listen to the movements of their hearts and dream their dreams by listening to the gentle voice within. They commit themselves to excellence, and armed with their dreams as a blueprint for their lives, they go out onto the stage of life chasing their rainbow, living life passionately. Aided by a mysterious and miraculous power that I can describe only as the grace of God, they make their dreams come true.

Life is too short to be lived halfheartedly and far too short to lose yourself in the day-to-day drudgery and the hustle and bustle. Dedicate yourself to the things that deserve your dedication.

Life is short, and you are dead an awfully long time. Live life passionately.

PART TWO

◊◊◊

FINDING
YOUR GENIUS

The Gentle Voice Within

There is a gentle voice within each of us.

When we are children, we hear this voice with great clarity and we live by what we hear. So we are immensely happy.

As we grow older, we become aware of all the other voices that surround us—the voices of parents, siblings, friends, critics, television, strangers, and experts.

All these other voices have the strength and confidence of experience, so we become fascinated with them. And as we enter into this fascination with all these other voices, they begin to distract us from the gentle voice within.

As we begin to listen to all these other voices, we begin to doubt, question, and ignore the gentle voice within. And gradually, the one true voice within each of us grows fainter and fainter.

Finally, when the gentle voice within us has become so faint that we can hardly hear it anymore in the midst of our daily activity, we are told that we have grown up, that we are adults, and that we are now ready for life.

Nothing could be further from the truth.

The gentle voice within is your truest guide. It has absolutely no self-interest. That is what sets it apart from every other voice in your life. The gentle voice within you is interested in only one thing, helping you become the-best-version-of-yourself.

Whether you call it your "conscience" or give it some other name, we all have this gentle voice within us. It is our true self, directing us toward our essential purpose. It is the-best-version-of-ourselves talking to us.

Take a moment to think about it. When was the last time you obeyed that gentle voice within you and it made you miserable? When was the last time the gentle voice within led you to become a-lesser-version-of-yourself? It may lead you to the pain of discipline and self-sacrifice, but always in the quest to help you embrace more fully the-best-version-of-yourself.

It is only when we ignore the gentle voice within that we find ourselves in places of misery and quiet desperation.

What we must do above all else is to learn once again to listen to the gentle voice within us. Only then will we have the peace that we all seek, but that only a rare few ever find.

Understanding Our Legitimate Needs

My first college experience was as a marketing major in Australia. I will never forget my first lecture. It remains indelibly engraved upon my memory.

The professor walked into the auditorium, placed his notes on the podium, and began, "Marketing is about creating needs in consumers. It's about creating a desire in people that in turn makes them feel that they need your product or service. It's about making people feel they need things even if they don't." He put it in such crude terms and with a straight face. But worse than that, the people around me didn't even seem to bat an eyelid. I was stunned. I was amazed. I looked around the lecture hall, which held six hundred people and was full beyond capacity. Everyone was writing down what the professor had just said—drinking from the well of wisdom before them.

My father had given me my first education in business many years earlier. Dad had always taught me that the secret to good and prosperous business was to provide a good (or service) that satisfied a real human need. If it was a repetitive need, so much the better.

With all their seduction, deceit, and psychobabble, the modern marketing industry has done a marvelous job of redefining the concept of need.

You may need shoes, but you certainly don't need a $350 pair of running shoes with a certain brand label on them. You may

47

need a car, but you probably don't need a $120,000 turbo-charged European convertible. I am not saying that we shouldn't have these things. I like nice things as much as the next person. All I am saying is, let's not confuse them with needs.

Now, these may be extreme examples depending on the person, but in all of our lives there has been a great blurring of the line between needs and wants. We do have real and legitimate needs, but they almost never have anything to do with consumer goods.

∽ ∽ ∽

Our legitimate needs are best understood in relation to each of the four aspects of the human person—physical, emotional, intellectual, and spiritual. These needs exist not only in these different areas, but also on different levels.

There are some things we need simply to survive. We call these primary needs, and this category includes the fundamentals that are necessary to sustain human life. Examples of primary needs would be food to eat, water to drink, and air to breathe. Without these primary legitimate needs, our lives would very quickly be brought to a grinding halt. Our primary needs are fundamental to our existence. We need them just to survive.

But this book is not about surviving, and neither is life. This book is about thriving, about becoming the-best-versions-of-ourselves.

Our secondary needs are not critical to our survival. We can survive without them for years in many cases. But they are essential if we are going to thrive in any (or all) of the four aspects of our lives. When our secondary needs are being fulfilled, we begin to blossom and bloom as human beings. The satisfaction of our secondary needs allows us to achieve and maintain optimum health and well-being. Among them would be needs such as regular exercise, a balanced diet, and healthy relationships.

Every day we attend to our primary needs—those things necessary merely to sustain our existence. In many cases we do this without even thinking about it. You don't have to remind yourself to breathe, you just breathe. You have made a habit of breathing. You do it now by instinct. Similarly, you eat and drink several times a day. You probably don't have to think too much about it. Eating and drinking have also become a habit for you. You are in the habit of surviving. You take care of your primary needs, because you have to.

On the other hand, we often neglect our secondary needs, either because we are too busy or too lazy or we simply don't consider them urgent.

The question is, are you satisfied being in the habit of surviving, or are you ready to get into the habit of thriving?

For a moment, think about each of the four areas: physical, emotional, intellectual, and spiritual. Which are you thriving in and which are you just surviving in?

Our secondary needs are the key to thriving. They may not seem urgent in light of the 105 things you have on your to-do list today, but they are probably more important than anything on that list.

The first step in our quest to become the-best-version-of-ourselves is to define our legitimate needs. The second step is to create a lifestyle that fulfills those legitimate needs.

We all have legitimate needs. The fulfillment of these needs is one of the very practical ways we can learn to embrace our essential purpose. If we are wise enough to seek their counsel, our legitimate needs will advise us what is necessary to maintain health of body, heart, mind, and spirit.

PHYSICAL NEEDS

Our physical body is the vehicle through which we experience life. Our bodies are both very fragile and extremely resilient. Our legitimate needs are most basically understood in relation to our physical well-being, because our primary needs exist in the physical realm.

If you don't have food to eat, you will die. If you don't have water to drink, you will die. You may not die today or tomorrow, but you will before too long, and as a direct result of not eating and drinking. Eating and drinking are primary and urgent needs. We have an even more urgent need for oxygen. If you don't have air to breathe, you will die almost instantly. Other primary needs include sleep and shelter (to a greater or lesser extent, depending on your environment and its climate).

Beyond our primary physical needs, we also have a number of secondary physical needs. Our primary needs are those we need simply to survive. Our secondary needs are those we need to thrive.

If we are to thrive physically, we have to bring these secondary needs into focus in our daily lives. Nothing tunes the body like regular exercise and a balanced diet. When we work out and fuel our bodies with the right types of food, we have more energy, and we are stronger, healthier, and happier.

Too often in our culture, food is seen a source of entertainment or comfort, instead of as a source of energy. Let me ask you something. If you owned a million-dollar racehorse, would you let it eat at McDonald's? Of course you wouldn't. If you had a million-dollar racehorse, you would control that horse's diet so that it was in absolute peak condition. I guess the question becomes, how much do you value your own body? Most people wait until they get cancer or have a heart attack before they remember that they have bodies.

Last year we spent more than $30 billion on diet products. How many diets have you been on? How many diets have people you know been on? I am amazed at how much people talk about diets—how this one works and that one doesn't.

Let's have a little bit of truth. Most of us do not need any other diet than a little bit of discipline. The average person knows the things that are good for him or her, and the things that are not. All we need is the discipline to choose the foods that fuel our bodies and give us energy, strength, health, and happiness.

But we don't want discipline. No, we want someone to stand in front of us on television and tell us that we can eat whatever we want, whenever we want, and as much as we want. As long as we take this little pill . . . or do this special workout for twenty minutes twice a week . . .

Our bodies are glorious creations and should be honored and respected.

Regular exercise, a balanced diet, and regular sleep are three of the easiest ways to increase our passion, energy, and enthusiasm for life. They are among our simplest legitimate needs and contribute massively to the well-being of the whole person. Physical well-being is the foundation upon which we build our lives. Unless we attend to our legitimate needs in relation to the physical aspect of our being, our capacity in all other areas of our life will be reduced.

EMOTIONAL NEEDS

In the emotional realm, it can be much more difficult to pinpoint our legitimate needs, because they are not necessary for our immediate survival. It is not too common to read in the newspaper about someone dying of emotional starvation. Our emotional needs are in many ways subtler, but certainly no less important if we are to thrive.

Emotional starvation, while not life threatening, does have some symptoms. For some of us, emotional starvation can lead to radical mood swings, for others to general lethargy, for others yet, to anger, bitterness, and resentment. The heart suffers and the body cries out. Most of all, emotional starvation leads to distortions in our character and prevents us from becoming the-best-version-of-ourselves.

This is certainly one of the areas I have neglected from time to time.

In the fall of 1997, after four years on the road and more than one million miles traveled, I took a three-month break from speaking and traveling. I spent that time in Austria, just north of Vienna, in an old monastery that was now being used as a college campus.

In Austria, I quickly realized that I had been severely neglecting the emotional aspect of my life. Over the previous four years, I had isolated myself. During this time I was now living in the United States, and my family and childhood friends were all in Australia, ten thousand miles away from this new life that mostly kept me in the northern hemisphere. On top of all that, I had become increasingly skeptical about people's motives for befriending me in this new time of my life. This was an insecurity that was born out of some bitter experiences. Besides, I was rarely in a city for more than a day, which isn't the most conducive lifestyle for forming or maintaining friendships.

Apart from the European students, there were more than a hundred American students on campus, enjoying what they called their "European experience." Every weekend, as soon as classes were over they would go—to Poland, Italy, France, Belgium, Holland, Germany, Greece, Ireland, and any number of other destinations in Europe. They would travel all night on trains for barely a glimpse of these great European countries. Each week as the weekend drew near, you could sense their passion for travel surging.

Most of the American students went to Austria just for the chance to travel. The studies were a means to an end. It seemed strange. I had gone there to escape travel. I had no interest whatsoever in traveling. I was happier than I had been in a long time just staying around the old monastery on weekends. On occasion, though, I would take the train into Vienna on a Saturday afternoon, sit in one of the squares, drink hot chocolate, and read.

But a few weeks into the semester, a friend I had met a couple of years earlier at college in the United States asked me to join him on a trip to Switzerland. Stuart was from Canada, and he had a unique sense of humor and an enormous appetite and propensity for fun. I hesitated at his invitation—not because of him, but because I had loosely resolved that I wouldn't travel during these three months. "Come on. We'll have a great time, we can stay with some friends of mine, we won't travel with a crowd, it will just be you and me, and we'll be back by Sunday night," he pressed. I relented. It was one of the best decisions of my life.

When classes were over on Friday afternoon, we hitched a ride to the local train station and went into Vienna. From there we took the overnight train to Geneva. We just talked, told stories, ate some bread and cheese, drank some wine, and traded songs on our Walkmans. The next day we had lunch on the lake, wandered for hours through the old city of Geneva, and then had dinner with his friend Alex and her family.

It was the strangest sensation—acceptance free of expectation. I felt like any normal twenty-four-year-old discovering Europe. I had been to Europe more than thirty-five times, but never like this. For forty-eight hours I was completely intoxicated with normality. It was refreshing. Exhilarating. Comforting. My relationship with Stuart rose to a completely new level, and he taught me again the great value of friendship. I was reminded that weekend of the age-old lesson that no man is an island unto himself. We are social beings—and relationship brings out the best in us.

⋄   ⋄   ⋄

For most people, their legitimate emotional needs include spending time with family, friends, a spouse, a boyfriend or girlfriend, colleagues at work, and perhaps a spiritual director or mentor.

Spending time with these people helps us to develop a sense of self, teaches us to participate in the fulfillment of other people's needs, and reminds us of our deep connection with the human family.

One of our most dominant emotional needs is our need for acceptance. We all need to feel we belong. In the face of rejection, we may put on a brave face and pretend that we can survive without acceptance. And that is true; we can *survive* without the nurturing acceptance provides. But we cannot *thrive* without it.

We all have a great need to feel accepted. It is one of the forces that drives human behavior. Our need to be accepted is powerful, and it is astounding what most people will do to gain some sort of acceptance or sense of belonging.

Peer pressure takes full advantage of this need to be accepted. Under the influence of peer pressure, people do things that they would not do if they were alone (and in many cases would prefer not to do), simply because they do not want to be excluded from a certain social circle. There is perhaps no greater example of our need to belong, our need to feel accepted.

We seek this sense of belonging in hundreds of different ways at work, at school, within our family, in the context of our intimate relationships, and by joining clubs, churches, and committees. Some of the ways we try to have this need met are healthy and help us to pursue our essential purpose. Others are not healthy and can prevent us from becoming the-best-version-of-ourselves.

I have always been fascinated with how many different churches there are in America and the criteria people use to choose a church. For several years I have been asking people, and I am amazed how similar their responses are. Most of them say something like "From the minute I walked in there five years ago, I just felt so welcome" or "I just feel like I belong there."

We have a great need to be accepted. We need to belong.

With this in mind, it is easy to understand why so many people join gangs and cults. From time to time, you may hear a story

about a gang or a cult, and those of us who live in a relatively se-
cluded world may wonder why anyone would get involved in these
things. Simple. Just like you and me, people who join gangs and
cults have a legitimate need for acceptance and a sense of belonging. They just don't have the options you and I have.

Young people who grow up in an inner-city environment join
gangs because they see it as their best option. The gang provides a
sense of belonging, the feeling of acceptance, and allows them to
feel that they are not alone in what must be a frightening world.
The gang tries to fill the emotional needs that a family should be
satisfying. But in many cases, the parents (or parent) are caught up
in drugs, alcohol, and crime. Or, in perhaps the best-case scenario,
they are doing all they can to pay the bills and keep food on the
table. People don't join gangs because they see a great future in it.
They see them as a way to survive. People join gangs because it
gives them somewhere to belong.

People join cults for the same reason. We all have a need to belong, a need for acceptance. A cult is just a more sophisticated
form of a gang.

Our needs are powerful. In many cases, if they are not fulfilled
in healthy ways, they will seek their own satisfaction in self-
destructive ways.

The next of our legitimate emotional needs is our need for dynamic friendship. While we certainly need acceptance, we also
have a need to be encouraged and challenged to change and grow.
Once you become dedicated to becoming the-best-version-of-
yourself, the people you will most enjoy spending time with are
not those who agree with you in everything you say and tell you
that you should be a little easier on yourself . . . and have that second slice of cheesecake! If you are dedicated to your essential purpose, the people you will want to surround yourself with are
people who inspire and challenge you to become the-best-version-
of-yourself.

The truth about friendship is this: We learn more from our

friends than we ever will from books. Sooner or later, our standards come to rest with the standards of our friends. Nothing influences us more than our peer group. The people you surround yourself with tell me something about who you are or something about who you will shortly become.

If you hang out with a group of people who want only to watch television, drink beer, eat pizza, and play video games . . . chances are you will adopt their lifestyle. On the other hand, if you surround yourself with a group of people who work out at the gym four times a week and fill their weekends with outdoor activities . . . chances are you will adopt their lifestyle.

If you hang out with people who are always going to the drive-through for burgers, fries, and sodas . . . guess what? But if you surround yourself with people who are interested in looking and feeling healthy . . . you guessed it, you will become more interested in your own health and well-being.

The people we surround ourselves with either raise or lower our standards. They either help us to become the-best-version-of-ourselves or encourage us to become lesser versions of ourselves. We become like our friends. No man becomes great on his own. No woman becomes great on her own. The people around them help to make them great.

We all need people in our lives who raise our standards, remind us of our essential purpose, and challenge us to become the-best-version-of-ourselves.

~*~ ~*~ ~*~

Our greatest emotional need is for intimacy. Beyond the primary needs for food, water, sleep, and air to breathe, intimacy is the greatest need of the human person.

Life is a self-revelation. Life expands in direct proportion to our ability to reveal ourselves to others and to the world around us. Yet most people spend most of their lives hiding their true selves and pretending they are somebody that they are not.

We want intimacy. We need intimacy. But we are afraid. We are desperately afraid that if people really knew who we are and what we are capable of, they would reject us. As a result, our fear of rejection (driven by our need for acceptance) and our need for intimacy are constantly at odds with each other.

We must ask ourselves these questions: "Do we provide a nonjudgmental environment for others to reveal themselves to us?" "Do we affirm those we love by complimenting them and expressing gratitude, not only for what they do, but for who they are?" "When others make mistakes, are we quick to judge and ridicule, or do we acknowledge it as a learning experience and part of their journey?" "Are we willing to take the first step and make ourselves vulnerable by beginning to reveal our true selves to others?"

Create an environment where people feel safe to be themselves and reveal themselves, and together you will drink from the springs of intimacy.

All relationships can be measured by our ability to share ourselves with others. We must press beyond the clichés of our common conversation and the facts of our daily lives. If we are to reveal ourselves and enjoy intimacy, we must learn to share and discuss our opinions, our hopes and dreams, our deepest feelings, our legitimate needs, and our fears, faults, and failures. The more two people are able to share and accept without judgment, the more intimacy they will enjoy.

Intimacy is measured by self-revelation. The more you share yourself with others (and vice versa), the more intimacy you will have. The more you hide yourself from others (and vice versa), the shallower your relationships will be. If you are unwilling or unable to share your self, you must resign yourself to low-level relationships.

Nothing satisfies the human person like intimacy.

ↄ ↄ ↄ

We live in the age of communication. The communications revolution has been driving the world economy for decades, and our lifestyles are constantly adjusting to the latest advances. Yet the communications revolution clearly has not increased our ability or willingness to communicate on a meaningful level.

The reason we neglect most of our legitimate needs is that they require our rarest resources: time and energy. Relationships are no different.

Relationships thrive under one condition: carefree timelessness. Quality time is now the discredited fantasy of an age that wanted more of everything except the things that really mattered. You cannot schedule quality time with your spouse or with your children. If you want twenty minutes of quality time with someone you love, schedule three or four hours with him or her one afternoon, and chances are, somewhere in the middle of that three or four hours you will have your twenty minutes of quality time.

When I was sixteen, I had a friend back home in Sydney. From time to time he would call me and say, "Let's waste some time together one day this week." That was his line, and what a wonderful lesson that one line taught me. We used to go out and have coffee or dinner. We would just talk, and laugh, and share stories. Sometimes we would even share a passage from a book one of us was reading. Were we wasting our time? No, of course not. Those times we shared were anything but a waste of time.

In our busy world, there is a tendency for us to try to contain our relationships in little boxes on our schedules. Too often the time we do set aside for relationships is on the perimeters of our already busy lives, so we approach our relationships without the energy they demand in order to be fruitful and fulfilling.

Relationships don't thrive under the pressures of our modern-day schedules. All of life's important relationships thrive under the condition of carefree timelessness. Learn to waste time with the people you love.

INTELLECTUAL NEEDS

Ideas shape our lives. Ideas shape history. We all have a need for a constant flow of ideas that inspire us, challenge us, illumine our minds, teach us about ourselves and our world, show us what is possible, and encourage us to become the-best-version-of-ourselves.

We need a diet of the mind just as much as we need a diet of the body. The ideas we feed our mind today tend to form our lives to-morrow.

Think of it in this way: We become the stories we listen to. It - doesn't matter if we get those stories from movies, music, television, newspapers, magazines, politicians, friends, or books—the stories we listen to form our lives.

If you want to understand any period in history, simply ask two questions: "Who were the storytellers?" and "What story were they telling?"

Winston Churchill, Francis of Assisi, Charlemagne, Napoleon, Charlie Chaplin, Adolf Hitler, Bob Dylan, Mother Teresa, Mahatma Gandhi, Abraham Lincoln, Marilyn Monroe, Nelson Mandela, and Jesus each told a story.

If you want to know how your nation will be different tomorrow from the way it was yesterday, find out how the stories your nation is listening to are different from the stories of yesterday. If you discover that the stories we are listening to have less meaning, contain more violence, and, rather than inspire us and raise our standards, appeal more and more to the lowest common denominator, you can be sure that in the future our lives will have less meaning, contain more violence, and be more focused on the lowest common denominator.

We become the stories we listen to. But perhaps the more important question is, what stories do you listen to? What stories are forming your life?

∽ ∽ ∽

Our intellectual needs are never urgent, so it is easy to overlook them. When was the last time you said to yourself, "I urgently need to read a good book today"? It doesn't happen. Why? For one, our intellectual needs are not primary needs. If we neglect them, we won't die. But mental vitality leads to physical, emotional, and spiritual vitality. Everything in our lives begins as a thought.

The reason people neglect their intellectual development is that they associate books and learning with school and work. Most people have very little leisure time, and they don't want to spend that time doing what they perceive as "work." One of the great tragedies of modern education systems is that they are failing to instill a love of learning. All too often, learning is seen only as a means to an end. It is necessary to pass an exam, or get a degree, or gain a promotion. Learning, like so many other aspects of modern living, has been violently disconnected from our essential purpose.

Some may argue that intellectually we are more advanced than ever before. This is certainly true, but the nature of our knowledge has become increasingly more specialized. The trend is for our professional knowledge, and in many cases training, to become more and more specific. A narrower base of knowledge necessarily creates a narrower worldview.

Add to all these factors the fact that most people feel exhausted by the intellectual demands being made upon them in the workplace, and it is easy to understand why a large proportion of people like to dump themselves in front of the television for hours each evening after work.

When we take all of this into account, it is easy to understand why most people neglect their legitimate need for personal intellectual stimulation.

At the same time, to neglect our phenomenal abilities to think, reason, decide, imagine, and dream is to enormously limit our potential.

We all have intellectual needs. Our intellectual needs may vary significantly from person to person, and while many are involved in intellectually engaging occupations, we all need other types of intellectual stimulation. In fact, the greater our professional intellectual stimulation, the greater need we have for other forms of intellectual nourishment to create a balance. Besides, it is highly unlikely that our professional intellectual efforts suit our individual needs at each time and place in life's journey.

In the category of personal intellectual stimulation, we could read magazines about fashion, gardening, sports, finance, music, or any other area of interest. We will be entertained, but it is unlikely that we will be challenged to raise our standards and become the-best-version-of-ourselves. To really stretch ourselves, we must delve into the wisdom writings. Selections could include a variety of philosophical texts, the writings of countless spiritual leaders past and present, and the scriptures. It is in these writings that the intellect comes face-to-face with the most profound questions and truths about the world, creation, God, humanity, and our individual journeys. Wisdom writings constantly hold before us a vision of the-best-version-of-ourselves. These writings seek not to entertain us, but to reveal to us who we are and why we are here. The wisdom writings gently call us out of our comfort zones and challenge us to improve, develop, grow, and live life to the fullest.

Our intellectual needs are many and varied. Most of us have a need for a professional intellectual focus. We all need different forms of entertaining intellectual stimulation. But we must challenge ourselves to move beyond these intellectual comfort zones and to embrace writings that challenge us to ponder the deeper questions, truths, and mysteries of our existence. As Mark Twain wrote, "The man who does not read good books has no advantage over the man who cannot read them."

Books change our lives. I believe that with my whole heart. I like to ask people what was the greatest period of transformation in their life. They tell me it was five years ago or seven years ago, they tell me it was when they got cancer or lost their job, they tell me it was in the town they grew up in or in a city where they didn't know anyone. "What were you reading at that time of great transformation?" I like to ask them next. Nine out of ten times, their eyes will light up, and they'll say, "I was reading ———— and that book changed my life."

In the room where I write in my home, I have more than a thousand books. But on the top shelf of one of the bookcases, at eye level, I have thirty-seven books. Each of those books has had an enormous impact on my life. I can tell you where I bought them, what city of the world I was in when I read them, and what the circumstances and situations of my life were at the time. There are books about philosophy, theology, psychology, business, and history. There are some incredible novels and biographies, and there on that shelf you will find some of the greatest spiritual and inspirational classics of all time. It is in a sense my own Great Books collection.

From time to time, when I become discouraged, confused, lonely, fearful, or simply begin to doubt my life, and myself, I go to that bookshelf. I glance along that row of books, and one of those books calls out to me. I take it from the shelf and rediscover the inspiration that first earned it a place on the top shelf.

Our bodies need regular exercise and a balanced diet, and so do our minds. You have a legitimate need to nourish your mind. If you choose the right diet of the mind, your life will be directed by ideas of excellence and greatness. If you allow the media and secular culture to select your intellectual diet, your life will be formed by distraction and mediocrity.

Books change our lives. Begin your own Great Books collection. Choose books that will help you to achieve your essential purpose and become the-best-version-of-yourself. Make daily reading one of the defining habits of your life.

SPIRITUAL NEEDS

Only here in the area of spirituality do we come to understand most fully our other legitimate needs—physical, emotional, and intellectual—and gain the insight to live a life that enriches, upholds, and protects our well-being in each of these areas.

Our spiritual needs have a tendency to change as the seasons of our lives change. Each of us has a unique spiritual journey. In different stages of the journey, we have different needs. And yet, there are some needs that are unchanging and necessary in all seasons of our lives—silence, solitude, and simplicity. The way we seek to experience these habits of the soul may change, but all the same, they remain essential to our spiritual diet if we are to find lasting joy in this changing world.

The noise of the world is preventing us from hearing the gentle voice within that always counsels us to embrace the-best-version-of-ourselves. We will begin to hear this voice again only when we make a habit of withdrawing from the noise of the world and immersing ourselves in silence. We needn't spend hours in silence each day, but nothing brings priority to our days like a period of silence each morning.

Every day life poses questions. We all have a need to search our hearts for answers to those questions. Every day we are faced with a myriad of choices and opportunities. We need time away from all the other voices to discern which of these choices and opportunities will enable us to become the-best-version-of-ourselves and which are merely distractions. It has been my experience that these exercises are performed most effectively alone, in the precious solitude of the classroom of silence.

It is also in silence and solitude that life's preeminent challenge is proposed to us. Brother Silence and Sister Solitude unveil the person we are today with all our strengths and weaknesses, but they also remind us of the better person we know we can be.

In the silence, we see at one time the person we are now and the person we are capable of becoming. In seeing these two visions at one time, we are automatically challenged to change and grow and become the-best-version-of-ourselves. It is precisely for this reason that we fill our lives with noise, to distract ourselves from the challenge to change.

Commitment to the purpose of becoming the-best-version-of-ourselves is the singular key to living life meaningfully and passionately.

Silence has been a great friend to the extraordinary men and women of every age. Many of life's great lessons can be learned only in the classroom of silence, especially those that teach us about our individual talents and how we can use them to fulfill our destiny.

For centuries and millennia, the wise people of every culture under the sun have sought the counsel of silence. Pythagoras, the Greek philosopher and mathematician (ca. 580–500 B.C.), wrote: "Learn to be silent. Let your quiet mind listen and absorb." Writing about the importance of silence and solitude, Blaise Pascal, the seventeenth-century French philosopher, scientist, mathematician, and writer, wrote: "All of man's miseries derive from not being able to sit quietly in a room alone." Franz Kafka, the Czech-Jewish novelist, philosopher, and poet, wrote: "You need not leave your room. Remain sitting at your table and listen. You need not even listen, simply wait. You need not even wait, just learn to become quiet, and still and solitary. The world will freely offer itself to you to be unmasked. It has no choice; it will roll in ecstasy at your feet."

Learn to be quiet. Learn to be still. These are among the most valuable lessons in our journey.

ဢ ဢ ဢ

We come now to the spiritual need of simplicity. Simplicity is one of the governing principles of the universe, yet with every passing century humanity looks to greater complexity to solve its problems and improve its life.

Who among us needs a little more complexity in their lives? None of us! What our lives desperately need is the liberation of simplicity.

If we learn once again to listen to the gentle voice within, we will hear it counseling us many times a day to simplify our lives. When the voices of the world propose the multiple complexities of modern living, the gentle voice within will whisper: *Why complicate your life?* Over time we will learn to turn our backs on a multitude of opportunities in order to preserve the peace in our hearts that is born from the blessed simplicity that the world despises.

Simplify. Simplify. Simplify your life and you will find the inner peace that the poets and saints of every age have coveted more than any possession.

Silence. Solitude. Simplicity. Three great friends! They may be the subtlest of our legitimate needs, but when they are honored our spirits soar to unimaginable heights, and we are left only to wonder how or why we ever followed the promptings of all the jeering voices of this world.

When we attend to our legitimate spiritual needs, everything else seems to fall into perspective. Only then are we able to let go of the past, wait patiently for the future, and live with an intense passion for life in the joy of the here and now. We feel healthy. We feel more fully alive. Our lives fill with vitality, and life becomes an exciting adventure instead of the day-to-day drudgery of counting the minutes away.

The fulfillment of our legitimate spiritual needs leads us to place our essential purpose at the center of our daily lives. When silence, solitude, and simplicity become a part of the fabric of our lives, we are much less inclined to neglect our other legitimate needs. Only with the focus, perspective, and vitality that are born from the spiritual disciplines will we ever learn to transform each moment and experience of our lives into opportunities to become the-best-version-of-ourselves. Spirituality brings clarity, direction, continuity, and integrity to our lives.

You already have everything within you that you need to make the journey. You must simply begin to honor the truth you already possess.

We all have needs. We need air to breathe, water to drink, and food to eat. We need to love and be loved. We need to accept and appreciate others and to be accepted and appreciated by others. We need to learn, to change, and to grow. We need to remember who we truly are and what matters most. We need.

This is our common bond as human beings. We are not as strong as we think we are. We are fragile. We are not as independent as we pretend to be. A day is coming when we will realize that independence is a myth. We are *interdependent.* We need one another, and only with and for one another can we live. We are one in our need. We are beings of need.

Our health and happiness are intimately connected. Our legitimate needs are the secret language that unites the two. When we acknowledge our legitimate needs and base our lifestyle decisions upon them, we necessarily live healthier and happier lives.

Life should be a rich and rewarding experience. Our lives should be filled with moments of wonder and inspiration. Life is an expression of abundance and should be lived passionately.

Know your needs.

Beyond Our Wants

The reason most of us neglect our legitimate needs is that we are too busy pursuing our *illegitimate wants*. We ignore our legitimate needs because we erroneously believe that if we get enough of our illegitimate wants, it won't matter that we are not taking care of our legitimate needs. This is a fallacy of monumental proportions, because you never can get enough of what you don't really need.

That's right. You never can get enough of what you don't really need.

Fulfillment comes not from having more and more of everything forever into oblivion. Fulfillment comes from having what you need. The whole world is chasing illegitimate wants with reckless abandon. We use all of our time, effort, and energy in the pursuit of our illegitimate wants, hypnotized by the lie that our illegitimate wants are the key to our happiness.

At the same time, the gentle voice within us is constantly calling out to us, trying to encourage us not to ignore the wisdom we already possess.

We must learn to move beyond our superficial wants and begin to discover our deepest desires.

The difference between our wants and our deepest desires is meaning. A desire is a want with meaning. Our deepest desires are things we want because we know they will help us become the-best-version-of-ourselves.

The problem is, we are all so busy wanting that we have forgotten why we want whatever it is we want. We have disconnected our wants from our reason for wanting them.

∽ ∽ ∽

For thousands of years in myths, legends, stories, fairy tales, and parables, the heart has been defined as the place from which our desires emerge and the place where our feelings reside. Our hearts are as individual and unique as our fingerprints. I cannot presume to know or understand the movements of your heart, nor you mine, but each of us must seek to discover and know the movements of our own hearts.

What we are about to discover is that our needs and desires are divinely and providentially linked. If we can get beyond our shallow and superficial wants, we discover that our deepest desires are for the things we legitimately need. Beneath the multitude of wants that plague the surface of our hearts, we desire good things for good reasons. These are the deepest desires of our hearts. They are good because in them we hope to better ourselves, the world in which we live, and others. They are the deepest desires of our hearts because their fulfillment leads us to become the-best-version-of-ourselves, and every being yearns to become all it is capable of being.

We would do well to learn to listen to these deepest desires of our hearts, and we should follow them wherever they lead us regardless of the cost or sacrifice involved.

Our fulfillment and happiness, our wholeness and holiness, depend upon us living out of the deepest desires of our hearts. Our deepest desires are directly linked to our legitimate needs. The careful pairing of our deepest desires and legitimate needs leads to the fulfillment of the human person—physically, emotionally, intellectually, and spiritually. The result is a life of unimagined balance and harmony, peace and prosperity.

PHYSICAL DESIRES

Many of our physical desires fall into the category of wants. Every day we have dozens of physical wants that have no meaning beyond the attainment of pleasure. Now, be assured, I enjoy pleasure as much as the next person. Our culture has in many ways promoted pleasure as the ultimate end in life or as the supreme good. But pleasure is not the ultimate end in life. We don't find our meaning and purpose in pleasure. The modern world proposes pleasure as the road to happiness. But wherever you find men and women who ascribe to the hedonistic view that pleasure is to be sought for its own sake at every available moment, you find people who are overcome with laziness, lustfulness, and gluttony. They are not free or happy. They are enslaved by a thousand different addictions, and the end produced by their philosophy is not pleasure, but despair.

Our deepest physical desires are for the things we need.

Each day at around lunchtime, for example, I have a desire for six chocolate doughnuts. It is a desire, but a shallow one. It's a want, a desire without meaning. If I listen to the gentle voice within me, it will remind me that I have a deeper desire to look and feel healthy.

The first desire for the six doughnuts arises in response to my legitimate need for food. But the best way to respond to that legitimate need for food is not by devouring half a dozen chocolate doughnuts. The best way for me to respond to my legitimate need for physical sustenance is by enjoying a healthy, balanced, and satisfying meal.

The shallow desire has only one thing in mind, the instant gratification of pleasure. Our superficial wants are not even able to take into consideration the future pain that a present pleasure may cause us.

The deeper desire of the heart—the desire to be healthy and

physically fit—takes into account the whole person and views the situation with our essential purpose in mind.

The only way to say no to the six doughnuts is to have a deeper yes. The only way to say no to anything is to have a deeper yes.

In this case, the deeper yes is for physical fitness, health, and well-being. But if you are not in touch with your deeper yeses, you will spend your whole life living out the shallow and superficial desires of your heart.

What we truly "need" we deeply desire, but not at the shallow levels of our hearts.

EMOTIONAL DESIRES

People will go to extraordinary lengths attempting to fulfill their emotional desires. In the emotional realm, to have a need and desire fulfilled today, we had to start preparing for that months or years ago. It's an idea that many struggle to come to grips with in a society where instant gratification isn't fast enough.

Physically, if you discover your deepest desire is for health and well-being, all you have to do is start exercising and adopt a balanced diet. Intellectually, if you discover your deepest desire is for greater wisdom about yourself and your purpose in life, all you have to do is set some time aside and begin to read and study the wisdom writings. Spiritually, if you discover your deepest need is for simplicity, all you have to do is have a spring-cleaning session and get rid of all the excess material possessions that clutter your wardrobe, garage, and basement and learn to say no to some of the many things that distract you from your essential purpose.

Each of these will deliver a relatively immediate satisfaction of your desire and fulfillment of your need. But if you discover today that emotionally your deepest desire is for intimacy, unless you have previously invested in this area of your life, it could take

weeks, months, and even years before you begin to see the fulfillment of your need and the satisfaction of your desire.

It is in the emotional realm that we are reminded more than
ever that we are not independent. We are interdependent. We rely
on one another for the fulfillment of our legitimate needs and
the satisfaction of our deepest desire. Life is not simply about the
selfish pursuit of the-best-version-of-ourselves. Rather, the more
we contribute to helping others become the-best-version-of-
themselves, the more progress we make in the attainment of our
essential purpose.

⌇⌇ ⌇⌇ ⌇⌇

While I hope someday to write an entire book about intimacy and
the power of relationships that are focused on the mutual fulfillment of our legitimate needs, this is not that book.

What we discover as we move through each of the four aspects
of the human person is that there is a strong connection between
our needs and our deepest desires. When we are truly in touch
with ourselves at the deepest levels, we discover that we deeply desire what we need for optimum health, happiness, efficiency, and
effectiveness.

The problem is that our everyday lives distract us from our
deepest desires. We get busy and tired, and fatigue makes cowards
of us all. Once fatigue sets in, we seek instant gratification and
begin to operate from our shallow wants again.

A common example in the emotional realm is our desire to
share certain experiences of our lives with others. When good
things happen to us, we want to share them with someone else.
The sharing magnifies the joy these good events have brought to
our life. Conversely, when something bad happens to us, we also
want to share it with someone else. The sharing diminishes the anguish and heartache.

Let's use the example of a bad day to expand a little. Everyone has a bad day from time to time, and when we do most of us need to talk through it with somebody else. But whom you choose to open up to is of paramount importance.

You may unload on an uncooperative salesclerk by saying, "You know, I have had a really lousy day, and I don't need you to treat me in that way." You will fulfill your desire to express your feelings, but your need to be heard, loved, accepted, and understood will go unfulfilled.

Your desire to express your feelings is only a tiny aspect of your deeper need to be heard, loved, accepted, and understood. This deeper need will be met and fulfilled only if you are able to express your feelings to the right person in the right setting.

If you are a mother and wife and you've had a terrible day, you may be tempted to say to your misbehaving children, "Listen, kids, I've had a terrible day, and I don't need you to be misbehaving." You will have fulfilled your desire to express how you feel, but the deeper need that this desire represents will remain unfulfilled.

In time we come to understand that when we feel a need to express ourselves, it is critical that we choose the right person. The salesclerk doesn't know you sufficiently and probably doesn't care, and your children are too young to respond appropriately.

The fact that you had a lousy day may be a small issue for you, but the bigger the issue, the more important it is for us to open up to the right person. If we share our feelings with the wrong person, it is unlikely that person will honor and respect our feelings in the way that is appropriate and necessary. Choose the wrong person and the most likely outcome is that we come away feeling frustrated and violated rather than comforted and understood.

⸲∞ ∞ ∞

We all have a need for a trust relationship, a person in our lives we can talk to about anything—a relationship with a person who will honor our feelings and reverence our struggle with the circumstances of our lives; someone who will listen without trying to fix, change, or move us; a person who is able to sit with us in our pain and dance with us in our joy; a person in tune with him- or herself enough to speak with compassion, encouragement, and honesty.

We all have a need for such a person, but they are all too rare to find.

For some people, this person is a spouse; for others, it is a close friend or a spiritual guide. For others, this person is God, and their emotional need and desire in this area is met through their spirituality. For most people, it is a mixture of their relationship with God and one or two special human friendships.

In the earlier stages of our lives, we may pass through many of these relationships—classmates, members of sporting teams, relatives, a family doctor, an older family friend, girlfriends and boyfriends, teachers, a priest, pastor, or rabbi, and maybe even a mentor or a coach.

One of our real challenges emotionally is that when we most need these people, they are very rarely just around the corner waiting for our emotional need and desire to coincide.

Experience has taught me that we express ourselves too little and we can express ourselves too much. It is easy to share too much with the wrong person and too little with the right person.

When life throws us a curveball, our instinct is to react by picking up the phone and calling five of our friends to vent. We almost invariably regret this as the dust settles. Our first response should be to take the situation and our feelings about the situation to the classroom of silence. Sharing a situation with God in prayer can often ease our sadness and anxiety. I have never known anyone who felt violated after pouring his or her heart out to God.

We have a legitimate need and a deep desire to share the triumphs and trials of our lives. We also have a desire and a need to be on the other end of a trust relationship. As is so often the case in the emotional realm, our needs and desires complement the needs and desires of those with whom we are making this journey.

The more we delve into the depths of our hearts, the more we discover that we have a legitimate need and a deep desire to be the person people can talk to about anything, without feeling judged or pitied. We yearn to be a person who will honor other people's feelings and reverence their struggle with the everchanging circumstances of their lives. We long to be that someone who can listen without trying to fix, change, or move the other person; a person who is able to sit with another in his pain and dance with him in his joy; a person in tune with herself enough to speak with compassion, encouragement, and honesty.

Our emotional needs and desires are vast and varied. It is one area of our lives that we must approach cautiously and that requires patience. Instant gratification has no place in the emotional realm. The fruits of the emotional world are reserved only for those willing to participate selflessly.

INTELLECTUAL DESIRES

When we get too busy and too tired, we tend to lose touch with our intellectual desires very quickly. But allow yourself several lazy Sunday afternoons in a row, unencumbered by technological stimulation, and you will find yourself thinking, I've always wanted to learn how to play the piano or the guitar, or, Wouldn't it be neat to learn Spanish and then take a trip to Spain. . . . I would love to master the game of chess. . . . I've always wanted to understand how the body transforms food into energy. . . . Perhaps I should read a little more history or research my family tree. . . . Maybe at this time in my life I should keep a journal. . . .

Leisure ignites our intellectual desires; fatigue banishes them.

We are born with intellectual desire. You may have lost touch with it, but you have it. Over the years, you may have buried it or it may have become distorted by some childhood experience, but intellectual desire is natural and abundant in us all.

Intellectual desire is best understood in the example of a child. Children have a curiosity that brings a natural sense of wonder to their lives. What are children always asking? Why? They are naturally curious. From the moment they can think and speak logically, one question dominates their inner dialogue (thoughts) and their outer dialogue (conversations). Internally and externally, they are constantly asking, Why? They are naturally curious, eager to understand, and they yearn for knowledge.

Intellectual desire is one of the great signs of human vitality. Are you thriving or are you just surviving?

If you are not in tune with your intellectual desire, what happened? Maybe when you were a child your parents used to yell at you when you asked questions. Perhaps you always wanted to learn to play the piano, but your friends told you it was only for sissies. The simplest things can cause us to shrink back and bury ourselves. You asked a question in class as a child, all the other children laughed, and the embarrassment buried that natural desire.

Life doesn't spare any of us from these and other bitter—sometimes brutal—experiences. Still, we have to get back up and move on. In this case, that means rediscovering our intellectual desires. Leisure brings clarity to the mind. Allow yourself time to rest, relax, and be rejuvenated, and as you do, your intellectual desires will once again begin to emerge.

One of the greatest proofs of our intellectual desire is the number of books we buy. Visit a bookstore for an hour and tell me how many books you buy or would have liked to buy. Maybe you don't buy books anymore because you have bought so many that you have never read. Most of us keep buying them and piling them up. Why? Our intellectual needs are so great and our corresponding intellectual yearnings are so strong that we hope one day we will start to live in alignment with our legitimate needs and our deepest desires.

Feed your mind.

SPIRITUAL DESIRES

Our exploration of the various types of desires brings us finally to our spiritual desires. They lie hidden from superficiality and frivolity in the deepest recesses of the human heart. Our spiritual desires in some ways are the subtlest of all, yet they reveal the greatest of our legitimate needs.

Perceiving and responding to our spiritual desires is the most essential aspect of personal development. The yearnings of the senses call out to us with unerring consistency and draw attention to the needs and wants of our bodies, but our spiritual desires lie at the bottom of the deep, still waters of our being.

The deepest desire of our hearts is not to do something or to have something, but rather for peace. We yearn endlessly for peace. We all long for the peace of knowing that who we are, where we are, and what we are doing is essentially good. We need to know that we are contributing to the happiness of others and that, however slowly, we are progressing toward becoming the-best-version-of-ourselves. This is the prescription for peace.

The needs that correspond with our desire for peace are silence, simplicity, and solitude.

Do you ever feel you just need a little time to yourself? Do you find yourself questioning the way you are living your life? Do you have questions about what is best for you now? Do you feel overloaded or overwhelmed?

All of these are signs that you need a little silence, solitude, and simplicity. These feelings and questions are our spiritual desires trying desperately to be heard.

Depending on our situation in life, some of these will be easier to meet than others. A mother with young children may find it very difficult to find silence, solitude, and simplicity. We must remember that we are not talking about the constant silence, solitude, and simplicity of a monk. What we need and desire are small pockets of silence and solitude and a general structure of simplicity.

It is also critically important that we treasure the time we do have to be alone. If we respond to our need for solitude by going shopping by ourselves, our need for solitude may be partially satisfied, but the distractions of music, other people, and the host of desires that will arise from "the mall experience" will prevent us from drinking from the well of solitude.

In order to achieve the soul-searching that we desire and legitimately need, it is important to find a quiet place to be alone. Only in that silence and solitude are we able to remember that we already know the things that will bring us lasting happiness.

It would be lovely if our souls growled every time they were hungry the way our stomachs do. But they don't. The voice of the hungry soul is confusion, questions, and a general sense of being overwhelmed.

HARNESSING THE
POWER OF OUR NEEDS
AND DESIRES

Once we learn to understand the language of our legitimate needs and our deepest desires, we can begin to harness their power in our everyday lives to increase our energy, vitality, and love for life.

If we make a point of observing ourselves in different situations, little by little, we will become more aware of the people, places, and activities that invigorate us and those that drain our energy and destroy our passion for life.

Our desire for food, exercise, sleep, relationship, study, and quiet times of prayer and reflection are all responses to our legitimate needs for the people, places, and activities that work together to make us whole. Our deepest desires lead us to the satisfaction of our legitimate needs, which in turn produces health and harmony within us. All this is part of the divine engineering set in motion within you to assist you in the fulfillment of your essential purpose.

Our desires and needs are very closely linked. We desire deeply because we need deeply. The careful matching of our deepest desires and our legitimate needs requires and demands careful discernment. Your health and your happiness depend almost entirely on the development of this ability.

There is a profound and providential connection between our

needs and our desires. To ignore our needs and desires, and their relationship to each other, is to ignore our very self. Your body, heart, mind, and spirit all yearn for you to be healthy in every sense of the word. They collaborate with one end in mind, that you may become the-best-version-of-yourself.

EVERYBODY IS A GENIUS

Albert Einstein wrote, "Everybody is a genius. But if you judge a fish by its ability to climb a tree, it will live its whole life believing that it is stupid." The question I have for you at this part of our journey together is, "What is your genius?"

You see, I believe that we are all capable of doing one thing better than any other person alive at this time in history. What is your one thing?

I know what you may be thinking. You may be thinking quietly to yourself that you don't have a genius. You may be tempted to doubt the idea and think that I am talking only about the extraordinary people. No. Everybody is a genius; what is your genius?

Who are the extraordinary people, anyway? Are they the only ones who possess genius? Surely we cannot count only those who achieve world acclaim and success.

If genius belongs only to those who invent things that change the whole course of human history, create masterpieces that draw crowds to art galleries for centuries, imagine symphonies that live on in our hearts forever, or become great presidents of great nations or great CEOs of great corporations—if we count only people who set world records and win gold medals, people who capture our imaginations and raise our spirits playing Major League Baseball or Basketball, those who win Oscars and Grammy Awards, and people who receive enormous public attention for going to heroic lengths to serve humanity—then what is to become of the rest of us? Are we to march off quietly and join - Thoreau's masses and simply lead our lives of quiet desperation?

I think not.

Let me explain from another point of view.

My mother lives in Australia, and probably nobody will ever write a book about my mother. She doesn't live in the right suburb on the right street, she doesn't drive an expensive car, and she - didn't go to the right college. My mother doesn't make a lot of money, she doesn't have a lot of money, she doesn't wear expensive clothes with fancy labels on them, she doesn't vacation in all the right places every year, and she hasn't had a job outside of the home since she gave birth to my oldest brother.

My mother hasn't invented anything that will change the whole course of human history, she is not the creator of artistic or musical masterpieces, and she has not, and is not likely to, become the great president of a great nation or corporation. Mum doesn't have any world records, gold medals, Oscars, or Grammy Awards, and she can go to the supermarket without being bothered by the paparazzi.

By all the world's standards, my mother is a complete failure. But let me assure you, my mother is an absolute genius.

I remember as a child coming home from school. Every afternoon at three-thirty my seven brothers and I would descend upon the family home like some sort of invasion. Some of us had experienced triumph, and some of us had experienced tragedy. My mother was able to instantaneously console the tragedy and celebrate the triumph.

As one of eight children, I never felt as though I were being treated as just part of the crowd. Both my mother and my father had a phenomenal ability to draw the best out of each of my brothers and me.

No. There will be no books about my mother. And as I said, if judged by all the world's standards, she is a complete failure. But you know what? My mother could not care less what the world thinks. Most people don't know her well enough to compliment her or criticize her. And she knows that. My mother could not care less what just about anybody thinks. Do you know why? Because my mother knows who she is, and she knows why she is here. She has no illusions about trying to be someone she is not. My mother has discovered her genius, pursued her genius, exercised her genius, and celebrated her genius. And if you and I can get even the tiniest taste of that peace—the peace that comes from knowing that who we are, where we are, and what we are doing makes sense regardless of the outcome or other people's opinions—then we have discovered our genius.

Have we simply been judging ourselves by all the wrong criteria?

"Everybody is a genius. But if you judge a fish by its ability to climb a tree, it will live its whole life believing that it is stupid."

What is your genius? We are all capable of doing one thing better than any other person alive at this time in history. What is your one thing?

Your one thing may be to love your spouse, raise your children, or be a kindergarten teacher. Your one thing may be to invent something that changes the whole course of human history or to become the president of a great nation. It doesn't matter so much what form your genius takes as it does that you embrace and celebrate it.

How will you know when you discover your genius? There are two signs: joy and a feeling of timelessness. When I speak and when I write, the hours pass without notice. This is not work, it is passion. Is it always like that? No, of course not. There are times when to squeeze a single coherent paragraph from my mind takes hours and hours. But when I experience the joy and the timelessness of sharing these ideas, I know that I was born to share these ideas as a fish was created to swim or a bird to fly. It is simply a part of who I am.

It is possible that you turned your back on your genius years ago. Many people cast aside their genius because it is not spectacular enough or because their family and friends wanted something different for them. All too often genius is abandoned because it - doesn't make us enough money.

ᔛ   ᔛ   ᔛ

We have seen the connection between our legitimate needs and our deepest desires; our unique talents hold the missing key. It is perhaps not possible to fulfill all our needs and desires, and it is not possible to completely develop and exercise all our talents. The challenge for each of us is to create a lifestyle that will allow our needs, desires, and talents to live in harmony. This dynamic collaboration is the key to living life to the fullest and becoming the-best-version-of-ourselves.

THE THREE CIRCLES

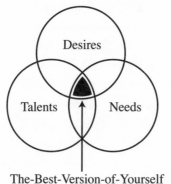

What You Are Passionate About

What You Were Born to Do

Desires

What You Need to Thrive

Talents   Needs

The-Best-Version-of-Yourself

In order to quickly and easily understand the three circles, imagine you were able to create a way of life (a lifestyle in the truest sense of the word) that would perfectly align with the following criteria.

First, you spend your days and weeks doing the things for which you have a particular genetic ability or God-given talent. When you apply yourself to these activities, you experience a great sense of joy and the rare feeling of timelessness. You are so connected with your self and your days that you feel you were born to do the things you are doing and live the life you are living. In every way, you sense you are becoming the-best-version-of-yourself.

Second, your physical, emotional, intellectual, and spiritual needs are each being attended to. You are immersed in a way of life that perfectly balances the four aspects of the human person. Rather than neglecting one or more of these areas for days or weeks, each day you allocate time and energy to each of the four areas of fulfillment.

Third, you are full of passion for life. You are passionate about what you are doing because you absolutely love who it is causing you to become. You love getting out of bed in the morning to watch the sunrise and greet a new day. You want for nothing other than to be all you are capable of being, and you consider anything that distracts you from that purpose as a waste of time, energy, and life.

The question is, who or what occupies the place created by the intersection of the three circles? You guessed it. The-best-version-of-yourself. The more you allow this one simple, crystalline concept to guide your life choices, the more you will drive toward *the zone* created by the intersection of the three circles.

Learn to live in that place and you will live a life uncommon.

At different times in our lives, we may have an intense experience of one, sometimes even two, of the circles in the way I have described them. Few people in our noisy, busy, distracted world ever experience all three. And even when we do experience one of the circles in an extraordinary way, we are often unable to sustain the experience because of the imbalance of our lives.

The three circles are the blueprint of the genius that lies within you.

Get to know your legitimate needs, your deepest desires, and your unique talents. They are the clues that God has placed within you to help you discover your destiny and become the-best-version-of-yourself.

A little later we will discuss what is missing in our lives and how we begin to build a life that allows the three circles to powerfully intersect in our daily lives. But now it is time to turn our attention to understanding the choices we make and why we make them.

PART THREE

THE-BEST-VERSION-
OF-YOURSELF

OVERWHELMED BY EXPERTS

○━━▶━━○

One of the characteristics of our age is an excess of experts. Everyone is an expert, it seems. Every day we are bombarded with opinions from these experts, and these opinions have a way of weaving their way into our lives and philosophies.

Take news and current affairs programs as an example. They have a habit of presenting experts who speak about the way your favorite foods are manufactured, the way you invest, how to raise your children, the latest statistics from a medical study, and a plethora of other topics that have an impact on your everyday life.

They start by running advertisements for this news item every fifteen minutes for the whole day, not only on their own television station, but also on regional radio stations. The wording of the advertisements invariably pulls you in by triggering a fear that causes you to question what you are eating, how you are exercising, the asset allocation of your 401(k) plan, how you are raising your children, whether or not you have the right health care plan . . . and so on.

The problem with the flow of this type of expert information is that it is presented in a rapid staccato form, with very little detail, is usually the result of some very narrow study, and is never followed up. If, two weeks later, the expert is proven to be blatantly wrong, they don't bring you another story apologizing for feeding you misinformation. They don't even stand corrected. They just move on to the next story that can create a fear in you great enough to get you to tune in at six o'clock.

This is just one of the ways expert information is being manipulated to create ratings and ultimately to make money. All the time, these expert opinions are massively affecting the everyday lives of millions of people. Expert opinions are one of the powerful voices that cause us to doubt the gentle voice within us.

When was the last time you saw anyone on CNN who wasn't an expert?

We are allowing too many experts into our lives. They are batting us around like a Ping-Pong ball, and in most cases they don't seek to educate and liberate us. Rather, they want to make us dependent on them. In more and more areas of our lives we know less and less and have become increasingly dependent on experts.

In an age where everyone is an expert, our base of knowledge is becoming narrower and narrower (so we can be experts in a field), but so is our base of common sense. As the number of experts in our lives increases, our ability to reason and make healthy decisions for ourselves seems to diminish.

Don't surrender your life to the experts. They are never going to care as much about your health, your relationships, your children, your education, your money, and your life as you do. And they very rarely consider the whole picture, the many aspects of your life.

Each of us must learn to make decisions consistent with the guiding principles that emerge from a clear and cohesive understanding of our essential purpose: to become the-best-version-of-ourselves.

ↂ ↂ ↂ

When I was a child, I never wondered what was the right or the wrong thing to do. I just knew. Something within me told me. It seems that most people can relate to a similar experience at some time in their lives. As children, we know deep within ourselves how we should act in certain situations. We don't always act that way, but we know. The most common name we give that gentle voice within us is conscience.

There is a lot to be said for a clear conscience. The idea doesn't get much airtime these days, but there is a tremendous tranquillity born from knowing that you are doing the right thing for the right reasons.

As we grow older, we seem to lose this gift of knowing which is the better way to act. Somewhere along the way, most of us seem to be conditioned to distrust ourselves. We stop listening to the voice of conscience and begin to seek out the opinions of the many other voices that distract us from the voice within. As a result, one of the real dilemmas that people face every day is the inability to look at a given situation and decide which is the best way to act.

When most people are faced with a financial decision, they consult a parent, friend, colleague, book, financial adviser, or combination of these. Most people, when faced with a personal or moral decision, consult their spouse, pastor, priest, minister, friends, or the scriptures. In all of these, however, there is no constant. Different opinions and different interpretations leave many people more bewildered than they were to begin with. But each of us, finally, after gathering as much information as is available, or as much as we choose to accept, is forced to make a decision and to act—understanding that even to make no decision is to act.

Between the gathering of information, the seeking of opinions, and the actions of our lives, another process takes place: decision making. Decisions cannot be made in a vacuum; they are made in space and time. To make an effective decision, we must have some goal toward which we are moving. If not, we find ourselves deciding because "Uncle Frank said it was the right thing to do" or "Reverend George told me it was best this way."

In some cases these advisers may very well be right, but in others they may not be. The point is, rather, that we should not make ourselves beholden to experts in our lives. We must seek to understand not only what is right, wrong, good, or best—but also why certain things are right or wrong. This does not mean that we do not seek the input from advisers and experts. It does mean that we assess what they say against the backdrop of our essential purpose and in light of the goal we are moving toward. It is also critical that we understand the effects and consequences of our actions.

These abilities are not easy to acquire. How is the ordinary person to know? Upon what criteria are we to base the decisions and actions of our lives?

Before we make a decision, particularly a large one (or before we give advice to assist someone else in making a decision), it is wise for each of us to take time in the classroom of silence to listen to the gentle voice within. Silence and solitude give a perspective to the situations of our lives that could not be gained by a thousand hours of conversation or a thousand pages of books.

Yet this thoughtful reflection also cannot take place in a vacuum. It must take place in relation to the space and time of our everyday lives by considering the matter at hand in light of our hopes and dreams, and with our essential purpose ever before us.

If you do not know where you are going, you will never get there.

Our ability to discern any question or opportunity in our lives depends primarily on our understanding of where we are and where we wish to go and, more important, our understanding of who we are and who we wish to become.

Most people don't know what they want. Most people don't know who they are. Most people don't know who they are capable of becoming.

These are three very large statements. Are they true? You decide. In any depth, beyond a little more money, a new car, and the vacation of a lifetime, do you know a lot of people who really know what they want from life? Do you know a lot of people who know what they want for themselves? How many people do you know who are intimately aware of and in tune with their legitimate needs? Do you know many people who are connected to the deeper desires of their hearts? Would you say most people know what their genius is and are using it as a guiding principle in their lives? Finally, do you think many people have a clear vision of what the-best-version-of-themselves looks like?

These are tremendous disabilities. When we don't know who we are, what we want, or where we are going and why, we are very susceptible to becoming pawns in other people's schemes.

Knowing who we are (strengths, weaknesses, needs, talents, and desires) and what we are here for (to become the-best-version-of-ourselves) is the knowledge that liberates us from the modern enslavement of a life of meaninglessness and gives our lives back to us once more.

Millions of people have lost their lives, and they don't even know it.

◡◡ ◡◡ ◡◡

In almost every moment of the day, we find ourselves being confronted with questions and opportunities. Our lives are a constant flow of decisions. What will I eat? What will I wear? Where will I go? Whom will I go with? What will I do? What will I buy? Where will I live? Life is always asking us questions. Often they seem small and insignificant, but in truth they can significantly impact our lives.

We have options. I could watch television for an hour every day or exercise for an hour every day. I could eat McDonald's every day for lunch or I can have soup and a salad. We choose between various options a hundred times a day, and our choices impact our health, happiness, well-being, and destiny.

In his classic poem "The Road Not Taken," Robert Frost describes coming to a fork in the road and having to choose between the two paths that lie before him. The poem closes with one of the most famous lines of modern literature: "I took the one less traveled by, and that has made all the difference."

Too often the poem is interpreted as being about one monumental moment, one enormous decision, that determines the outcome of a person's whole life. It is as if, once this one decision is made, all is well, and the rest of the road is smooth and slopes gently downhill.

The poem is not about one moment in a person's life. It is about every moment of our lives. We find ourselves constantly at a crossroads. No sooner do we make one decision and take three or four steps down either path than we come upon two roads diverging in a yellow wood . . . again!

The fork in the road is constantly appearing in our lives.

The ability to choose comes from a sense of purpose. Leaders are charged with the responsibility of making decisions, because they above all others are supposed to understand the *purpose* of the people or organization they lead. Direction comes from an understanding of where you are going. If you don't know where you are going, you are lost.

When we have a sense of our purpose, the decisions of our daily lives can be easily assessed with that purpose in mind. Direction emerges in our lives by bringing our decisions before the altar of our essential purpose.

If you make great decisions, you will live a great life. In my own life, I have found that the following model has been very useful in bringing clarity to the decisions I need to make every day and often under enormous pressure. When properly understood, this model serves as a compass to help us discern the opportunities that cross our paths. It is a simple but faithful decision-making tool that has served me well and that I hope will also become a trusted friend of yours.

Life cannot be confined to a model. Life should never be reduced to a model. But very often, models give us visual starting points that bring great clarity to our unique situations.

This model makes allowance for, and can be adapted to, the individual person and any particular situation.

I set this model before you as a starting point for discerning questions, decisions, and opportunities in your life. More than this, it bridges the gap between knowledge of acts that are right and wrong and the much superior knowledge of why a certain action is right, wrong, good, or best. This is one of the major distinctions that organized religion has failed to communicate, to larger or lesser extents, since the beginning of time.

Most people need to know not only if a certain act is right, wrong, good, or best, but also why a certain action is right, wrong, good, or best. If you can take people one step further and show them how a certain action will help or hinder them from becoming the-best-version-of-themselves, most people will then at least be filled with a desire to do what is good, true, noble, and right. Even if they are unable to convert that desire into action, you have at least given them a vision that will live with them always. This model helps bridge that gap.

Embrace this model. Call it to mind during the day when you are faced with a decision, and you will see that it delivers with unerring consistency a startling clarity.

This model has become a powerful practical tool in my journey, and I pray it serves you as well as it has served me.

The diagram below represents what is understood in the Christian tradition as "the path of salvation," or "the journey of the soul." At this very moment, we are all at point A.

Point A represents you (or me or any individual person) right

THE JOURNEY OF THE SOUL

The Person   The-Best-Version-
You Are Today   of-Yourself

now—here and today—with all your strengths and weaknesses, faults, failings, flaws, defects, talents, abilities, and potential.

Point B represents you (or me or anyone) as the person you were created to be—perfectly. If you close your eyes for a few moments and imagine the better person you know you can be in any area of your life, and then multiply that vision to include the better person you know you can be in every area of your life, that is the person you have become when you reach point B—the-best-version-of-yourself.

At every point along the path closer to point B, we more fully recognize, appreciate, and use our talents and abilities and are more dedicated to our development—physically, emotionally, intellectually, and spiritually. At each point along the path toward point B, there is a more harmonious relationship among our needs, desires, and talents. Through this process of transformation, we begin to reach our once hidden potential. At point B, through the dual process of self-discovery and discovery of God, we have overcome our fears and transformed our faults and failings into virtues.

Are you dedicated to your development physically, emotionally, intellectually, and spiritually?

Dedicate yourself above all else to becoming the-best-version-of-yourself. It is the best thing you can do for your spouse, your children, your friends, your colleagues, your employees, your employer, your church, your nation, the human family, and yourself. The best thing you can do is to become the-best-version-of-yourself, because it is *doing* with a *purpose*.

Embrace your essential purpose. Celebrate your best self.

ৎ৹ ৎ৹ ৎ৹

As you make the journey from point A to point B, you begin to allow the Divine Spirit to emerge from within. With every step closer to point B you allow the Divine Spirit to guide you in all your decisions and actions.

When you reach point B you have reached perfection, not in a robotic sense, but in the sense that you have become perfectly the person you were created to be. The journey has taught you to align your spirit with the Divine Spirit in everything, which brings you tremendous peace, happiness, fulfillment, and a focus that is awe inspiring to all those who cross your path.

The journey makes you "whole" once again. Here is the essence of the ancient term *holiness*—every element of your being is now working together in balance and harmony. Here, the power of the four fundamental aspects of the human person—physical, emotional, intellectual, and spiritual—have been harnessed and are being used to lead you toward perfection.

At every point along the path, there is a more intimate relationship among our needs, desires, and talents. Every major world religion holds that the meaning and purpose of our lives as human beings is to give glory to God. The Egyptian monk Athanasius wrote, "The glory of God is the perfection of the creature." There is no better way to honor life and God than to strive to become the-best-version-of-yourself.

Dedicate yourself to this journey—physically, emotionally, intellectually, and spiritually.

Use this simple model to guide you. It will reveal to you your essential purpose. It will help you to become fully aware of your legitimate needs. It will teach you to perfect the art of meeting your needs through the daily events of your life. As you dedicate yourself to the journey and progress along the path, you will begin to have less interest in anything that does not help you to become the-best-version-of-yourself.

Only then will you have the freedom of the seven dreams—when you are finally free in every situation to abandon the-lesser-version-of-yourself and choose your best self. It is a freedom very few men or women possess.

Choosing Happiness

＊

Happiness is not success. Happiness is not pleasure. Happiness is not fun.

Too many people equate happiness with success, physical pleasure, and fun. These are the myths that distract us from pursuing true happiness.

Happiness is not success. What level of success do you imagine will make you happy? I promise you, the happiness born from the achievement of that success would be very short-lived. Once you have climbed that mountain, you will cast your gaze to the peak of another, higher mountain. I have met enough successful people to know that success cannot be equated with happiness. Some of them are tremendously happy, others are desperately miserable. It seems that those who were happy before they became successful are still happy, and their success has perhaps increased their happiness. But those who were not happy before their success are still not happy, and in some cases they are unhappier than ever before.

Success contributes to our happiness only inasmuch as it helps us become the-best-version-of-ourselves.

Happiness is not physical pleasure. What physical pleasure can be sustained? How long can you enjoy the pleasure of food before it turns to pain? How long can the pleasure of sexual intimacy be sustained? How long can you indulge in the pleasure of alcohol or drugs before the high turns into a low? Physical pleasure is fleeting and when detached from our essential purpose leaves emptiness as its aftermath.

Physical pleasure creates lasting happiness in our lives only when it helps us become the-best-version-of-ourselves.

Happiness is not fun. Most people believe that the more fun experiences they have, the happier they will be. Children are the perfect example. It is inconceivable for them that happiness is something other than fun. Believing that the more fun we have, the happier we will be, we also tend to choose friends we think will contribute to the fun factor. How important is fun to your conception of happiness?

Close your eyes for a moment and imagine a scene filled with happy people.

Most people conjure an image of people laughing, eating, drinking, or partying. Very few people conjure a picture of a woman sitting quietly on her porch swing, enjoying a great book; a man just as quietly enjoying his vegetable garden; a couple married for thirty-five years walking hand in hand; or a young couple raising their children.

Our conception of happiness is often fatally flawed by the belief that fun equals happiness. Don't get me wrong; I'm not suggesting you should spend your life avoiding fun. Fun is an important part of a healthy and happy life. But fun for fun's sake rarely leads to any type of lasting happiness. The challenge is to learn to have fun doing the things that matter most.

Fun increases our happiness when it is infused into those activities that help us become the-best-version-of-ourselves.

Your ability to experience happiness will be limited only by your ability to grasp the meaning and purpose of your life.

In every decision, we choose happiness or misery. When we choose to become the-best-version-of-ourselves we choose happiness, and when we choose by default to become a-second-rate-version-of-ourselves we choose misery.

There is only one question: Will what you are about to do help you become the-best-version-of-yourself? If the answer to that question is "Yes," do it without hesitation.

⚭ ⚭ ⚭

The journey of the soul is difficult. Life is difficult. It is those who imagine that life is easy or should be easy who end up the unhappiest. It is the friction of life, the challenges of life, the ebb and flow of the unexpected, that all work together to help us fulfill our essential purpose and destiny.

Along the way, there are many barriers and obstacles to be overcome. In the diagram on page 95, the symbol ⚭ represents the obstacles that confront us along the way—disappointment, failure, loss, fear, addiction, discouragement, fatigue, anger, hatred, laziness, and the struggle between good and evil.

Everything in our lives should be seen in relation to this path and embraced or rejected accordingly. It may seem simple. It may seem oversimplified. Genius is the ability to capture complexity with a simple vision. Simplicity is the key to perfection. Embrace this simple vision and it will help you unveil and celebrate your genius.

The shape, form, and content of our lives are determined by our decisions. Some of our decisions are small, while others are large. Yet to some extent, each decision impacts not only what we do, but also who we become.

Life comes down to a series of choices and decisions. We find ourselves constantly at a crossroads.

There are a thousand possible paths. You must decide which path is best for you. It is not a decision that you must make today. Take the time necessary to become familiar with your legitimate needs, deepest desires, and talents. Start to make the small decisions of your day-to-day life in alignment with your essential purpose. By honoring the meaning and purpose of your life in the small things, you will discover that the larger questions looming in your life become clearer and clearer.

⚭ ⚭ ⚭

Happiness eludes all those who seek it for its own sake. True happiness is the by-product of the journey.

In our earlier examination of the happiness paradox, we explored each of the four aspects of the human person—physical, emotional, intellectual, and spiritual—and the activities in each of those areas that caused us to experience happiness.

What do all the things that cause us to experience a true and lasting happiness have in common? They all assist us in our quest to fulfill the purpose of our lives. They are all activities that help us along the path toward the-best-version-of-ourselves.

When you eat well and exercise regularly, how do you feel? You feel more fully alive. You feel healthier. You have more energy. You feel fantastic. What is happening to make you feel that way? Not just the activity of eating well and exercising, but activity with meaning. Activity empowered by purpose. When you are eating well and exercising regularly, physically you are becoming a-better-version-of-yourself. You are moving along the path from point A toward point B.

When you fall in love, or when you give priority to your existing relationships by investing some carefree timelessness in them, how do you feel? Amazing, energized, inspired, moved, capable of anything. What is happening to make you feel that way? You have engaged your essential purpose and are moving from point A toward point B. You are making the journey. Your ability to love is increasing, and your ability to be loved is increasing. Your heart is expanding its capacities. You begin to think of another person before yourself. Emotionally, you are growing, changing, developing—becoming the-best-version-of-yourself.

When you read a great book and discover dynamic ideas and ancient truths, how do you feel? More mentally vital, more vibrant, more alert. Why? Your mind is expanding. Intellectually, you are growing, changing, developing—becoming the better person you know you can be.

When you have a spiritual encounter or experience, how do

you feel? As though the whole world could fall apart and it - wouldn't matter. Why? Your spirit is expanding and you are beginning to see things with proper perspective and priority. Spiritually, you are growing, changing, developing—becoming the better person you know you can be.

This journey is life.

Happiness is merely a by-product of the journey.

Dedicate yourself to the journey. Develop a strong, uncompromising commitment to becoming the-best-version-of-yourself. Make the decisions of your life with that purpose and goal in mind.

Take time each day to visualize that person you are capable of becoming. If you cannot visualize the better person you wish to become, you cannot become that better person. The more specific your visualization, the faster and more effectively you will be transformed into that better version of yourself. Visualize particular ways of acting in certain situations. Imagine a situation with a particular person where you are normally impatient. Visualize the perfect way to respond to that person, over and over again in the empty moments of the day, and before too long you will begin to respond to that person in the way you have imagined.

All great change is first an idea in our minds. The first expression of every great achievement in history has been in the wonder of the imagination. Visualize the changes you wish to achieve.

If you do not, you will not.

Philosophers hold that the being of something changeable consists not only of what it is, but also of what it still can be—that is, its potential. So, in the philosophical sense of being, as a person you consist not only of who you are now, but also of who you are capable of becoming at any moment in the future. It is the vision of the potential within us that leads us to become the-best-version-of-ourselves.

Recognize your potential. You already have everything within you that you need to make this journey.

Life is choices. Choose the-best-version-of-yourself in each moment.

Choose happiness.

THE ENEMY OF
EXCELLENCE: MINIMALISM

❦

Very often our old habits get in the way and, to a certain extent, can prevent us from choosing happiness. These habits may manifest as eating too much, drinking too much, watching television instead of exercising, hanging out with the wrong crowd, or any number of behaviors that cause us to become a-lesser-version-of-ourselves. But they all begin as habits of the mind. If we want our lives to change, we must first examine and alter our mind habits.

One of the greatest obstacles in the modern psyche to achieving our dreams, becoming the-best-version-of-ourselves, and embracing our destiny is minimalism. Consciously or subconsciously, the minimalist is always asking, "What is the least I can do?" Minimalism is a mind-set, a habit of the mind that can affect any area of our lives.

The litany of the minimalist is never ending.

What is the least I can do and still keep my job? What is the least I can do and still get reasonable grades in school? What is the least I can do and stay physically fit? What is the least I can do and raise my children? What is the least I can do and keep my spouse from nagging me? What is the least I can do and still get to heaven?

The minimalist wants the fruit of a certain toil but does not want to toil.

Minimalism breeds mediocrity. It is the destroyer of passion. Minimalism is one of the greatest character diseases of our time. It is the enemy of excellence and a cancer on society. The problem is, culturally we encourage minimalism.

Our education systems foster, encourage, and reward this attitude. The final exam is the main test of what a student has or has not learned. This allows, if not encourages, students to cram knowledge into their minds for an exam, knowledge they will almost immediately forget once the exam has ended. If you pass, you move on; if you fail, you must repeat the process. At the end of the course, you receive a piece of paper—the reward.

The word *education* comes from the Latin word *educare,* which means "to draw out." We do not teach our children the love of learning. We do not hold knowledge before them as a powerful tool for personal development.

We don't produce broadly educated, well-rounded leaders for tomorrow. We teach more and more about less and less. We don't draw out the individual. We impose upon the individual—systems and structures. We don't reverence individuality, we don't treasure it, we stifle it and try to stamp it out. We don't educate, we formulate. We abandon the individual in his or her own need and uniqueness and "impose" the same upon all.

We provide an education in specialization. We produce clones for the modern world. We throw people into a mold, which we call an education system, to form cogs for the global economic wheel, all the time dangling the golden carrot before them as incentive and reason.

Truth be told, our modern education systems crush the very spirit they claim to instill.

We need to return to the ancient Greek ideal of educating the whole person and crown that ideal with our modern understanding of spirituality, as we strive to nurture every aspect of the human person—physical, emotional, intellectual, and spiritual.

Minimalism is born from a lack of passion for the things we do. Wherever you find people doing things that they are not passionate about, you will find minimalism.

Our legal systems and our modern interpretation of law are another prime example. Today, people tend to interpret the law such that they consider whatever they can get away with as right and whatever they cannot get away with as wrong (in many cases perhaps not even wrong—just "against the law," or inconvenient).

Speeding is a prime example. The speed limit is fifty-five miles per hour, but you know that the police will not stop you unless you are doing more than sixty-four miles per hour.

The law obliges us only to the minimum. The problem is that obliging people only to the minimum breeds minimalism. And once in our system, this diseased mind-set creeps into other areas of our lives, takes a grip on our character, and significantly affects our work and our relationships.

The effects of minimalism are many. Minimalism eats away at the character of a person, and therefore society, just as a disease eats away at the body one cell at a time. The minimalist suffers from dreadfully low self-esteem. His low self-esteem is not the result of failure, but the consequence of not even trying. The minimalist - doesn't strive to excel; he strives to survive. The minimalist forgets that it takes just as much energy to avoid excellence as it does to achieve excellence. A person gripped by the mind-set of minimalism becomes very self-seeking and contributes little to the common good of his community or society. The minimalist quickly becomes unfulfilled and miserable, but with no plan to change, he goes on, minimally, doing what he has always done and spreading the dissatisfaction and misery that he has created for himself to everyone he meets. The minimalist just goes through the motions. He is a prisoner and victim of the day-to-day drudgery that stifles the greatness of the human spirit.

The truth is that we probably all suffer from minimalism in one form or another. To larger and lesser extents, we are all minimalists in different areas of our lives. It is good that we are able to recognize this, because minimalism is like a cancer: it spreads. The good news is, there is a cure for minimalism.

In every age there has been a group of people who have escaped this diseased mind-set and risen above minimalism. These people are successful in many different walks of life. They are achievers. They got the job done. They are leaders, heroes, legends, champions, and saints. They didn't ask themselves, "What is the least I can do?" and then proceed to lead dispassionate, boring lives of misery and dissatisfaction. Rather, they asked themselves, "What is the most I can do?" With the vision inspired by this question, they then set out to do the most they could. Not merely activity, but activity driven by a deep sense of purpose. They did the most they could to the best of their abilities in a single lifetime.

When we look at their lives, we find men and women who had a commitment to excellence. They knew how to dream, and they were not afraid to dream the big dreams. They were filled with courage, and that courage was born from knowing who they were and why they were here. There was boldness and brilliance in the way they lived their lives. As we look on as spectators, we are continually amazed by the passion, enthusiasm, energy, and excitement they filled their lives with. Their achievements are so many that they can only be summarized. And the greatness of these achievements will never be fully known to us—or them—for the effects of their vision and goodness continue to impact the lives of people every day.

Do not ask, "What is the least I can do?"; rather, in every situation, ask yourself, "What is the most I can do?" If you are willing, this one question will introduce you to your better self and change your life forever.

Somewhere right now, someone is training for the next Olympic games. Can you imagine an Olympic athlete asking herself, "What is the least I can do and still win the gold medal?" Champions don't take shortcuts. Champions give everything they have to training, preparation, and competition. That is what makes them champions. On the day of competition, the day that really counts, every shortcut taken in training comes to haunt the athlete.

Your character is your destiny. Building character is a task only for the brave and dedicated. There are no shortcuts when it comes to building character. If you wish to cure minimalism in your own life, to develop a complete commitment to excellence and an absolute rejection of mediocrity, the question you need to start asking yourself is, "What is the most I can do?"

Give this question a permanent place in your inner dialogue, and you will be well on the way to achieving your dreams and becoming the-best-version-of-yourself.

ARE YOU FREE?

Histsory has taught us that the one thing men and women of every place and time have always been willing to fight for, and indeed die for, is freedom. Freedom is the cornerstone of all great nations. Freedom is the pinnacle of spirituality. And freedom is the most basic and essential human right.

While at this time in history there appears to be no military threat to our freedom, I believe it is crucially important for us to reassess what makes us free.

What is freedom? What does it mean to be free? This is one of my favorite topics when I speak in high schools. I begin by posing the question to the students, and one inevitably replies, "Freedom is when you can do whatever you want, wherever you want, whenever you want, without your parents or teachers telling you to do otherwise."

Consciously or subconsciously, this is how most people view the concept of freedom in the world today. Freedom is viewed as the power, the strength, or merely the convenience to choose. This notion is false.

Freedom is not simply the circumstances that allow you to do whatever you want. Freedom is not only the opportunity to choose. Freedom is the strength of character to choose and to do what is right. With that in mind, ours is not an age of freedom, but an age of slavery. It is subtle, but it is real. The foundation of freedom is not power or choice. Freedom is upheld not by men and women in government, but by people who govern themselves.

Self-discipline is the foundation of freedom. This self-discipline, this mastery of self, is acquired only by the practice of self-denial and is acquired always from within. Discipline can never be imposed upon a person; it must emerge from within a person. Self-discipline is the foundation of greatness, achievement, success, heroism, leadership, sanctity, and vibrant and flourishing communities and nations. There is no liberty where there is no self-discipline.

Speaking in an interview about discipline, Julie Andrews commented, "Some people regard discipline as a chore. For me, it is a kind of order that sets me free to fly."

If you examine the lives of men and women who have achieved little or nothing with their lives, people who are miserable, mean, and dispassionate, you will discover that it was not other people who destroyed their lives. Destruction always comes from within. It is true for a nation, and it is true for people.

In 1838, with a prophetic voice, Abraham Lincoln said, "At what point is the approach of danger to be expected? I answer, if it ever reach us, it must spring up amongst us. It cannot come from abroad. If destruction be our lot, we ourselves must be its author and finisher. As a nation of free men, we must live through all times, or die by suicide."

On another occasion Lincoln said, "Our defense is in the preservation of the spirit which prizes liberty as the heritage of all men, in all lands, everywhere. Destroy this spirit, and you have planted the seeds of despotism around your own doors." In the later part of the twentieth century, we "planted the seeds of despotism" around our own doors with one creed, message, and motto: "If it feels good, do it."

In a day and age where there is little real threat of our freedom being attacked by foreign forces, we have become slaves. The threat is not foreign, but local. Internal. We have become our own worst enemies. The people of these modern times have become slaves to alcohol, drugs, food, pornography, gambling, sex, violence, shopping . . . Our slavery is the result of a complex of addictions that we often refuse to acknowledge or challenge. These addictions attack and take over not only our bodies, but also our minds, hearts, spirits, and checkbooks.

Addiction is the enemy of self-discipline. Addiction is the enemy of freedom. Addiction robs us of self-discipline, freedom, and indeed our very dignity.

During the last five years, I have had the opportunity to travel all over the world and to experience dozens of different cultures. But my fascination lies with the United States. I am continually amazed as I witness the influence that America exercises culturally, economically, politically, and socially in almost every nation.

The foundation of this nation we call America is the simple yet practically complex notion of "liberty for all." Freedom!

Never was a nation founded on ideals and principles as pure as those the founding fathers laid down for this great nation. They envisioned a land where men and women could live together in harmony and peace. They imagined a prosperous land, one where the people would help and encourage one another to lead good lives in service of the common good. A land where people would rather help you up than pull you down, a land where men and women could pursue their dreams. They had in mind a nation governed by men and women from all walks of life, with different views, but dedicated to their common purpose of affirming the highest values of the human spirit. Has their vision been realized? Has their dream been forgotten?

Mottoes and philosophies such as "If it feels good, do it" and "To each his own" are destroying the founding fathers' vision and robbing us of our freedom. Such philosophies lead us to have one more beer or one more shot—because it feels good. These attitudes lead us to cheat on our wives, even if it is her best friend— because it feels good. Then, before you know it, children start walking into classrooms and shooting their teachers and classmates—because it feels good. After a while, our children are hungry and have holes in their shoes—because the thrill of gambling feels good. And it goes on, and on, and on, reaching into every corner of our lives and our society.

Where did it all start? Where did we get lost? What went wrong? How do we make it right? The foundation of great nations is freedom. The foundation of freedom is not strength, but character. The foundation of character is discipline.

The moral decay of our modern Western culture began when we put aside self-discipline, when we stopped expecting it of ourselves, and when we failed the tests of friendship, parenthood, and leadership and stopped expecting it of the people around us.

Our lives and times are plagued and characterized by innumerable addictions. We are addicted, and inasmuch as we are addicted, we are slaves.

The human spirit has extraordinary abilities and was created to soar. There is nothing more devastating than the stifling of the human spirit. Addictions take a grip on us from within. They suck the strength from our will and render us useless in any worthwhile cause. People who are enslaved by addiction have a weak will. Their mind is plagued by doubts, fears, and all manner of negative thoughts. They have no self-control and are not capable of taking the initiative. Those who are paralyzed by addiction follow sheepishly wherever the flock leads. And they will do anything to avoid taking a good, long, hard look at themselves.

Quite the opposite is a person who is free. The free man or woman is quietly confident and peaceful. Aware of both his strengths and weaknesses, he seeks self-analysis to improve himself. She is a woman of integrity, and her word is better than a signed contract. His mind is constantly filled with gratitude, appreciation, and all manner of positive thoughts. She is a leader who is prepared to take the initiative. He is a man of character, self-control, and firm will. She lives by bringing happiness to other - people's lives. He has been an addict of one thing or another—

perhaps many addictions have plagued his life—but he has over-come them and now guards carefully against new addictions.

Are you free?

I love chocolate. It's just one of those things that I have to watch in my life, otherwise I can get carried away.

During the months I spent in Austria in 1997, I was sharing a room with a fine young man from Slovakia named Juraj. One af-ternoon, I was resting after an overwhelming morning of classes when he came unexpectedly through the door. I was lying on my bed, reading *To Kill a Mockingbird* and eating a small half-pound bar of chocolate.

I think he had noticed the empty chocolate wrappers around the room in the weeks before that day, and he looked at me and said, "I think you eat too much chocolate." I humored him and admitted that he was probably right. But then he said to me, "Are you free from it?" I looked at him as if to say, "What are you talk-ing about? Relax. It's just chocolate." He saw that thought cross my mind, and he asked again, "Really, are you free from it?" Not waiting for an answer, he then picked up a book from his desk and went back to his class.

I immediately began to think about it. I couldn't answer the question. I didn't know if I was free from chocolate. It had become such a regular part of my life, I couldn't remember the last time I went for more than a couple of days without chocolate. So I de-cided to answer that question in the only way I knew how. I de-cided that beginning the next day, I would not eat any chocolate for one month.

Then it began. The excuses, the crying out of the body, those tormenting urges of the flesh demanding to be satisfied. I lasted about sixty hours before I found myself devouring a small half-pound bar of chocolate.

The next day I resolved to try again. I tried and failed. Tried and failed. Three times I failed. Only on my fourth attempt did I succeed. On my fourth attempt I was able to give up chocolate for more than three months. It was then, and only then, that I knew I was free from chocolate. I knew it was my servant and not my master.

I discovered that chocolate had become a part of my everyday life. In some ways I had even begun to live my life around it. Now it is an occasional joy in my life, and I enjoy it more than I ever did when I was eating a pound at a time as part of my everyday routine. I taste it now. It sounds silly, but back when I was eating chocolate constantly, I don't remember tasting it beyond the first bite.

Those of you who have experienced and overcome an addiction will notice the classic symptoms in my thinking and behavior.

If you think you are addicted to something, there is only one way to find out. They say twenty-eight days is the critical period for breaking addictions. The only way to know if you are free is to say no. Give it up. If you can, you are not addicted. If you cannot go without it, whatever it is for you, then there is a good chance you are addicted.

Aldous Huxley observed, "Addiction is an increasing desire for an act which gives less and less satisfaction."

We all have addictions. Some are much more serious than an addiction to chocolate, but the effect is the same. Addictions weaken the will, which in turn weakens our character, which weakens our ability to achieve and succeed in any area of our lives, and ultimately weakens our ability to choose the-best-version-of-ourselves in the moments of our days. Every area of life is weakened by addiction. Mahatma Gandhi once wrote, "Man cannot do right in one department of life whilst he is occupied in doing wrong in another department. Life is one indivisible whole."

How do we acquire these addictions? Addiction is simply the result of taking the path of least resistance. Too often we live by the mottoes "If it feels good, do it!" and "What is the least I can do?" In doing so, we begin to form certain habits. In forming these habits, we become addicted to certain patterns of behavior that are ultimately self-destructive.

We are creatures of habit. It is simply the way we are made.

The important thing is that once we have recognized this truth about ourselves, we should begin to use this self-knowledge to our advantage. The power of habits can be harnessed to help us to become the-best-version-of-ourselves, or the power of habits can be used to help us become a-second-rate-version-of-ourselves. It's the same power, but how we apply it to our lives can be radically different.

If a child learns to quit every time he is unsuccessful, his character will never bear the jewel of perseverance and he will form the self-destructive habit of quitting. If a person's character is scarred by this trait, what will he achieve in life? Nothing.

On the other hand, if a young girl learns to be patient with her little brother, even though he is slower and clumsier, she will quickly develop the empowering habit of patience. When this girl becomes a woman and comes up against obstacles in her life, her preexisting habitual response will be patient perseverance. If a - person's character is marked with this trait, what will she achieve in life? Great things. We are indeed creatures of habit. And yes . . . we choose our habits.

‿✑ ‿✑ ‿✑

Addictions are acquired by practicing a certain type of behavior often and excessively. Character is acquired by practicing certain types of behavior often and excessively.

We break addictions in the same way we form them. An addiction is a pattern of behavior. It is not enough merely to give up a certain type of self-destructive behavior. That simply does not work. We must crowd them out. In the place of the self-destructive habit, we must plant a self-empowering habit.

Addictions stifle our personal development. They prevent us from changing, growing, and becoming the-best-version-of-ourselves. Deep within you there is a very strong desire to become your best self, and living out of that desire is the key. Desire is a great motivator. If you can see how overcoming the addiction will give you a richer, fuller life, and constantly remind yourself of this fact, your desire for a richer, fuller life will become greater than your desire for the addictive behavior.

As always, we must live with the path in mind. The journey from point A to point B shows us clearly that any addiction we have in our lives is going to become an obstacle that will keep us from fulfilling our essential purpose.

Once we are convinced that our addictions are going to stop us from becoming the-best-version-of-ourselves, we need a strategy. There has been no strategy for overcoming addictions more successful than the 12-step program of Alcoholics Anonymous. Although it is not a guide to overcoming and recovering from all types of addictions, it gives us an idea of the type of strategy needed to overcome any addiction in our lives. The program was developed by two alcoholics in the United States and is unquestionably the most successful approach for treating addictions in history. The program began simply as the story of these two men and their struggle to overcome their addiction to alcohol. Beyond that, they pinpointed the ways they deceived themselves and others and formulated twelve steps to help other alcoholics recognize and overcome their self-destructive dependency on alcohol. It is an example of how powerful our stories can be, to ourselves and to others. The story of AA has empowered millions of men and women to wrest their lives back from the haunting powers of addiction.

The program is centered on the following twelve steps, but it is dependent upon the recovering alcoholics who continue to share their own stories every day in thousands of cities around the world.

STEP ONE

We admitted we were powerless over alcohol—that our lives had become unmanageable.

STEP TWO

Came to believe that a Power greater than ourselves could restore us to sanity.

STEP THREE

Made a decision to turn our will and our lives over to the care of God, as we understood Him.

STEP FOUR

Made a searching and fearless moral inventory of ourselves.

STEP FIVE

Admitted to God, to ourselves, and to another human being the exact nature of our wrongs.

STEP SIX

Were entirely ready to have God remove all these defects of character.

STEP SEVEN

Humbly asked Him to remove our shortcomings.

STEP EIGHT

Made a list of all persons we had harmed, and became willing to make amends to them all.

STEP NINE

Made direct amends to such people wherever possible, except when to do so would injure them or others.

STEP TEN

Continued to take personal inventory and when we were wrong promptly admitted it.

STEP ELEVEN

Sought through prayer and meditation to improve our conscious contact with God as we understood Him, praying only for knowledge of His will for us and the power to carry that out.

STEP TWELVE

Having had a spiritual awakening as a result of these steps, we tried to carry this message to alcoholics, and to practice these principles in all our affairs.

Addiction is not confined to areas such as alcohol, drugs, and gambling. The truth is, we all have addictions. Some of our addictions are large and serious problems; others are small and more minor issues. But whatever the addiction, the effect is the same. The great Spanish mystic and monk John of the Cross wrote: "Whether a bird is held by a chain or a thread, still it cannot fly."

Addictions drain us of our willpower and tend to make cowards of us. Some people are addicted to having the remote control in their hand when they are watching television. Take it from them, and their reaction will have addiction written all over it. Some people cannot survive, they think, without coffee first thing in the morning. Others are addicted to having everything in their house, office, and car exactly in the right place and perfectly tidy. Others are addicted to cigarettes. The point is, we all have addictions. We all have habits that enslave us. There are areas in our lives that have become *out of control.* Areas in our lives where external realities or illusions determine how we act or what we do. We all have areas of our lives where we are not masters of ourselves.

In the beginning, we form our habits. After a while, they begin to form us. If we do not conquer our bad habits, sooner or later they conquer us. What areas of your life have become out of control? From time to time, we all have to wrestle with different things. What are you wrestling with? You had better get rid of it, or it is going to get rid of you. That is the very nature of addiction. You are not wrestling for a can of beer or a piece of chocolate; you are wrestling for your very self.

It would be convenient if we could isolate our addictions to one area of our lives, but they will not be contained. Born in our minds, addictions spread through our minds to every area of our lives. They deprive us of our well-being and rob us of our personal freedom. Addictions are a serious drain on our efficiency and effectiveness. They cloud our judgment, cause us to lose sight of our essential purpose, and hold us back from becoming the-best-version-of-ourselves.

All true spirituality seeks to free us from any type of slavery that prevents us from moving along the path and becoming a more loving and lovable person. A valuable exercise to make a regular part of our prayer, reflection, and self-analysis is to seek out and identify areas of addiction and slavery in our lives. They will not go away simply by ignoring them. Every day they will become more powerful until we confront them.

Nothing compares to the freedom of being able to choose the-best-version-of-yourself in the moments of the day. I want that freedom in all things. It is a liberation that nobody can ever take from you. It is the freedom to choose what is good, true, noble, beautiful, and right. I find myself agreeing with Charles Dickens when he wrote, "I only ask to be free. The butterflies are free."

FOLLOW YOUR STAR

I have always been fascinated with the story in the Bible about the Magi following the star. For years I have spent hours reading and reflecting upon this story, because I believe it teaches us a lot about what makes certain people successful.

It is first of all important to acknowledge that it was not the chief priests, or even the high priest of that year, who recognized the signs that accompanied the coming of Jesus. It was, rather, the three simple Magi. The star rose in the east, and they fixed their gaze upon the star and followed it with unwavering persistence.

One Christmas a couple of years back, I was driving past a church on the East Coast of America and outside was one of those message boards. It read, "Wise men still seek Jesus today." That simple message had an impact on me and renewed my interest in the story. My reflection leads me to ask these questions: "What was the difference between the Magi and everybody else on the planet at the time that Jesus made his entrance into the world?" "What was the difference between the three wise men and the chief priests?"

When someone shares a remarkable insight or a rare piece of knowledge, you will sometimes hear people say, "Oh, isn't she wise!" Yet there is an enormous difference between knowledge and wisdom. The chief priests had knowledge. They knew everything there was to know about the coming Messiah. They could have recited every passage from their sacred scriptures that related to the coming of the Messiah, including the place of his birth. The Magi - didn't have anywhere near as much knowledge as the chief priests did regarding the coming of the Christ, but what they did know they lived by. Therein lay the key to wisdom, and that is why we call the Magi "the wise men" and the chief priests "the chief priests."

Wisdom is not the amassing of knowledge. Wisdom is truth lived.

പ പ പ

The Bible doesn't tell us how old the Magi were. Nor are we told how long they had been following the star. In fact, contrary to popular opinion, the scriptures do not even state that there were three of them. We all have a star to follow in our lives. Some of us follow it from a very young age, and others take a few years to recognize the star in the sky of their lives. And yet, one thing is certain: It takes time to develop the understanding and awareness necessary to recognize your star when it rises. The Magi had probably been waiting and preparing for many years.

The first lesson in finding and following your own star is patience. Many people lose their chance at greatness by chasing after the first star that rises. We should wait and prepare patiently for *our* star to rise. It will not rise early. It will not rise late. It will rise in the fullness of time—at the most appropriate moment. You need not worry that you will not be ready. It will not rise until you are. You need not fear that you will miss it or fail to recognize it. It is looking for you even more than you are looking for it. It will help you to fulfill the purpose of your existence, and your whole life is leading you toward it.

As you wait for your star to rise, there is much preparation to be done. Dreams come true when opportunity and preparation meet. Now is your time to prepare. Do not say, "I am too old." Do not say, "I am too young." Now is your time to prepare. You are where you are right now for a reason, reading what you are reading right now for a reason.

During this time of preparation, you must search your heart

and become intimately aware of your legitimate needs, your deepest desires, and your talents. When your star does rise, you will know it is your star because you will have a burning desire to follow that star—not on a whim, but through careful consideration. In following that star, you will put your talents to use for the service of others and for your own fulfillment and satisfaction. This employment of your talents will lead to the fulfillment of all your legitimate needs—physical, emotional, intellectual, and spiritual—and help others to fulfill their legitimate needs. Follow your star and it will lead you to the-best-version-of-yourself.

∾ ∾ ∾

Since my teenage years, I have been fascinated with famous and extraordinary people—great achievers in all walks of life. I love to watch them being interviewed. I love to watch footage of their day-to-day lives. One thing that has always struck me, and I do not consider it in the slightest way to be coincidental, is that great men and women always believed that they were destined to be great. From this day on, begin to foster a belief that you were born for a reason, and although you may not have yet discovered the specifics of that reason, you are being prepared to fulfill it in every moment.

In general terms, you know that your essential purpose is to grow, change, develop, and become the-best-version-of-yourself. The details are simply that, the details. It is this process of growth that makes life interesting, exciting, rewarding, and fulfilling. Dedication to this process of growth is greatness. Greatness should never be confused with fame, fortune, status, or power. These are only passing illusions. Greatness is to become more fully your self with each passing day.

A chance for greatness awaits you—your own chance at greatness—and it will involve the unique and providential blend of your needs, talents, and desires. The pursuit of your chance at greatness will reveal you to your family, friends, colleagues, spouse, children, and everyone who crosses your path. It is the attuning of your personality. Life is a revelation of self. Life is an unfolding story. Your life is your story. Life is a gift to you and for you—and yet, in a paradoxical but complementary way, it is also your chance to serve your neighbor, to touch and enrich the lives of others, and to make a difference in this sometimes weary world. This is the mystery of God—to lead you toward your perfection and fulfillment, while at the same time using your journey to lead others toward their perfection and fulfillment.

∞ ∞ ∞

We must each learn to trust that we are here for a reason and that, no doubt whether we are aware of it or not, things are unfolding just as they should be. The right circumstances will emerge. I prefer to think of them as opportunities. The right opportunities will emerge. The most unexpected circumstances often hatch opportunities that enable us to follow our star. The circumstances of our lives perfectly and providentially prepare us to become the-best-version-of-ourselves. Charlie Chaplin is a great example.

CHARLIE CHAPLIN

Charlie Chaplin was born to a very poor family in London in 1889. While Charlie was still a child his father left his mother, which only exaggerated their poverty. Mrs. Chaplin couldn't find work, couldn't pay the rent, and couldn't afford fuel to heat their small apartment, and most nights Charlie and his brother ate fish-head soup—nothing but the heads of fish in warm water with a little bread. Miserable circumstances, I'm sure you'd agree. But from that misery was born one of the greatest talents humanity has ever known.

Chaplin developed his humor and comedy to rise above the depressing circumstances of his childhood. He put together all types of acts to make his mother and brother laugh. He later recalled wanting to make them laugh so much that they would forget how desperately hungry they were.

By 1918, Charlie Chaplin was twenty-nine years old and indisputably the most famous man in the world. He continued to write and direct until his death in Vevey, Switzerland, on Christmas Day in 1977. Over a lifetime he wrote and directed eighty-one films, founded his own studios in California, and made more people laugh than anyone else in history. Charlie Chaplin is a legend. His path was not an easy one, but he followed his star. The circumstances of his childhood prepared him to recognize the star when it rose, and rise it did.

∾ ∾ ∾

Following your star is about discovering who you are and what you are capable of. Following your star is about learning to be yourself. You must be prepared to dare to be different in a world where uniformity is safe and rewarded. Search yourself. Discover something deep within that is yours and no one else's.

Uncover your uniqueness. Your chance at greatness is intrinsically linked to being yourself. Become a champion of selfhood and you will meet with unimagined success.

Everyone is good at something. We all have talents and abilities that are unique and different. These gifts are the key to great happiness in our lives and on occasion are leading indicators in the search to discover our vocation or mission in life. But first we must seek out these gifts and talents. So often people say to me, "But I am not good at anything." This I cannot believe. I can believe, however, that a person has not yet found that one area in which he or she has a special gift.

Frustration and the sense of failure tend to follow us wherever we go until we find our own area in which to work, our own gift to develop, our own niche, our genius. Don't despair. Have a little faith. It can take some time, but the active search brings a sense of fulfillment in the interim. It is only when we give up the search, believing that we will never find that special talent or that we simply do not possess one, that frustration and depression take hold of us.

Hold firm. The search is noble. Avoiding the search is cowardice. Sometimes we think we have found that special talent and what we have found is only a stepping-stone.

Ten years ago, I was studying at university in Australia toward a degree in business with a major in marketing. I thought I had found my gift. I was wrong. It was just a stepping-stone. My true gift, I now believe, is my speaking and my writing. Was the time I spent studying business a waste of time? Absolutely not. I can clearly see the hand of God in that part of my life. In many indirect ways, God was preparing me then for what I am doing now. In the future I may discover that this is just another stepping-stone to something else, somewhere else.

George Washington was first a surveyor. For many years, Norman Vincent Peale was a newspaperman. Garth Brooks wasn't always a musician. Peter was first a fisherman, Matthew a tax collector. Sting was first a schoolteacher. Harrison Ford was a carpenter. Before Somerset Maugham began writing, he graduated from medical school. John Denver worked for an insurance company before embarking on his journey to become an internationally acclaimed entertainer and songwriter.

As you seek out your dominant talent, your genius, it is important to remember that everyone wasn't born to be in the spotlight. Here are two of this century's greatest examples.

BRIAN WHO?

Have you ever heard of Brian Epstein? Have you ever heard of the Beatles?

At lunchtime on November 9, 1961, Brian Epstein walked

into a dark, crowded, smoky club in his hometown of Liverpool, England. The club was called the Cavern, and Epstein had gone there to hear a local group, four young men who called themselves the Beatles.

At that time, Brian Epstein managed and operated a small record store, which his father owned. His curiosity was piqued when in one day six people came in asking for a record by the Beatles. When he tried to order the record, Epstein discovered that no such record existed. This is what drew him to the Cavern.

Two weeks later, Epstein offered to manage the Beatles. He confessed to them that he had no experience, but that he truly believed they had what it took to be "the next big thing." The Beatles agreed to let Epstein manage them despite his lack of experience. John Lennon later recalled, "We had nothing to lose, we had already been turned down by every major recording label in the country. Brian was enthusiastic about our music and about our future. All we wanted to do was play music. We had everything to gain and nothing to lose."

For the next seven months, Brian Epstein went knocking on doors in London, playing the demo tape for every recording company he could get to listen. They all said the same things: "These boys will never make it" or "It just won't work" or "Their sound is just too different." Epstein's reply to each of them was the same: "These boys are going to be bigger than Elvis." The record executives just laughed at him. At the time, this was an altogether absurd claim. Elvis was at the peak of his popularity, and a British group - hadn't made it big in America for years.

It wasn't until June 1962 that Epstein finally broke through. The Beatles recorded their first session at EMI studios in London—two songs, "Love Me Do" and "P.S. I Love You."

The Beatles's first British record was released on September 11, 1962, and entered the charts forty-eight hours later at number forty-nine. It peaked after two weeks at number seventeen, and the Beatles had their first top twenty hit with "Please Please Me."

The door was open, and within twelve months they had a record succession of British number one hits. From there they took Europe by storm, and in no time word spread to Asia, America, and Australia as anticipation of their world tour began to build.

The Beatles came to the United States for the first time on February 7, 1964, and although by that time they had reached a certain level of fame in Europe, nothing could have prepared them for what was about to happen. When those four young men stepped off the plane on that early February morning, there were ten thousand screaming fans at New York's John F. Kennedy Airport to meet them. Whether they were aware of it or not, their lives changed forever that day.

By May of that same year, the Beatles had become a worldwide phenomenon, like nothing any of us will ever see again. And yes, they had become bigger than Elvis.

The absurd had become a reality. When their fifth record, - "Can't Buy Me Love," was released in America, it went immediately into the number one position on the charts, topping five other Beatles's records that were occupying the first five places on the charts. Are we ever again likely to see a group occupy the first six places on a *Billboard* chart?

Who was Brian Epstein? He was the man of insight, passion, courage, vision, integrity, fortitude, and marketing genius—the friend, manager, uniting force, and tireless worker who made the Beatles the worldwide phenomenon that they were and the historical legends that they will always remain.

Brian Epstein believed that those four young men had something incredibly unique and special, and because of his belief the world came to know the Beatles.

Perhaps your talent is to help others find and share their talents.

THE IMG STORY

Today, sports agents, endorsements, and sports management are all a big thing, but it wasn't always so. In fact, forty years ago they - didn't even exist. What changed to bring about this whole culture of sporting celebrities, sports agents, and incredible endorsements? Let me tell you, all of this is the result of one man following his personal star.

In 1960, Mark McCormack was a reasonably successful marketing executive in Cleveland. In November of that same year, he saw a young man play golf in a way he had never seen anyone play. It wasn't just his swing, and it wasn't just the way he struck the ball, it was everything. And not the least of it was this young man's personality. McCormack looked into this young golfer's eyes and he saw the potential for greatness.

On that day, Mark McCormack saw a way he could help this young golfer, and at the same time he saw his own star rising. He had a vision. No more than a dream. He saw something that was not yet, but that could be. Some people said McCormack's vision was impossible. McCormack said it was inevitable. He approached the young golfer and inquired as to whether or not he had a manager. The golfer told him that no such person existed in his life, and McCormack offered to fill the gap.

Filling gaps has made more people successful and wealthy than anything else. You could call it freak luck or mere chance, but I prefer to think of it as preparation meeting opportunity.

The young golfer's name was Arnold Palmer. He became Mark McCormack's first client. That day, the concept and organization now known as International Management Group, or IMG, was founded. IMG's first three clients were Arnold Palmer, Gary Player, and Jack Nicklaus. These three golfers began to win everything in sight and in time became the famous "Big Three."

Today, IMG has offices in sixty countries, more than two thousand employees, and a client list that includes Pete Sampras, Joe Montana, Wayne Gretzky, supermodels Niki Taylor and Tyra Banks, Formula One driver Michael Schumacher, Itzhak Perlman, Michael Johnson, Andre Agassi, Nick Faldo, and more than one-third of the top thirty golfers in the world.

For thirty consecutive years, IMG's first client, Arnold Palmer, was the highest-grossing athlete in the world in terms of income from endorsements. Only in 1991, at age sixty-four, was he surpassed by Michael Jordan. Arnold Palmer still ranked second until the late 1990s, when Tiger Woods overtook him.

It all began with one man following his star.

It takes a little time sometimes to find that one ability and talent that makes you unique. Don't give up your search.

∾ ∾ ∾

We must each follow our own star in our own way at our own time. It helps me to read the stories of other great men and women. It is the stories of the leaders, heroes, legends, champions, and saints that taught me to wait patiently for my star and continue to teach me to pursue it with unrelenting dedication.

If you have heard me speak, you know of my great love for stories. There is something very powerful about stories—each listener hears something different according to his or her own place on the journey.

Stories help us discover who we are and who we can be. Stories are important. To poison a person, poison the stories you tell him. To demoralize a person, tell her demoralizing stories. You will always be as confident and healthy as the stories you read, listen to, and tell yourself. We become the stories we listen to, read, and tell. That is the power of a story.

Conrad Hilton, founder of the Hilton Hotel empire, used to tell this story.

A very poor Greek man once applied for a job as a janitor in a bank in Athens. "Can you write?" demanded the discriminating head of employment.

"Only my name," said the fellow.

He didn't get the job—so he borrowed the money required to travel steerage to the United States and followed his dreams to the "land of opportunity."

Many years later, an important Greek businessman held a press conference in his beautiful Wall Street offices. At the conclusion, an enterprising reporter said, "One day you should write your memoirs."

The gentleman smiled. "Impossible," he said. "I cannot write."

The reporter was astounded. "Just think," he remarked, "how much further you would have gone if you could write."

The Greek shook his head and said, "If I could write, I'd be a janitor."

∽ ∽ ∽

Follow your star. Wait for it to rise, and while you are waiting, prepare yourself. Become intimately familiar with your needs, talents, and desires. Remember, circumstances, whether they appear to be good or bad, are opportunities. When you see a star rise on the horizon of your life, and you are filled with a burning desire to follow it, and you perceive that by following it you will use your talents and fulfill your legitimate needs—follow it.

Once you begin to follow it, let nothing distract you from it.

Every leader, hero, legend, champion, and saint in history has followed his or her personal star; by doing so, these people grasped their chance at greatness—and left those around them awe inspired and amazed.

CELEBRATING YOUR UNIQUE SELF

There is only one you. It may sound a little absurd, but it is true. Most people spend their whole lives running away from themselves or hiding themselves from others. I believe that life should be a process of self-revelation. As we live, we reveal ourselves to the people we love and to the people who cross our path as we make our journey. We can put up barriers and put on masks, or we can let people see us as we really are.

What concerns us about the latter is that others might see our faults. In our concern, we forget that we all have faults. The people who are able to love and admire us have faults and flaws. The people who criticize and express anger and hatred toward us have flaws and failings. As human beings, one of our common bonds is our brokenness. It is a great wisdom to be able to see yourself in other people. It is this insight that empowers us to love everyone, everywhere, at all times, and in all circumstances.

We all want to be loved and accepted. The danger that emerges from this desire is that we may fall into the trap of doing or saying things just to please others. Each time we walk this path, we abandon a portion of our self. There is a part of each of us that is weak and can be bought. There is also a part of each of us that is strong and cannot be bought at any price. Ignore the former and nurture the latter. But most of all, befriend that part of you that cannot be bought at any price, because it will tell you who you are.

In truth, nobody is loved by everybody. Even the greatest men and women in history have critics. Even people who have dedicated themselves and their lives selflessly to assist others have critics and detractors. You are no different. Some people are going to like you, some people are going to love you, some people are not going to like you at all, and some people may even despise you. You might as well be yourself. That way, at least you will know that the people who like you, like you for who you truly are.

෴   ෴   ෴

The great men and women of every age that we have spoken of and will speak of further throughout this book—the legends and saints who fill our history books, the heroes and champions who fill our hearts and minds with inspiration—all listened to the inner voices of need, talent, and desire.

Their greatness was not the result of luck or freak chance. They were not singled out at the beginning of time to be special or favored. They laid the foundation of character and listened to these inner voices. Then with passion, belief, commitment, courage, and perseverance, they followed their star.

Their lives reveal the secrets of love, success, achievement, heroism, leadership, and holiness. It would be a mistake to imitate what one of these men and women did with his or her life. It would be a mistake not to imitate the way they lived their lives. The difference may seem subtle, but it is great. The spirit by which they lived should be imitated, but you have your own path to walk and your own star to follow. Imagine if Beethoven had tried to be another Mozart or if Picasso had tried to be another Michelangelo. What beauty and wonder will you deny the world if you abandon your self?

This section has been an exercise in discovering what possibilities exist for you and me as individuals. Every happiness in life comes from discovering who you are as a unique individual and being true to your own self.

The following is a brief passage from the diary of Dag Hammarskjöld:

"At every moment you choose yourself. But do you choose your *self*? Body and soul contain a thousand possibilities out of which you can build many *I's*. But in only one of them is there a congruence of the elector and the elected. Only one—which you will never find until you have excluded all those superficial and fleeting possibilities of being and doing with which you toy, out of curiosity or wonder or greed, and which hinder you from casting anchor in the experience of the mystery of life, and the consciousness of the talent entrusted to you which is your *I*."

∽ ∽ ∽

Who are you? In many different ways, people try to discover who they truly are as individuals. Some go off into the mountains, some travel to distant lands, others go to monasteries and convents, some walk up and down the beach early each morning, and still others seek to discover themselves through writing or music. I have even heard people use "finding themselves" as an excuse for leaving their husband or wife.

You may try any path you wish. You may try to find yourself in a thousand different ways, but in a wonderfully profound and mysterious way, it is only through self-donation—giving ourselves to others—that we discover our true self.

There is no greater gift than the sincere gift of self. It is the essence of relationship and life. It is not something that I completely understand, nor is it something I can clearly and definitively explain. But at the times in my life when I have been able to summon the strength of character it takes to give of my time, energy, and resources to make a difference in other people's lives—I have experienced an unquenchable sense of fulfillment and happiness.

There is more to life than getting, grabbing, having, and receiving. Life is as much about giving as it is about receiving. Learn to give the one gift that you were born to give—yourself. The meaning of life is mysteriously revealed in this act. There is no faster way to happen upon the purpose of your life than to embrace life's daily opportunities to serve those around you.

Life is an adventure of self-discovery. I hope this book is the beginning of a journey that lasts your whole lifetime. You are different. Not better or worse, just different. You are unique and special. You are a wonder and a marvel. Be all you can be. Be yourself.

In every moment, choose your best self. If you do, you will be choosing happiness for you and for all those you touch in this life. You are the best gift you can give to yourself and to the world.

Celebrate the one life you have by becoming the-best-version-of-yourself.

PART FOUR

DISCOVERING
THE RHYTHM OF LIFE

WHY ARE WE ALL SO BUSY?

B y now, you are perhaps wondering what causes someone to sit down and write a book like this at such a young age.

This book is based upon personal crisis. My own. It is said that a crisis brings out the best in people. They say if it doesn't kill you, it makes you a better person.

It didn't kill me.

I must confess, I am anything but comfortable writing about myself. I think I fear being perceived as prideful or self-important. In my other writings I have tried to avoid it wherever possible, but many of my friends and colleagues have often commented, "You need to give the reader more of Matthew Kelly." In this case, the only way to avoid writing about myself would be not to write—and at the same time, I feel I must write about these things. A little betwixt, I sense that I am writing as much for myself as I am for you.

I grew up in Sydney, Australia, with my brothers: Mark, Simon, Andrew, Brett, Nathan, Bernard, and Hamish. Having seven brothers meant bunk beds, hand-me-down clothes, and never a dull moment. Apart from the fact that I had seven brothers, until I was nineteen I lived what I think could be described as a fairly normal life.

For nineteen years, I had been floating along just fine. Throughout high school I had gathered a handful of close friends, thrived on the sporting field, dated some wonderful girls, held an afternoon job at a drugstore delivering packages to the elderly, and had even grown to quite enjoy my studies. I had also fallen for the classic modern lie—life is about success, and success is the fast car, the big house, the important job, and lots of money. Believing that, I was in college studying toward a degree in marketing, preparing for my ascent to the upper realms of the corporate world. It was at this time that extraordinary things began to take place for me.

All of a sudden, I began to think about life—and death, greed, fear, love, God, society, suffering, forgiveness, history, and particularly whether or not I was put here for any real purpose. Our lives change when we stop merely replying to questions and begin to ask them. I started asking questions.

In no time at all, life started responding to my questions. And as my reflections grew deeper, I noticed that I was beginning to approach everyone and everything in my life differently. I was discovering a sense of the miraculous in the everyday. It was as if I had found some coveted treasure or secret. I felt a fire within me—an intense passion for life and, at the same time, an unshakable peace.

On the outside, little had changed. On the inside, I was developing an exciting new awareness.

Later that same year, an opportunity emerged for me to give a talk to a small group of people at a home in Castle Hill, a suburb of Sydney. It wasn't something that I felt particularly comfortable with, but I had a real desire to share some of the ideas that my soul-searching had given birth to during the preceding months.

Although I was unaware of it at the time, speaking to a handful of people on October 8, 1993, was to become a very significant event. It was one of those events that cause our lives to completely change direction.

The following week I found myself giving four talks, the week after that, six—and it was then that life invited me down unimaginable paths.

I discovered my gift, and my life changed.

Between October 1993 and August 1997, I gave almost seven hundred talks and seminars in forty-one countries to audiences that totaled over 750,000 people. I was twenty-four years old, had published four books in six languages, had a constant barrage of invitations to speak all over the world, was appearing regularly on television and radio programs, and received more than one hundred letters a week from readers and listeners. Publishing companies were clamoring over my books; I had just received my first serious offer to do my own radio show; and I was being courted by two television networks. I was constantly meeting the most extraordinary people, and every opportunity was being laid before me.

It had all happened so quickly.

ى ى ى

On the outside, everything seemed fine. On the inside, I was deeply troubled. I wasn't a sign of contradiction; I was a walking contradiction. The authentic life I aspired to, and wrote and spoke about so passionately, had been lost somewhere along the way.

One Tuesday morning early in August 1997, I woke at about eleven o'clock. I had slept through the alarm and was literally unable to drag myself out of bed. It was not the first time. In fact, for months I had been sleeping for ten, twelve, sometimes fourteen hours a day. I was completely exhausted.

I rolled over and slept until about four o'clock that afternoon.

When I finally did get out of bed, I called the doctor, and over the next several days I went through the physical, emotional, and mental anguish of medical tests. I was then told that there was nothing wrong with me other than the fact that I was suffering from chronic levels of fatigue and exhaustion.

It had been coming for some time. I had seen it coming and ignored it. I suppose I didn't want to admit something was wrong. I was in denial.

My life was a complete mess. Nothing was right. Although I was still constantly hopping from continent to continent, I was now based in America. Everything seemed to bother me, and confusion and chaos were the only regular feelings I could express. I felt overwhelmed. Everything important to me was slipping away, and the people I loved were the very people I was disappointing and hurting. I had never felt more alone. I was miserable. I had lost my roots.

My diet was atrocious, I could count on one hand the number of times I had exercised in the past six months, and my sleeping pattern was appalling.

Physically I was exhausted. Emotionally I was confused and hurting. Intellectually I had lost my bearings. And spiritually I was as dry as the Sahara desert.

The well was empty.

My lifestyle had caught up with me. I was too young to feel this old. I had fallen victim to my own misplaced priorities. I was forced to admit that the general day-to-day structure of my life was fatally flawed.

I had lost the rhythm of life.

∽   ∽   ∽

My doctor suggested a break from speaking, writing, and traveling. He sat me down in his office and gave me a long speech, explaining that he felt I should take at least three months off. Impossible, I thought.

At the time, my schedule was being booked twelve months in advance, my fourth book had just been released, and a very large fall speaking tour had long been planned.

I explained this to the doctor, who told me, with no hesitation and the greatest ease, that I was a fool. "If you don't take time to re-cover now, you could develop problems that will last a lifetime," he said. And he continued, "Matthew, you are only twenty-four, and you can go on speaking and writing for fifty years, but you need to take care of yourself. And right now, that means taking three months off."

That was a turning point in my life. A moment of salvation. In that moment, assisted by some mysterious grace, I got off the merry-go-round that was my life.

᠎᠎᠎᠎᠎᠎᠎᠎᠎᠎ ᠎᠎᠎ ᠎᠎᠎

Two weeks later, in the fall of 1997, I took three months away from my speaking schedule and went to Europe to study. I spent that time in what was once a monastery, in the small village of Gaming, Austria. My experience there became one of reflection, refreshment, and renewal.

In the classroom I was studying German and medieval history. Outside the classroom, I was learning a lot about myself. But my exhaustion and pain continued to haunt me, and I began to won-der whether the intense passion for life that had emerged four years earlier would ever return. I suppose that's what makes a crisis a crisis, the fact that you don't know when it will end, what the outcome will be, or even if it will end.

As the days and weeks passed, my reflections led me to take a good, long, hard look at my lifestyle, the world in which we live, and myself. It was then that I made some discoveries so important that they have changed my approach to life forever—truths I had overlooked my whole life.

The first of these discoveries was my legitimate need. It dawned on me that I am a human being—not a machine that writes books and gives talks—and that I have some basic but legitimate needs. This is not selfish, as I had previously believed. It's life. Some of my legitimate needs are as simple as oxygen to breathe and water to drink. Others are as complex as my need to love and be loved.

Examining the various difficulties and heartaches I was experiencing led me to see that these "legitimate needs" fall into four categories—physical, emotional, intellectual, and spiritual. I also came to realize that when these needs are satisfied, I am necessarily a healthier and happier person.

In this realization, I was now face-to-face with all the flaws in my lifestyle of the previous four years. Many of my legitimate needs had been almost completely neglected. I had fallen into a common trap. My life had gathered a momentum of its own. I was just being carried along. My legitimate needs had never been considered in the creation of that lifestyle. My scheduling was never done with my legitimate needs in mind. How could it be? I wasn't even consciously aware that I had legitimate needs.

Delving into my past, I discovered that the times I had experienced a sense of peace, joy, and fulfillment—and still achieved and excelled—were times when I had a certain consistency and rhythm to my life. They were the times when I had been attentive to my legitimate needs—physically, emotionally, intellectually, and spiritually. At those times, all the major elements of my being were working together in harmony and moving toward a common goal.

As I looked back over the four-year period, I could see that gradually I had allowed the hustle and bustle of the world to distract me, to affect me, to disorient me. It had all happened so subtly that I could not even pinpoint the time when this demise had begun.

What surprised me the most was the cause of the personal crisis I was then experiencing. It was not bad things that had led me to this lonely place of brokenness—but, rather, good things. Good opportunities were destroying me. I always considered an invitation to speak to a group of people as something good. Objectively, of course, it was. But recalling one day when I had traveled from New Orleans to San Francisco to Cleveland in the same day, I learned that too many good opportunities can become a danger-ous situation . . . even when they are opportunities to do good. Es-pecially when they are opportunities to do good.

Good opportunities are very hard to refuse. I also came to real-ize that just because something is good doesn't mean it is good for you or right for you.

For four years I had become increasingly busier doing "good things." So much so that they had become bad for me. They had worn me down to the point of exhaustion, and my schedule pro-vided no opportunity for me to recover. I had adopted a lifestyle that didn't make allowance for my legitimate needs. My exhaus-tion led to confusion, my confusion to frustration, my frustration to poor decisions, my poor decisions to chaos, and this chaos to disappointment.

I discovered that I was going to have to learn to say no—even to good opportunities, even to opportunities to do good.

ᑐ ᑐ ᑐ

During my time in Austria, each afternoon when my classes were finished I would take a walk. Often I would go down to the store in the middle of the village to buy some chocolate. Nothing com-pares to European chocolate. Just beyond the boundaries of the monastery was a small park. In the middle of the park stood one very tall, strong tree.

Each day I would look at this tree and notice that despite its imperfect forms and crooked branches, it had a perfection of its own.

One night there was a fierce storm. For two hours I lay awake in my bed watching the lightning flash across the sky and feeling the thunder crash. The next day when I went walking, there was debris everywhere. The trees around the monastery had lost lots of leaves, huge branches had been torn from others, and some had even been uprooted and pulled from the ground. But in the middle of the park, even though it stood alone, the great tree still stood tall, virtually unaffected by the storm. It had lost some leaves, but no major limbs, and the storm certainly hadn't uprooted it.

I learned many lessons from that tree.

A tree with strong roots grows strong. A tree with strong roots bears much fruit. A tree with strong roots bears good fruit. A tree with strong roots can weather any storm. If a tree is uprooted and replanted often, it will not be able to sink its roots deep into the earth and therefore will not grow strong or be fruitful.

All of this is true not only for a tree, but also for a person.

The tree helped me to see that my physical, emotional, intellectual, and spiritual roots were neither strong nor deep.

∽ ∽ ∽

The crisis didn't last forever, and there was no complex solution to the problems I had been experiencing. Quite the opposite, it was the simple things that restored me to health.

As the days and weeks passed, I dedicated myself to becoming more and more attentive to my legitimate needs. As I did, my withered roots began to grow and I could feel them stretching out and sinking themselves into the rich, moist earth of life. I began to eat regularly, to sleep regularly, to exercise and pray regularly, to study regularly, and I started to make time for rest and relaxation on a regular basis.

Then one day I heard myself laugh again. Really laugh, and I - don't think I had laughed like that in a long time. The restlessness and exhaustion had dissipated. The dissatisfaction and depression had lifted, and I was once again feeling peaceful, happy, energized, excited, and passionate about life.

I started waking up to an old familiar feeling and to thoughts like, "It's good to be alive." When I looked in the mirror, something seemed different. People began to comment, "You are looking really great!" or, "You seem so happy these days!" The color was back in my face, and the sparkle had returned to my eyes. The simplest acts began to bring me the most intense satisfaction. Life was good.

There in the mountains, a couple of hours outside of Vienna, I rediscovered the rhythm of life.

◌◍◌ ◌◍◌ ◌◍◌

When I returned from Austria, I noticed that the difficulties I had experienced over the previous four years were not unique to my life or situation. In fact, I discovered that very few people are not suffering from identical or similar lifestyle problems.

The world is full of men and women who work too much, sleep too little, hardly ever exercise, eat poorly, and are always struggling or failing to find adequate time to spend with their families. We are in a perpetual hurry—constantly rushing from one activity to another, with little understanding of where all this activity is leading us.

Modern parents find themselves in a perpetual rush—hurrying from work to school to day care to baseball to hockey to ballet to the doctor to the supermarket to the mall to church . . . Even college students—living a life of leisure, in the truest sense of the word—are always complaining about how busy they are and the stress and pressure they are under.

The world has gone and got itself in an awful rush, to whose benefit I do not know. We are too busy for our own good. We need to slow down. Our lifestyles are destroying us.

The worst part is, we are rushing east in search of a sunset.

We know this truth, but we don't know what to do about it. More and more demands are made upon us every day. We feel as though our lives have a momentum of their own. This momentum continues to carry us forward at an alarming pace . . . but to where? . . . to what end?

Is all this activity that clutters our lives helping us, or is it hurting us?

We have more money and more choices, but less time. Less time to do the things that nurture well-being and less time to spend with the people who invigorate us.

What we have gained is clear. But what have we lost? Are we aware of the real cost? Have we even begun to measure the real cost?

You cannot measure the cost of everything in dollars and cents.

∽ ∽ ∽

As I reflect on the world in which we live, it isn't any wonder that I fell so blindly into the traps I did.

We live in a world obsessed with noise, speed, and activity. We live in an age plagued by greed, lust, and violence and paralyzed by fear. The climate of our age is seductive. The effects are so gradual that we hardly notice them from day to day, but over time they are dramatic, even devastating.

We live in a troubled time, in many ways an age of confusion and crisis. Not only in a personal sense, but also from a social and cultural perspective. It is my belief that any adequate solutions to the challenges that face us in the world today must be both accessible and applicable to everyone, everywhere, regardless of age, color, creed, or culture. Furthermore, the practicality of these solutions must impact and be deeply intertwined with people's day-to-day living.

My experience and reflection lead me to believe that one of our greatest challenges in the modern world is lifestyle. In today's hectic world, we often push ourselves to the limit—sometimes forgetting that our bodies, hearts, minds, and spirits all need time to refocus and recharge. Striving for a balanced lifestyle—one that enables us to maintain a natural state—will ensure optimum health and well-being.

We need a new way of living. We need a new way of life. Our lifestyles are self-destructive. We need a way of living that brings out the best in us. We need a way of life that honors our legitimate needs. We need a lifestyle that helps us to become the-best-version-of-ourselves.

∽ ∽ ∽

The rhythm of life is a passport to achieving this balance.

The rhythm of life is a way of life. It is a lifestyle that integrates all of our legitimate needs—physically, emotionally, intellectually, and spiritually.

The rhythm of life is the perfect combination of rest, activity, and pace; it ennobles us to become the unique individuals we were created to be, enables us to excel in all we do, and empowers us with a certain clarity of mind and peace of heart.

The rhythm of life is the antidote for our busy age.

I believe life should be lived passionately and that the day-to-day drudgery that stifles the greatness of the human spirit should be avoided at all costs. I do not despise simple daily tasks, but I believe their place is in building us up, not in tearing us down.

As we venture into this new millennium, the challenge life presents to us all is to develop a balance between activity and thought. But, particularly, to fill our lives with action that springs forth from contemplation and an understanding of our essential purpose.

Look at the world. Look at yourself. Look at your lifestyle. Ponder these things. Our chaotic world and complex lives are crying out for a little order and simplicity.

Most people stumble through life believing that one day they will find the pace of life and variety of activity that will create the rhythm of life that is conducive to optimum health, happiness, efficiency, and contentment. They will not. The rhythm of life must be desired and created.

We make a thousand lifestyle choices every day. Those decisions either create or destroy the natural rhythm of life.

Life is not a hundred-meter dash; it's a marathon.

There is more to life than increasing the speed. Faster isn't always better, bigger isn't always better, louder isn't always better. More isn't always the solution. Life is not a competition to see who can collect the most expensive toys. The best things in life are not things—and sometimes less is more.

Find your rhythm . . . and you will flood your life with passion, creativity, and energy.

What Can Creation Teach
Us About Ourselves?

There is a natural rhythm to life. Every element of creation has its own unique rhythm. The seasons have their cycles—the darkness, death, and cold of winter give way to the warmth, joy, and new life of springtime. The universe finds rhythm through time. The darkness gives birth to the light of a new day as the sun rises in the east, and then, at the end of each day, the sunset surrenders us to rest. The waves crash on the beaches and the tides rise and fall, attuned to a rhythm. The whole process of growth, development, and fruition of plants—photosynthesis—is centered on a rhythm. Our hearts beat to a rhythm, pumping our very lifeblood around our bodies. And particularly, rhythm is the key to the powerful role a woman's body plays in reproduction. The rhythm brings forth life. Creation is ordered by rhythm. Rhythm is important.

All the elements of nature were created in harmony. As I ponder the mysterious realities of nature, they remind me of a greater overall plan. I can then appreciate the harmonious workings of the universe as one whole, despite the apparent chaos. I find comfort in the rhythm and harmony of nature. In nature, despite its complexity and vastness, there is rhythm, and the rhythm creates harmony.

If we can discover the rhythm of our own lives, that rhythm will in turn create a harmony and balance that will give birth to a deep and abiding peace. And it is that peace, the fruit of harmony, that allows the highest levels of effective and abundant living.

Perhaps you have heard of the king of ancient times who, so inflated with pride, thought he could hold back the tide simply by commanding it to do so. After all, the tides were part of "his kingdom" and therefore subject to his rule. Late one night, the king gave orders for his throne to be placed at the water's edge during low tide. Early the next morning, the king went to the beach and sat on his throne. Just before sunrise, the people of his kingdom began to crowd the beach. As the sun came up, so did the tide. The king commanded the tide to recede, but his command was ignored. Not willing to have his reputation damaged, the king drowned commanding the tide to recede.

You cannot hold back the tide. Nature has an unmatched strength and persistence. Wisdom is harnessing the strength of our own better nature by working with it. We do this by discovering and adopting the rhythm of life. If only we could develop an understanding of our nature as human beings and harness the power of that nature by working with its strength. It is then that unimaginable achievements would be recognized in our lives.

What great lessons can nature teach us about ourselves? Nature whispers messages to us each and every day: "Great things are achieved little by little. Discover the rhythm of life and align your life with this rhythm. The more you do, the more you will enjoy peace and prosperity."

The truth of this message is displayed all around us in thousands of ways every day. The waves roll onto the shore, washing against the rocks, and erosion occurs. You do not see it with the first wave or with the second or third, but over the years you realize that slowly and steadily the waves are wearing the rock down. Who would think of water as stronger than rock? Persistence has strength.

The rhythm of life is a powerful thing.

∾ ∾ ∾

The creation narratives from the Judeo-Christian scriptures offer some profound insights as we seek to understand our place in creation. There is order to all of creation. Despite the constant change, there is order and consistency. Everything was created in harmony. This order and harmony are in some way a reflection of - God's personal qualities. Creation is a message from God. Creation is a natural revelation. In every instance, God's work reveals something of God, and in every revelation there is a lesson for humanity.

Two of the valuable insights we gain as we read the account of creation in Genesis are the rhythm God intended for our lives and our place in creation:

On the first day God created light. He separated the light from the darkness and called the light day and the darkness night. Then He reflected on His work and saw that it was good.

On the second day God made a vault to divide the waters of heaven from the waters of earth.

On the third day He created the dry land and filled it with trees and plants, and all types of vegetation. Then He reflected on His work and saw that it was good.

On the fourth day He placed lights in the heavens "to divide day from night" and to "indicate festivals, days, and years." Then He reflected on His work and saw that it was good.

On the fifth day He filled the sea and the air with all types of creatures. Then He reflected on His work and saw that it was good.

On the sixth day God created the animals of the earth, the man, and the woman. Then He reflected on His work and saw that it was good.

"Thus the heavens and the earth were finished, and all their multitude. And on the seventh day God finished the work that He had done, and He rested on the seventh day from all the work that He had done. So God blessed the seventh day and hallowed it, because on it God rested from all the work that He had done."

One by one, each day of creation reveals another level of humanity's dependence on the other elements of nature. We are dependent on the sun for light and energy. We are dependent on water. We are dependent on trees for fresh air, on plants and vegetation for food and nourishment.

Humanity is dependent on the other elements of nature. It makes sense that God created us dependent on them, so that we would not abuse and destroy them. Perhaps the idea in the mind of God was, if we were dependent on the other elements of nature, we would respect and live in harmony with them.

From this narrative of creation I wish to draw attention to two themes: our dependency on the other elements of nature and the institution of rest as a divine pastime.

The actions of God so often are a response to the needs of humanity. On the seventh day God rested. God did not need to rest. He did, however, foresee our need for rest. And in foreseeing our need for rest, he established the Sabbath, the seventh day, as a holy day—to be set aside for rest and renewal.

By creating the Sabbath, by setting this time apart, God provided another tool to restore and maintain rhythm in our lives—the rhythm that restores the balance, harmony, and peace intended for us.

In part 5 we will discuss in detail the seventh day as an instrument for creating and maintaining the rhythm of life.

∽ ∽ ∽

The rhythm of life leads us to a deeper understanding of ourselves and our place and role in nature, empowering us to harness our own natural energies.

PRIORITIES

One of the strange and false ideas that are propagated in the modern world is that an important and successful person is always busy. Another of those strange ideas is that material success is the measure of greatness. Many people judge others, and are judged themselves, by how busy they are and how much money they earn. The result is that many rush around in a frenzy, dressed in designer label clothes, trying to give the appearance that they are busy and earning a lot of money—after all, these are the signs of success!

The cost of such a lifestyle is the loss of the necessary consistency and rhythm in our lives. The cost of this type of success is often the loss or failure to find one's very self—our truest and deepest desires, talents, dreams, needs, and the necessary pursuit of these. Sadly, with our focus fixed so firmly on these other, less important, almost inconsequential things, many of us are completely unaware of what we have lost or are missing.

We need to dedicate ourselves to our development as a person—body, heart, mind, and soul. There is nothing more important in life. I know it, you know it, but we let the things we do get in the way. We get carried away with doing. We become human doings. Life is about being and becoming. We must remind ourselves continually that there is nothing more important than our development as human beings.

I used to think I was busy, but then I met one or two people who were really busy. The thing I learned from these people who truly did have an enormous amount of work and responsibility is that they have order. They have a rhythm. They know their priorities and resist sacrificing their health—physically, emotionally, intellectually, or spiritually—merely for a couple of hours' extra work or a few more dollars.

Rhythm and order create harmony and efficiency.

∽ ∽ ∽

We do, of course, live in a time that is marked by tremendous technological advancement. Every time-saving device is available to us, and still no one has time.

Each morning my assistant presents me with a list of things that he thinks should be attended to that day. The list includes phone calls to be made, letters to be written, meetings to attend, and my travel schedule. On top of those things I need to set time apart to pray, write, exercise, and stay in touch with family and friends. Every day I go through the list and say to something, "I - won't have time to do that today." In itself, that is fine. Nobody can do everything. What is critical is what I decide to exclude and why I decide to exclude it.

When was the last time you said, "I don't have time!" either to an idea in your mind or to a person? What was it that you didn't have time to do? For most people it is something like spending time with the family or taking the time to look up an old friend and make sure that life is not treating her too harshly. For others it is exercise or that extra time it takes to eat properly. And at one point or another, for all of us, it is prayer. Yet if God appeared to you right now in a vision and told you that three weeks from today you would be making the journey from this life to the next, would you rush back to work to make your millions? Would you rush out to the mall to make sure you had the right clothes to die in? No. Most of us would spend time with family and friends and, in some way, try to prepare ourselves for that journey to the next life.

We do not know how long our lives on this earth will last.

Some things are more important than others. Prayer, reflection, meditation, and a life with rhythm remind us of this truth and help us to remain focused on the things that are really important.

∽ ∽ ∽

In my life I have found many things. As a boy I once found a beautiful soccer ball in the park just down the road from our home in Sydney. When I arrived home with the ball, my mother inquired as to where it had come from. I told her I had found it. She asked, "Where did you find it?" and I told her, "Down at the park." Then she said to me, "Did it occur to you that someone might come back for it, or that the person who has lost it is very sad right now?" She paused and then continued, "How would you feel if that was your soccer ball and you had lost it?"

I sat in a big green armchair in the corner of the dining room with the ball grasped to my chest while a few minutes of that deadly silence passed—the silence that even as a child you know means you have done something not altogether right. My mother kept about her business in the kitchen, preparing dinner, and then, knowing she had given me just enough time to think about the situation, said, "I think you should take the ball back to the park now and leave it where you found it."

After that I found other things. One day I found a watch, and at a carnival once I found $50. But I have never found time. It just never happens. Sometimes people ask us, "When are you going to do this?" or, "When are you going to do that?" I have discovered that when my reply to these questions is, "When I find time!" I never do those things. I never find that time. Even as a child I learned quickly that from the moment we are born into this life and placed on this planet, there is more to do than can ever be done, more to see than can ever be seen, and if something is important, we must make time.

We must decide what is really important, really necessary,

make it a priority, and make time. Otherwise the siren call of the world will always keep us busy and distracted from what really is important. What really counts?

There is a short prayer that I like to use often during the day, particularly during busy times: "God, help me to see that so few things are really important and to at least take care of these first."

Our priorities should not be based on a material goal. Rather, we should use our time and our talents to develop our whole person. Our own development should be our top priority. When we are fully alive, in every way, striving toward perfection, we experience the profound joy of life.

Finding the rhythm of life is largely about reassessing our priorities and reallocating our resources and energies according to those new priorities. The result is the whole person, a person fully alive, striving to grow, develop, and perfect the various aspects of our character.

∽ ∽ ∽

Once upon a time there was an investment banker. He lived in New York City, was phenomenally successful, and made a ton of money. But his life was busy, noisy, and very stressful.

So, once a year, he would leave the city and go down to a small coastal village in Mexico. For two weeks he would rest, relax, and allow himself to be rejuvenated.

One day he was standing on the pier just before lunch, looking out to sea, when he noticed a small fishing boat coming in to dock. He thought this was a little strange, because most of the fishermen used to stay out late into the afternoon so they could catch as many fish as possible, before coming in and preparing the fish for market.

Curiosity overcame him. So he walked over to where the fishing boat was about to dock. Looking into the boat, he saw just one fisherman and several large yellowfin tuna.

"How long did it take you to catch those fish?' he said to the fisherman.

"Not very long," the fisherman replied with a smile.

"Is there something wrong with your boat?" the American asked.

"Oh, no," the fisherman said. "In thirteen years I have never had a problem with the boat."

The American was a little perplexed, so he asked the fisherman, "Why don't you stay out there longer and catch more fish?"

The fisherman smiled again and said, "I have plenty for my - family's immediate needs. Some of the fish we can eat, and the others we can sell or trade for the other things we need."

"But it's not even lunchtime. What do you do with the rest of your time?"

"In the morning," the fisherman explained, "I like to sleep late. When I wake I fish a little, mostly just for the pleasure of fishing. In the afternoon I play with my children and take *siesta* with my wife. In the evenings I have dinner with my family. And then, when my children are sleeping, I stroll into the village, where I sip wine and play guitar with my *amigos.*"

The American scoffed and said, "I'm a Harvard MBA and I can help you."

The fisherman was a little skeptical, but nonetheless he obliged and asked, "How?"

"You should fish longer every day," the American counseled, "late into the afternoon. This way you will catch more fish, make more money, and you can buy a bigger boat. With the bigger boat you will catch even more fish, make even more money, and then you can buy another boat and hire another man to work the second boat."

"But what then?" the fisherman inquired.

"Oh, we are just getting started," the American volleyed. "With two boats you'll catch even more fish and make even more money, and before you know it, you'll have a whole fleet of boats and every man in the village looking for work will come to you."

"But what then?" the fisherman asked.

"Before too long, you can cut out the middleman, sell your fish direct to the cannery, and make more money. As your fleet of boats continues to expand, you can build your own cannery. And before you know it, you'll be able to leave this small coastal village, move to Mexico City, and manage your expanding enterprise."

"But what then?" the fisherman persisted.

"Well then, you can begin to ship your fish to different parts of the world. Down into Asia and Australia and up into North America. And as demand grows for your fish, you can leave Mexico City, move to Los Angeles, open a distribution plant there, and begin to ship your fish to Europe and every corner of the globe."

"But what then?" the fisherman asked again.

The American continued, "By then your business will be one of the great ventures of the industry. You can move to New York City and manage your empire from the epicenter of the business world."

"How long will all this take?" the fisherman asked.

"Twenty-five, maybe thirty years," the banker explained.

"But what will I do then?" the fisherman asked.

The American's eyes lit up like a Christmas tree. "That's the best part," he said. "When the time is just right, you can go down to Wall Street, list your business as a public company, offer an IPO, and make millions and millions of dollars."

"Millions?" the fisherman asked.

"More money than you ever dreamed you could earn in ten lifetimes," the American explained.

"But what then?" the fisherman asked.

The American didn't know what to say. He had reached his climax. He was stumped. But then a thought crossed his mind and triggered an idea, and he turned once more to the fisherman and spoke.

"Well then, you could move to a small coastal village. . . . You could sleep late. . . . You could fish just for the pleasure of fishing. . . . In the afternoons you could take *siesta* with your wife. . . . In the evenings you could have dinner with your family . . . and then you could stroll into the village and sip wine and play guitar with your *amigos*. . . ."

TIMING

One of my great childhood loves was golf, and although I do not get many opportunities to play these days, what I learned on the golf course through my midteenage years has had a lasting impact on my life. That knowledge seems constantly to have new applications.

Golf is a lot like life. If you are a golfer, you may know what I mean. If you are not a golfer, you may just want to pass me off as another obsessed sporting fanatic. But let me explain.

You can never have a perfect round of golf. There is always that shot that you could have hit a little farther or a little straighter. The secret to successful golf is tempo, timing, and rhythm.

When a shot doesn't go exactly as you wanted it to, you must control the disappointment and frustration. Otherwise it will affect your next shot. The frustration will lead you to tense up and want to hit the ball a little harder, so you will swing a little faster—and your rhythm is gone.

Swinging faster doesn't make the ball go farther.

Similarly, when you hit a great shot you must control the exhilaration. Otherwise in the excitement you may walk a little faster, which will make your heart beat a little faster, which will affect the timing of your swing—and again, your rhythm is gone.

Some evenings, as I reflect on the day that has just passed, I realize that I have spent the whole day in a rush. I look at what I achieved in the day, and often I come to the realization that I really didn't need to rush. All the rushing didn't help.

A small example of this are my routine trips to Pittsburgh International Airport. In the space of the year, I average more than one trip a week to the airport. From my home in southeastern Ohio to the airport is thirty-two miles. If I drive at the speed limit, which is fifty-five miles per hour, it will take me thirty-five minutes. If I drive at seventy miles per hour, I risk getting a ticket, subject myself to the anxiety caused by the possibility of being pulled over, expose myself and my passengers to the danger of having an accident—and arrive at the airport in twenty-eight minutes. Imagine the anxiety I have been prepared to cause myself for the sake of arriving seven minutes earlier!

If the rhythm is going to be sacrificed in a certain situation, make sure it is a decision that you make and not one that is forced upon you.

In this world that is always racing, we must learn to slow down. We must learn to create a pace for ourselves. We should learn to take control of—and maintain—the rhythm of our own lives. I have always enjoyed walking. To me, it is a time to think about whatever is happening in my life. Recently, I have been trying to walk like a man who doesn't have a worry or care in the world. I begin walking as I have for years now, normally quite quickly, with thoughts chasing through my mind one after the other. As each issue arises, I focus on it and decide whether or not I have done everything within my power regarding the matter. If I discover that I have, I surrender the situation. If I decide that I have not done everything that I should, I resolve to do so and then surrender the situation. I then move on to the next issue and do the same with all the major issues in my life that day.

As the time I spend walking passes, I feel the burden of these various issues lifting from my shoulders, and I find myself slowing down to a nice, steady, peaceful pace. I begin walking to a rhythm. In that rhythm I find a peaceful heart, quiet mind, and restful spirit.

Learn to walk like a person who doesn't have a care in the world.

When we are in touch with the rhythm of life, we are able to think about our lives as we live them, rather than as an afterthought or regret. It is good for the soul to live life reflectively.

Often on a golf course, as in life, you find yourself in places and situations you would rather not be in. In both golf and life, you just have to work your way out of them as best you can. Golf is a thinking game—it's not about strength or stamina. Many people have the talent to hit great shots—but to do it consistently and often requires a certain mental fortitude and a psychological strength and focus. To be successful in the game of golf, you must be a thinker. Nobody can focus his or her mind for five hours continually. The art of golf is to be able to focus your mind on the shot and relax your mind between shots. The same is true of life. Many people are gifted extraordinarily; very few use their gifts to the upper limits.

Upper-limit achievement is the fruit of disciplined, selective, concentrated focus.

A life lived reflectively is a life lived effectively.

Slow down to find the rhythm of life. Maintain the rhythm in your life and enjoy the harmony it produces. Once you discover that peace deep within you, protect it at all costs. For this peace alone is happiness, fulfillment, contentment, pleasure, and a sure sign that you are evolving into a glorious being. Reflection creates direction and inner peace. The rhythm of life allows us to maintain that inner peace even amid the turmoil of the world.

                    ∽ ∽ ∽

I believe that God is our Father. I believe He has wonderful plans for His children. Throughout history, no sooner have our needs arisen than He has responded to them. From the beginning, all He created He created in harmony and with order. Since then His gifts have been such that they help and encourage us to reestablish and maintain this order in our lives. God's gifts give rhythm to our lives. It is this rhythm, the rhythm of life, that binds heaven and earth, man and nature, the human and the Divine together in harmony, fulfilling the words so often uttered: "Your will be done on earth as it is in heaven."

Do you believe in the big bang theory? The idea that all the beauty, wonder, and complexity of nature that surrounds you, and is within you, is all the result of an unintelligible explosion caused by a random mixture of chemicals? No? Nor do I. Then why do we apply this theory to our lives?

Perhaps, on the other hand, you believe that God created the world, and the universe, and indeed all things, and that He created them in an orderly fashion with harmony and rhythm. Why don't we apply this truth to our lives?

Let us begin to live what we believe. Let us discover the rhythm of life.

PART FIVE

IT'S ALL
ABOUT ENERGY

OUR MOST VALUABLE RESOURCE

We don't need more time; we need more energy.

Let's face it! There are twenty-four hours in a day. Nobody gets more, and nobody gets less. It doesn't matter how much money you have, who your father is, or how well you can kick a football. Twenty-four hours is all you get. It is probably the only way the equality we speak so much about actually exists.

The differentiating factor is energy.

Energy is our most valuable resource, not time.

For too long we have been subscribing to myths. Stress is bad. Downtime is a waste of time. Money drives performance. These are but a few.

Stress isn't bad. Stress all the time is bad. Downtime isn't a waste of time. Too much downtime is a waste of life. Money doesn't drive performance. Passion and purpose drive performance.

Energy is created by a sense of purpose and a lifestyle that integrates our legitimate needs, our deepest desires, and our talents.

Our purpose is to become the-best-version-of-ourselves. The rhythm of life is the way of life that brings our needs, desires, and talents into harmony with each other. The result: passion and energy.

Life is the spending and replenishing of energy.

What level is your energy at?

The first level: depressed, exhausted, burned-out, and defeated.

The second level: angry, fearful, anxious, defensive, and resentful.

The third level: mellow and serene.

The fourth level: confident, joyful, enthusiastic, and invigorated.

You can't get more time, but you can have more energy. It is time to unleash the energy factor in your life.

How? With three simple but powerful instruments.

CREATING THE RHYTHM

E_{ven} now, several years beyond my struggle with chronic fatigue, it is still a daily challenge to maintain the rhythm in my own life. Some days I rise to the challenge, and when I do I feel more fully alive and I am a better person. On other days I fall into the same old traps. It is then that I become tired and frustrated. When I do, I try to learn from my shortcomings in order to avoid similar pitfalls in the future.

Each of us must find our own rhythm, the rhythm that allows us to thrive.

Finding the rhythm in our lives is difficult. To create the rhythm of life, we must first confirm in our hearts and minds that the rhythm is desirable. Once we desire the rhythm, we will use the daily activities of our lives to satisfy that desire. Desire is the greatest motivator.

The rhythm of life ensures our health and well-being—physically, emotionally, intellectually, and spiritually—by creating a lifestyle that fulfills our legitimate needs in each of these four areas.

The rhythm of life maximizes our efficiency and effectiveness in everything we do.

The rhythm of life lays the natural foundation for us to achieve our greatest dreams and achievements beyond what we have even dared to dream.

The rhythm of life leads to the satisfaction of the deepest desires of our hearts, which is the fulfillment of the will of God. The fruits of this alone are peace, joy, happiness, an increased ability to love, and an increased ability to be loved.

The rhythm of life is desirable.

Our lives are a material expression of our desires. Desire is the seedling from which everything in our lives is born—good and bad, enriching and destructive.

If you can teach yourself, condition yourself, to desire those things that are good for you, there is nothing you cannot achieve or become.

Desire is one of the greatest forces at work within the human being.

How do we condition ourselves to desire the things that are best for us? We desire the things we ponder. We desire the things we see every day.

Television is a perfect example. The combined audiovisual stimulus impacts us powerfully. We respond to the on-screen images with desire. What happens when you see something you like on television? You want it. In her book, *The Overspent American,* Juliet Schor describes a survey she conducted in 1998. Ms. Schor's research revealed that for every hour of television watched weekly, the consumer's spending rose by $208 a year.

We desire the things we ponder, the things we hold in our mind, and as such television is a form of pondering. Television drives consumer aspirations, not just through the commercials, but through the stylish clothing worn by actors and the affluent settings of many of the shows.

Great sporting champions ponder and desire victory. Great entrepreneurs ponder and desire financial wealth. Great saints ponder and desire intimacy with God.

If you begin to ponder the things that are good for you, you will begin to desire them. If you begin to desire them, you will soon begin to attain them.

THE THREE INSTRUMENTS

I wish to share with you the three instruments that allowed me to escape and recover from that difficult period in my life when I was so exhausted, overwhelmed, depressed, and confused.

My experience in Austria led me to anchor my life in these three simple instruments. The first instrument involves regular sleep. The second instrument deals with regular prayer and reflection. The third instrument delves into the ancient tradition of the seventh day as a day of rest, reflection, and renewal.

These three instruments impact the very philosophical foundation of our lives while at the same time they are rooted in our day-to-day activities. They are not rules and regulations. They do not rob us of our individuality, but rather help us to discover who we truly are and encourage us to become champions of selfhood.

The instruments shine the light of wisdom into the deep places of our hearts, minds, bodies, and spirits, revealing to us all of our strengths and weaknesses. They encourage us to look at the different areas of our lives and to examine different aspects of ourselves—to observe the ways we respond to certain events, activities, people, and circumstances.

From this we gain the self-knowledge we have spoken so much about. With this knowledge we are in a position to understand our unique legitimate needs in each of the four areas—physical, emotional, intellectual, and spiritual.

The three instruments therefore lay the foundation for these needs to be met. The result is a man completely in harmony with his self, a woman completely in harmony with her self. This harmony produced by the rhythm of life increases our effectiveness in our work; makes us more present in our relationships; and empowers us with a spiritual presence and focus—all of which gives birth to that deep and abiding peace, an inexpressible joy and satisfaction, and a sense of fulfillment that burns within us, igniting an excitement and passion for life.

SLEEP: THE FOUNDATION
OF ENERGY

Your aims and aspirations may reside in the upper realms of the intellectual life. Your dreams and goals may dwell higher than the highest peaks of this world in the spiritual realm. But no matter how high, noble, and spiritual your aspirations may be, you must build them on natural foundations. In the human being, that foundation consists first of physical well-being.

Have you ever been unemployed? Have you ever lived with someone who was unemployed? What happens? What changes? Most people suffer from an acute blow to their self-esteem, which produces depression in one form or another. A classic symptom of this depression is that when they don't have to get out of bed— they don't. Often when people lose their job, they tend to slip into the habit of sleeping in. After a while, they shave only every second day, then every third day. When they do get out of bed, they go down to the local store to get the newspaper and look for available positions. But by the time they call about the jobs, it is early afternoon—maybe late afternoon—and the positions are already filled. Before you know it, they shave only when they have a job interview, which is almost never, because they don't get out of bed early enough to make the calls in time.

They fall into a rhythm of life, a certain rhythm that grabs hold of them and takes them for a ride. We call that ride "a vicious cycle." Where does it take them? Nowhere.

This rhythm of life does not energize them or bring out the best in them; rather, it drains them of their energy and prevents them from achieving anything worthwhile. This rhythm of life that has kidnapped them does not support the fulfillment of their legitimate needs physically, emotionally, intellectually, or spiritually. This rhythm of life they have adopted is self-destructive.

That vicious cycle exists in one way or another in the lives of each and every one of us. We get caught up in certain patterns of behavior that are self-destructive, a rhythm of life that does not attend to our legitimate needs, a lifestyle that does not enrich and fulfill us.

Is your lifestyle destroying you?

ᔧᔧ ᔧᔧ ᔧᔧ

How do we escape these vicious cycles? Little by little. Small victories are the key. If you decide to become a marathon runner, you don't go out and try to run a marathon straightaway. You start by running one mile a day, then two, three, five, and seven. Over time you build yourself up, and as you strengthen and develop, you extend the distances. Many victories are won before a marathon runner's first race.

Can you do one hundred sit-ups? If you are not in the habit of doing sit-ups regularly, you probably think it is impossible to do one hundred sit-ups consecutively right now. But if you start today by doing twenty each day for a week, then thirty a day for a week, and so on, before too long you will be able to do a hundred sit-ups—and the impossible will have been made possible. That is the greatness of the human spirit—making the unknown known, making the impossible possible. Small victories, one upon another, are the making of every great champion.

These small victories build strength and confidence. The victory over twenty sit-ups builds strength, courage, and confidence to achieve the victory of doing thirty sit-ups the following week. If, on the other hand, you tried to do one hundred sit-ups every day, the first day you might stop after eighteen, the second day after twenty-one, the third day after twenty-five, the fourth day after twenty-six. After a week, most people would become so discouraged from failing over and over again, they would quit.

Set goals that stretch you but do not break you.

In the way that these small victories build strength, confidence, and courage in athletes, they can do the same for us in every area of our lives, whether in our professional work, our relationships, or our spiritual practices.

A large part of success in anything is victory. Success is mostly about victory over ourselves. The habitual and repetitious achievement of such victories produces the quality of self-discipline in a - person's character. This self-discipline is the founding ideal of all great nations and religions in history. It is the founding father of freedom and the foundation of the nation, culture, and dream we call America.

If you give your body a choice, it will always take the easy way out. Your body lies. It tells you it cannot when it can.

How did Michael Johnson become the fastest man in the world? By running when he felt like running? No. Michael Johnson tells his body what it is and is not allowed to feel and when it is and is not allowed to feel those things. His success comes from his mastery of his body. His higher faculties—intellect, will, spirit— reign over his lower faculties—bodily instincts. Each time his body says, "I can't," he pushes it a little further. The body has a natural capacity to increase its strength and abilities. The heart, mind, and spirit are all equipped with the same natural capacity.

Do Andre Agassi and Serena Williams hit tennis balls only when they feel like it? Did Bill Gates achieve what he has by sleeping in until one o'clock in the afternoon? Does Emmitt Smith show up to practice only when he is in the mood for it? Did Abraham Lincoln do only the things he felt like doing? Do you think Mother Teresa always felt like taking care of the poorest of the poor?

One thing is certain. If you do only what you feel like doing, your life will be miserable and you will be a failure.

∽ ∽ ∽

Victory over self leads to ever increasing levels of achievement in any field. Our first opportunity for victory each day is when the alarm clock goes off and it is time to get out of bed. This is the first victory of the day. Most people when they wake up would prefer to lie in bed a little longer. The body cries out, "Just ten more minutes."

Who is the master? Your lower faculties—bodily instincts—or your higher faculties—intellect, will, spirit? Do you do what your body tells you to do, or does your body do what you tell it to do?

If your dreams, goals, and purpose are not enough to inspire you to want to get out of bed in the morning, then you need to rethink your dreams, goals, and purpose.

Get out of bed. Grasp the day from the first moment. Achieve that first victory. Look at it as a victory. Affirm it as a victory. Victory encourages the human spirit to soar higher. Small victories are the mentors of greater victories. The human spirit responds to victory. Victory elevates the human spirit. We must learn to find victory in everything, even in defeat.

THE FIRST INSTRUMENT

⊙══╪══⊙

The first instrument for creating the rhythm of life is sleep: the foundation of energy. It sounds deceptively simple. In part 2, we began our investigation of legitimate physical need with a brief discussion of our need for food. If we do not eat, we will die. We have a legitimate need to eat and to drink. Our legitimate needs are those activities and things that are necessary for survival and allow us to maximize our health and well-being. These needs are an intended part of the divine plan. Sleep is also one of our legitimate physical needs. If you do not sleep, over time you will become delusional, and finally, over an extended period of time, sleep deprivation will lead to insanity. If you were forced to stay awake long enough, you would die.

Over the past twenty years, the study of sleep has grown considerably in popularity. These studies have sought to discover when we should sleep, for how long we should sleep, where we should sleep, and how we should sleep—in order to maintain optimum health and well-being.

To apply the first instrument to our lives, we must first ask these questions of ourselves: "When do I sleep?" "For how long do I sleep?" "Where do I sleep?" "How do I sleep?" But first, we must ask the question philosophers, scientists, and children have been asking since the dawn of human history: "Why?"

"Why do we sleep?" The common answer to this question is, "We sleep because we have to sleep." This is true. We must sleep. Sleep is essential for survival. However, this answer only displays an attitude toward sleep. It does not answer the question.

We sleep to be renewed. Sleep refreshes us. Sleep energizes us. Our sleep brings rest, renewal, and energy not only to our bodies, but also to our hearts, minds, and spirits. Sleep heals us from the stresses of daily life. When we view it from this very positive perspective, and consciously approach it with these things in mind, we maximize the effects of sleep.

Conscious living maximizes the enrichment of every activity and experience in our lives. Conscious living simply means knowing what you are doing while you are doing it.

When we approach sleep as something we must do, or as a burden and limitation, we reduce the refreshing, renewing, and energizing effects sleep has upon our bodies, hearts, minds, and spirits.

For a few moments now, pause and reflect upon your attitude toward sleep. You will gain very little from this discussion unless you take this important step and are therefore able to ask yourself the other questions: "When, where, and how do I sleep?" Many of us will not be able to answer these right away. To do so, we must seek this very important self-knowledge.

෴   ෴   ෴

The most important issue regarding sleep is when you sleep. Why do so many people feel they don't get enough sleep? People of all different sleeping habits seem to want more. The issue here is not the quantity of our sleep, but rather the quality of our sleep.

You may think sleep is sleep. Yet numerous studies have revealed that people who sleep at the same time every night are considerably healthier than those who do not. They are affected by common colds less than one-third as many times as people who do not sleep at regular hours. The incidence of depression is also significantly lower with people who sleep at regular hours.

To implement the first instrument in our lives, to be able to get out of bed refreshed and energized in the morning, some preparation must be done. Once again, this preparation involves self-knowledge. If you know you need to get out of bed at seven a.m. in order to get ready for your day in a calm and peaceful manner, and if you also know that if you don't get seven hours of sleep, you become grouchy and miserable, then be fair to yourself. Be kind to yourself, and use your self-knowledge. It is powerful to live by what you know about yourself. Make sure that by midnight you are in bed, despite what problems emerge—schedules, stresses, social situations, and poor habits. Often these are what hinder our ability to get the sleep we need.

For example, to be in bed and asleep at midnight every night, you will certainly find yourself leaving some social events early. The question is, for the sake of a couple of extra hours at a party, are you prepared to throw your life into chaos?

Yes, there are exceptions. No, you do not have to be in bed every night by midnight for the rest of your life. But in our lives the exception has become the rule. There is no consistency to our sleeping patterns, and that is costing us dearly.

You may need only six hours of sleep, and you may decide your time is from eleven p.m. until five a.m. Or you may need eight hours of sleep and may decide to sleep from ten p.m. to six a.m. Each person must decide how much sleep optimizes his or her energy. Only you can decide what are the best hours for you to sleep.

Sleep should be used offensively, not defensively.

Many of us have been falsely led to believe that sleep is an expendable element and that it can be used defensively. Sleep builds us up. Sleep is one of the indispensable natural elements of our lives. Sleep is one of our legitimate needs. Sleep is intended to make us stronger, more vibrant, more productive, more loving, and more alert individuals. Sleep is important and should be given priority.

Our modern world works against this in so many ways. For instance, a great number of people uphold lack of sleep as a source of pride. Some people believe that excessive dedication to waking hours overrules the necessity for rest and regular sleep. They convince themselves that to be successful in their chosen field they must sacrifice sleep and rest—they even believe this to be heroic. These ideas are particularly common in business. Perhaps they need to return to the business school textbooks, reconsider the concept of "long-term residual effect," and ponder it in relation to their own lives.

We have no greater evidence of the importance of sleep than in the habits of those who are highly successful. Recently I had the opportunity to meet Olympian Alberto Salazar after one of my talks in Oregon. He had a presence, the presence of a champion, a certain strength, and yet a profound humility.

Do you suppose when Alberto Salazar won the gold medal for the marathon at the 1992 Olympic games, he credited his success to sleeping less than all of the other athletes in his field? No, Salazar trained harder, rested more effectively, was more attuned to his dietary needs, was more in touch with his desire to win—and has been leaving parties early for years because he knows he has to get up early the next morning to train. If he doesn't train well, he won't compete well.

The truth is, people are walking around half-asleep all the time. Every day, people are exhausted. They are fatigued. Fatigue has become a pattern in our lives. This is a sad testament to how little we observe, know, and respect ourselves.

When was the last time you woke up and felt renewed, refreshed, and excited to get into your day? That is what I want you to experience—not occasionally, but every day.

On the other hand, do you remember the last time you had to get up early after a late night? How did you feel? Did you say to yourself, "I wish I didn't have to get out of bed this morning"? Or perhaps, "I am never going to stay out late again on a work night"? How was your day? Were you a picture of energy? Did you enjoy the day? Were you efficient? Effective? Happy?

The real question is, will you let it happen again? Each of us should know how much sleep we require in order to function at maximum efficiency—be it six, seven, or eight hours. When will we begin to use this valuable information to our own advantage?

In this era of lust, we lust even after knowledge. Foolishly we believe that wisdom is the amassing of knowledge. We want to know more, but we do not want to live what we already know.

∽ ∽ ∽

The first step is to sleep at the same time every night. In order to attune ourselves to the rhythm of life, we must adopt a regular pattern of sleep—going to bed at the same time and getting up at the same time. It really is quite simple, yet on occasions when I have shared this idea with people, they have looked at me as if I were asking the impossible. It is perhaps a testament to how complex and cluttered our lives have become. It is perhaps a testament to how out of control our lives are. Begin to take control of your life—adopt a regular sleeping schedule.

This is the most basic way I know to create the rhythm of life, and it is the essence of the first instrument. It brings a consistency to the general structure and organization of our lives. In the area of physical well-being, it is the first step toward maximizing our energy and therefore the first step toward increasing our effectiveness in everything we do.

I have seen it work in my own life, and I have seen it work in the lives of others. If you go to bed and get up at the same time every day, weekdays and weekends, in less than ten days you will feel like a different person. New energy, new enthusiasm, new passion for life.

It will be a challenge. It will be difficult at times. It will cost. It is simply a matter of priorities. This regular sleeping schedule will empower you to give your best to everything you do every day. You will no longer find yourself saying, "I just want to get through today and get home to bed!" That is no way to live. Every day should be savored. Being rested is not just about being awake—it's about being able to devote yourself completely to whatever is before you in every single moment of the day. It is about living life to the fullest.

It is also important that you give consideration to how long you sleep. The secret with sleep is the same wisdom that applies to just about everything that affects the body—guard against extremes. Too little sleep is not good for us, and too much sleep is not good for us. If we sleep too little, we wake up fatigued; and if we sleep too much, we wake up fatigued. Test different sleeping times for several days. Grow to know yourself and what amount of sleep allows you to function most effectively.

Consideration should also be given to where you sleep and the environment you sleep in. Once again, try different things and get to know yourself. If it is too hot or too cold, how does that affect the effectiveness of your sleep?

How you sleep can also make a radical difference—whether it's on your stomach, on your side, or on your back. Observe yourself. Know yourself. Use the knowledge you gain about yourself to live a happier, healthier, fuller life.

When I was eighteen and first in college under the spell of the "modern lie," I used to believe that eating and sleeping were a waste of time. Twenty minutes was the absolute maximum I would dedicate to sitting at table for a meal, and mostly I ate on the run. When it came to sleep—two, three, four hours a night, and some nights I would not go to bed at all. Over the past ten years, I have learned a lot about myself, and I know now that without seven hours of sleep each night, I am no good to anyone.

It is time we began to see sleep not as a limitation or burden, but as a gift. Embrace this gift. Treasure the gift. Cherish the gift. Enjoy the gift. Use the gift of sleep to its maximum advantage. Use sleep to begin to create the rhythm of life.

THE SACRED HOUR

Image or light, that is the question. We tend to spend our lives dedicated to the image, to the material. The image represents the body. The light represents the spirit.

Do you identify more with your body or with your spirit? The highest levels of living are experienced when we have an absolute disregard for the body beyond our basic needs and a complete adherence to the promptings of the Divine Spirit within us. It is then that we form our identity from the spirit within, when we let the sweet light within us shine.

Most of us, however, are dedicated to the body, to the image. We see and value ourselves not in terms of the spirit, but in relation to the body. We find our identity through the body. We form, and live by, an image made up of physical and sensory perception.

Do you find your identity through your body or through your spirit? Are you dedicated to the image or to the light? The image is an illusion. The light is truth.

A person who is completely dedicated to the light is capable of anything.

Prayer shifts our dedication from the image to the light.

❧ ❧ ❧

We live in an age that is obsessed and preoccupied with the material. We live in a time dominated by greed and lust. We live in the era of perpetual noise and motion, an age obsessed with speed.

These are the characteristics of our times. These are the trends, mind-sets, and structures that distract and prevent us from discovering the rhythm of life. Yet this is the world we must live in.

I want to live in peace. This is my single greatest desire. Perhaps it sounds simplistic, but when I have this peace I am happy and in love with life. Without this peace, life is a drudgery. I have experienced this peace. It is real. It is the most intense pleasure life has to offer. It heightens the sensitivity of all the senses and increases the intensity of all of life's other pleasures. It is both calm and exhilarating. It could be likened to taking a journey to the deepest places and the highest places all at once. It is a contradiction and yet perfectly in balance. It is the fruit of an intimate harmony among the physical, emotional, intellectual, and spiritual elements of the human person.

Peace is not the absence of pain or pressure. Nor is it the absence of activity. Peace is not lying on a beach without a worry in the world. Peace is not born by doing nothing.

This peace I speak of is a certainty in my heart and mind that I am using my life for a worthy purpose—that each day I am able to love more than the day before, that I am becoming a better person each day, that in my own way I am touching and improving the lives of others. It is maintained with the conviction that the way I am spending the energies of my life makes sense.

ᴄᴏ　ᴄᴏ　ᴄᴏ

A few months ago, I spent a couple of days with a very wealthy gentleman in Europe, a friend of a friend. This man has more money than you and I could physically count in a lifetime. All his life he has worked very hard, and his achievements in business are admirable. One morning at breakfast, it was just the two of us and he began to speak. "There is something different about you, Matthew. I don't know what it is, but it is special and rare. You make me ponder life." I said nothing, and he said nothing for several minutes. Then he continued, "I will tell you this because you are young and perhaps it will be of some use to you. I am a very wealthy man. I have more houses than ten families could live in, more boats and cars than I could ever use, more money than I could ever spend. Everywhere I go I am treated like royalty . . . but, I have no peace. Peace . . . and the funny thing is, I would give everything I have, the things I have spent my whole life building, for just a little peace. As a little boy I had it, but now as an old man, I have no peace." The most overwhelming sorrow and pity for this man welled up inside me, and I wondered how many others felt this way. I couldn't help but think to myself, It's not a "funny thing," it's a tragedy.

As time goes by, what I discover most about people is that we want to live in peace.

This is why in a time when so many people are turning their backs on prayer, I am trying to embrace prayer with my whole being. Prayer gives me that peace. Prayer teaches me to use my life for a worthy purpose. Prayer reveals that purpose. Prayer warns me when I wander from the narrow path. Prayer increases my ability to love and my ability to be loved. Prayer fills me with hope, and that hope is not the conviction that everything will turn out well, but rather the certainty that the way I am spending my life makes sense regardless of how it turns out. Prayer allows me to live my life in peace.

If you look into the eyes of the people you meet today, you will see clouds and storms, fear and doubt, confusion and worry, anxiety and restlessness. But very rarely, in this day and age that has turned its back on prayer, do you look into a person's eyes and see the calm, still, peaceful waters of a crystal-clear lake.

∽ ∽ ∽

Prayer is essential. Prayer cuts through and clarifies. Prayer reminds us of what is really important. Prayer awakens our awareness to our legitimate needs. Prayer is the great friend who introduces us to ourselves. Prayer is the great mediator that introduces us to God. Prayer is the faithful friend who points out who we are and who we are capable of being. Prayer reveals the deepest desires of our hearts and points out the path that was ordained for us from the beginning of time. Prayer whispers those golden words "That is your star, go now and follow it." Prayer gifts us with purpose and direction, and peace in that direction. Prayer is a journey and a destination. Prayer is a chance to become intimately familiar with the better person we know we can be—and that familiarity is the beginning of wisdom. Prayer helps. Prayer is important. Prayer is needed. We need prayer. Prayer doesn't need us, and God doesn't need prayer. Prayer doesn't help God, it helps us. It isn't something we must do, it is something we should do. I pray because I cannot help it. I pray because in every moment the need flows out of me. I pray because I am a better person when I do.

Pray.

THE SECOND INSTRUMENT

The second instrument I used to rediscover the rhythm of life I call "the sacred hour." Essentially it consists of an hour of prayer and reflection, but not necessarily in the way you may currently conceive an hour of prayer to be. If you are not in the habit of praying, the idea of praying for an hour may seem frightening or even impossible. Be open. Open your heart and your mind to a new understanding of prayer.

The purpose of prayer is to help you make the journey from point A to point B and to become the-best-version-of-yourself, which indeed is the purpose of life. The common mistake is to think of prayer as easy. I assure you, prayer is the most difficult thing in the world to do. In prayer we find ourselves standing on the edge of a deep, dark abyss—the world of the Divine, Infinite, and Eternal. In prayer we come face-to-face with ourselves and face-to-face with God, and at different times both of these encounters can be very frightening. Prayer is difficult. But those who learn to master prayer come to master themselves, and those who come to master themselves become the instruments of tremendous good and are able to master every other human activity.

In my life, I believe that everything good comes from knowing and living in the will of God. I believe that I was created for a purpose. I believe that there is a plan for each of us—a divine blueprint—a mission. That plan perfectly intertwines our talents, our legitimate needs, and our deepest desires—to bring about this perfect harmony among body, heart, mind, and spirit. In following

that plan, I believe we find peace and prosperity, freedom and fulfillment.

We may, of course, reject this plan, this blueprint, this mission.
And there lies the mystery of freedom and love.

The will of God is the perfection of the creature. The will of
God is that you make the journey from point A to point B. Each
step along that path forms an allegiance and bond with the will of
God. It is in this journey that we discover the glory of life. It is in
prayer that we discover the glory of God. And it is by living what
we discover in prayer that we become the glory of God. The will
of God is that you become the better person you know you can
be, the-best-version-of-yourself. Your unique personality, talents,
needs, and desires are what make your journey different from
mine. All of these are unveiled in the classroom of silence.

Prayer is the great classroom of silence. During my travels over
the past ten years, I have continually heard people whisper, "How
did he become so wise at such a young age?" Wisdom is not a mass
of accumulated knowledge. Wisdom is those little pieces of knowledge that have the power to change our lives. Wisdom is truth
lived. Wisdom is the fruit of a reflective heart. Wisdom is the fruit
of silence.

∽ ∽ ∽

When I was nineteen, God touched my life in a very powerful way.
It was at that time, leading up to when I first began speaking, that
I began to pray seriously—and that I felt God inviting me into the
classroom of silence. For almost six months every day I would sit
alone in silence, pondering and reflecting upon my life, the world,
God, and the scriptures for three, four, five, sometimes six hours at
a time.

You can learn more in an hour of silence than you can in a year
from books.

Noise is the mouthpiece of the world. Silence is the mouthpiece of God. It is in the classroom of silence that God bestows His infinite wisdom on men and women.

We live in a noisy world. People wake up to clock radios, listen to the news while they shower, watch television while they eat breakfast, get into the car and listen to the morning shows on the way to work, listen to music all day over the intercom, talk incessantly on the phone between any number of meetings . . . We need a break from the noise.

Everything great in history has arisen from silence . . . even great noise. Beethoven and Mozart closed themselves off from the world and inhabited silent rooms for days at a time in order to hear things that no one else could hear—sounds so glorious that they themselves would never hear in the midst of the world, and yet sounds that the world would never know if Beethoven and Mozart had not befriended silence.

USA Today conducted a survey last year in which people were asked to name the ten things they feared the most. The most feared was death, and then flying. After flying . . . silence—followed closely by public speaking, dogs, snakes, and spiders. Why do we fear silence? Why do we avoid silence?

Silence introduces us to ourselves—for better and for worse. Silence convicts, suggests, and challenges—yes. But silence also consoles, heals, comforts, clears the mind, and gives courage to the weary heart. Peace is the fruit of silence.

Why do we fear and avoid silence? The truth is, most people believe that everything within them is worthless and embarrassing. That is why we live in a world terrified of silence and full of people dedicated to imitating other people instead of developing the unique individual that they are themselves.

Befriend silence. I am not suggesting that you spend four, five, six hours a day in silence. Drop by a church during the day when it is empty and quiet. Find a quiet corner and a comfortable chair at home. Leave the radio off in the car on the way to work. Have a television-free evening once a week. Try it. It works.

I close my eyes so that I may see things that I could never see
with my eyes open, things that would never come to be if I did not
close my eyes. I enter the classroom of silence to listen, and there I
hear things I would never hear in this noisy world, the murmurings of my heart and soul that lead me to my future.

⌒o ⌒o ⌒o

What are you prepared to do to significantly increase the level of
peace, happiness, and fulfillment in your life? How far are you prepared to go? How much are you prepared to give? Are you prepared to give one hour a day?

I would like to encourage you to set aside one hour a day. This
time becomes another landmark in our day and helps us to restore
and maintain the rhythm of life. It's difficult to set aside one hour
a day, I know, but I'm going to try to convince you that it is worth
making the effort and initial sacrifice.

For this one hour I want you to pray. I do not want you to go
into your church and mindlessly repeat prayers that you were
taught as a child until you either fall asleep or are bored out of your
brain. I would like you to discover the joy of prayer. I want this
time to be a joy for you.

If prayer were something you loved and longed for, you would
have no difficulty spending one hour a day in prayer. The secret to
prayer is discovering dynamic ways to make it something you love
and long for, something you know and are comfortable with.

Prayer is like a great love. When you start dating the silence can
be awkward, but as you grow to know each other you can sit in silence for hours and just being with each other is a great comfort.
When you are dating you don't go to the same restaurant every
time and eat the same food and have the same conversation. Variety brings vitality to relationship. Love is creative. Just as we must
be creative in the ways we spend time with those we love, we

must be creative in the ways we spend time with ourselves and with God.

Over time all relationships develop certain rituals and staples, but these remain vibrant only when they are surrounded by dynamic variety. The same is true in our prayer life. Our spiritual diet may consist of certain rituals and staples, but there is a constant need for dynamic variety.

What is missing in your life?

Whatever it is, the first step to finding it or regaining it is time for you. Most people don't have fifteen minutes' time for themselves each day.

One of the first things we established in part 1 was that we know the things that make us happy. We just don't do them. Why? We forget. We get distracted. We need this time for ourselves to remember. Remember what? Time to remember what matters most.

Give this hour to yourself each day as a gift. Make it a habit in your life, a ritual in your day. Give it priority over all the little things that distract you and drain you. Discipline yourself to do it. Every disciplined effort has its own multiple rewards.

༄ ༄ ༄

There are hundreds of ways to pray, and in time you will discover which ways work best for you. Some are more active, and some are more passive. Some forms of prayer draw upon nothing but the murmurings of our hearts, and others draw upon the scriptures and other inspirational writings. Some days we pray best in a quiet church, and other days we pray best walking a sunny beach.

My intention here is merely to share some ideas with you, to construct a collage from some of my personal experiences of prayer in the hope that they may be helpful and insightful to you.

Sometimes my heart is tormented by restlessness and anxiety. Sometimes my mind is distracted by a hundred little problems.

Sometimes my spirit is burdened, and I feel the weight of the world upon my shoulders.

It is often at these times that I find myself wandering into a church and sitting quietly in the presence of God.

Prayer allows me to put into words exactly what is troubling me. I sit in a quiet place, close my eyes, and in a gentle mental dialogue I tell God what is on my heart and mind. I explain what is bothering me. I explain the situation. I tell him how I feel and why I feel that way. When I am finished I sit there in silence and listen. Usually, by the time I am finished explaining, I know what it is I need to do.

Most of us know what we should and need to do. But that knowledge gets buried beneath the messages of the world and the opinions of family and friends. Sometimes we just need someone to talk to or someone to listen to us. How often do we begin to talk to someone about a problem and before we are finished explaining the situation to that person, we see things much more clearly in our own mind, and we know what we should do? God is the great listener.

∽ ∽ ∽

Some days I am so distracted by the happenings of the day that I am simply unable to concentrate enough to engage in this dialogue. On those days I like to use some reading material to bring me into focus, to help me concentrate.

I am fascinated with the life of Jesus—a leader who for himself wanted nothing, which in itself is a great sign of sincerity and honesty. I am fascinated with the Gospels, which tell us of his life and teachings. They are so simple and yet deeply profound and potent. Very often I use the life of Jesus in the Gospels during this sacred hour. Slowly, deliberately, reflectively, I read over a short passage. Once, twice, three times—trying to delve into and extract some of the mystery and wisdom.

Reading can be a very powerful tool to bring us into focus during prayer. Read slowly, savor the words, ponder what they mean to you in your particular circumstances. There are hundreds of books that would serve as good companions for the sacred hour.

∽ ∽ ∽

On other days when I find myself entering the sacred hour restless and anxious, I use the meditation of the red rose, which I have spoken of so often in my talks and seminars.

I begin by sitting in a quiet place, sitting comfortably, sitting still, and closing my eyes. Then, in my mind's eye, I envision before me a single red rose. In the Middle Ages, the single red rose was a symbol of Christ. If you travel through Europe, you will often find this image in the stained-glass windows of the great cathedrals. You will also find it was used to decorate many of the manuscripts of that period. For you it could be any image that leads you to focus your attention on God and the perfection you seek.

With my attention now focused on the rose, I slowly allow all other thoughts to flow out of my mind. Distractions are inevitable. When I realize that a thought or idea has reentered my mind, as soon as I am aware that I have been taken hostage by a distraction, I free my mind once again by returning to the single red rose in my mind's eye.

Over a few minutes, my mind is able to still and my heart and soul begin to heighten in awareness. I find myself in the presence of God. Some days my whole time of prayer can consist of this exercise of stillness and focus. It is one of my favorite ways to spend my time on planes. On most days I use this meditation for a few minutes to begin my prayer before moving on to one of the other forms of prayer we have discussed.

We must learn to turn from the outer life of noise and confusion toward the inner life of silence and serenity.

ᴄᴑ ᴄᴑ ᴄᴑ

One of the classic counsels from the Bible is, "Be still and know that I am God." The stillness is important. In this stillness we are able to contemplate the things of the spirit. The stillness frees us from the limitations of the body and sets the spirit free to soar. The spirit within us is fearless. The spirit within us does not doubt, it knows.

In the stillness we form a connection with the spirit within. Through this practice, over time, we come to perceive ourselves as a spiritual being having a physical experience, rather than just a physical being.

In discussing the rose meditation, I mentioned that I would sit still. When I say still, I mean completely still. No movement whatsoever, not even a fraction of an inch. The only movement is the gentle rising of my chest as I breathe.

Sit up straight, but not forced. Erect, but relaxed. Place both feet flat on the ground, spaced comfortably apart. Rest your hands in your lap. And now, sit still. Completely still.

Let me warn you, if you try to practice this method of prayer, there are some common traps. Within thirty seconds of making yourself comfortable and resolving to be still, your body will object and inform you that it is uncomfortable. Thirty seconds ago you were reasonably comfortable. A more comfortable position is only an illusion. If you move to find a more comfortable position, you will spend your entire time of prayer shifting and moving—approximately every thirty seconds—and once again the body will have triumphed.

If you are able to ignore the temptation to search for the position that is perfectly comfortable, you will overcome the first obstacle, inform the body who is master, and move to a deeper level.

Your next hurdle will come within two minutes. You will have an itch. Perhaps on your hand, your neck, your nose, or just under your eye.

Your body will beckon you to scratch the itch. To do so you will have to move, which will break the dominance of mind and spirit over body. Don't. Acknowledge the itch and ask yourself: Is it bearable? Will it kill me to ignore it? Of course it is bearable, and it certainly will not kill you. Stay still. Ignore it. Once you resolve not to respond to the call of the body, the itch will increase in intensity for a few moments. Then, as your resolve not to respond builds, the itch will fade. Throughout this, you will be progressing to new levels of stillness, silence, solitude—all leading you to oneness with the spirit within.

Another danger is that as we become silent and still, our minds clear. The calm produces clarity of thought. You will be reminded of things you had forgotten, things you need to do. All of these are temptations to stop.

For me, I find that as soon as I come into the stillness and silence, this calm produces all types of writing ideas. My temptation is to stop praying and to write. But I find that if I ignore those initial temptations, I am led to even deeper ideas later in my prayer.

These temptations will reemerge occasionally—itches, discomfort, distractions, the temptation to stop, to scratch, the temptation to shuffle into a more comfortable position. I tell myself it won't kill me, and I ignore it. It irritates for a few moments, sometimes minutes, but then it goes away, and with that victory we are taken to even higher places of contemplation.

It is in those places that I have experienced the most glorious moments of my life. The experience cannot be described, but if you are able to taste it for a moment, just once, you will long and yearn for it every day—and then prayer will become your passion and pleasure. You will go to the classroom of silence every day for peace and guidance, to discover who you are, and to summon the strength to be true to your self. Only then will the words I have placed on the pages of this book take on their full meaning for you and your life. You will reread these lines and discover layer upon layer of meaning.

You are about to discover how difficult it is to sit still. If you persevere, you will discover the unfathomable power of stillness and silence. Only in this state, I believe, can we come to truly know the deepest needs and desires of our being.

Prayer is a contraction. In prayer we close ourselves off from the world, from people, places, and possessions, we abandon the seduction of noise, and close our eyes. But from this contraction is born the most remarkable expansions, and we are empowered by the Divine Spirit to see things before unseen, to hear things before unheard, and to become an unimagined creation.

Prayer is a contraction that produces an expansion.

Be still and know that I am God.

Be still and know that I am.

Be still and know.

Be still.

Be.

ᴔ ᴔ ᴔ

There are days when I like to spend the sacred hour taking a long walk in a quiet place. I like to walk slowly, making sure not to lose my breath. I like to try to walk like a man who hasn't a care in the world, as I described in part 4.

It is amazing the difference the way you breathe can make. For example, if you are in a pressure situation, or you are frustrated, how are you breathing? Heavily and quickly—short breaths. Now, concentrate on your breathing. Breathe slowly and deeply. Within minutes your whole demeanor can be changed and controlled.

Another example: You get into the shower and the water turns freezing cold. You are stunned. Your reaction is to gasp, taking in short breaths of air. Breathe deeply and you will be able to tolerate the cold water.

How you breathe during prayer is important. When you first begin your prayer, pay attention to your breathing. Breathe slowly and deeply. This will help you to calm down, relax, and surrender to the peacefulness of prayer.

We eliminate stress and invite relaxation by returning our focus to the basics of life. There is nothing more fundamental than breathing. Breathe. Don't forget to breathe. The way you breathe can change your state more quickly than any other controllable physiological aspect of the human person.

∽ ∽ ∽

On other days, particularly when I am visiting my family and friends in Australia, I like to spend my sacred hour sitting on a quiet beach, listening to the waves roll in and out. The rhythm of the waves has a calming, soothing quality. There is a sacred connection between God and nature. It is mysterious, but real.

When I was a child, my parents often took my brothers and me to the beach. We would swim and build sand castles. We used to go to Manly Beach. I always go there when I return to Sydney. There is something powerful and wonderful about the places of our childhood. In a mystical way they remind us of who we once were, which brings into focus who we are now. They remind us of our story. Everyone has one, and our own story is an indispensable tool in the journey to grow and change. I like to visit Manly Beach, to eat in restaurants I ate in on special occasions, to walk on the soccer fields I once played on.

Visit the places of your childhood. That would be a sacred hour well spent.

∽ ∽ ∽

Prayer is a time to share our joys and troubles with God, but it is so much more than just that. Prayer is a time to dream and visualize.

There is one thing my golf coach told me that I have never forgotten. He used to say, "If you cannot see the shot, you cannot hit the shot. Stand behind the ball. Look at the ball and then look at the hole. Visualize the shot you want to hit. See it flying through the air and landing where you want it to land. If you can't see the shot, you can't hit the shot."

It is true for just about everything. Van Gogh was able to stand before an empty canvas, unlock his imagination, and see something that wasn't there. Thomas Edison was able to see things that didn't even exist—yet. Martin Luther King Jr. was able to see something that wasn't before him but that he knew should be.

Van Gogh once wrote, "The thing has already taken form in my mind before I start it. The first attempts are absolutely unbearable. I say this because I want you to know that if you see something worthwhile in what I am doing, it is not by accident but because of real direction and purpose."

The first attempts at prayer are also often unbearable.

This principle of visualization is also true for our most important work in this life. If you cannot see the better person you know you can be, you cannot be that better person. Prayer is the place and time to visualize the ways in which you can become the-best-version-of-yourself. Prayer is an opportunity to join your heart and mind to the heart and mind of God and to visualize everything you dream, hope, and wish to achieve and everything you long to be. Here lies the power of prayer. Make no mistake, prayer unleashes the unfathomable potential of the human spirit—the power to visualize and engage unrealized potential.

Would the same idea work for a young man who wanted to become the greatest basketball player in history? Michael Jordan once said, "I visualized where I wanted to be, what kind of player I wanted to become. I knew exactly where I wanted to go, and I focused on getting there."

∽ ∽ ∽

It is also by prayer that God empowers us to overcome faults, addictions, and vices. For example, suppose there is someone who really annoys you at school or at work. Over and over the same situation arises, and you become frustrated, annoyed, even angered. That one situation, and others like it, can destroy your peace for a whole day, even for days at a time.

Do not let that person rob you of your peace. Imagine the situation. Visualize it as it has happened before. Now, imagine the perfect way to respond in that situation in order to remain calm and peaceful. How long does it take to visualize that response? Ten seconds. In the empty moments of the day, between tasks, while you are walking from one place to another, imagine that situation. Visualize it over and over again. Visualize your response, your perfect response, over and over again. Imagine yourself remaining calm and peaceful in that situation. Visualize yourself responding to that situation perfectly twenty times a day. It will cost you less than three and a half minutes of twenty-four hours, and within two weeks I promise you will be responding in exactly the same way you have visualized.

Thought determines action. Do not let your whole life be a reaction to the things that happen around you each day. Let your life be an action.

∽ ∽ ∽

The sacred hour is a time of renewal and refreshment. It is a time of spiritual nourishment. It is a time to slow down and remind ourselves of what is really important. The sacred hour is an opportunity to bring focus and direction to our lives. A time to dream and visualize. Yet our prayer should not be confined to this one hour each day.

At the end of my sacred hour each day, I feel peaceful. I feel confident I can handle the events and situations that are before me. But after five minutes back into the hustle and bustle of daily life, it is so easy to lose that peace and focus.

I try to sustain the effect of the sacred hour by using a simple and ancient spiritual technique. I repeat to myself a simple phrase or word over and over again, hundreds of times throughout the day. This technique is known as a mantra and has been used for centuries in several different religious traditions. The phrase I like to use is the first line of a prayer attributed to Francis of Assisi: "Lord, make me an instrument of your peace."

Throughout the day in those empty moments between tasks, in those minutes driving from one place to another, at times of frustration, pressure, anger, disappointment—I repeat this phrase over and over again. Slowly. Thoughtfully. I allow it to reach down to the depths of my being.

After a while it becomes second nature to respond to certain situations internally first before responding externally. To reflect rather than speak or shout.

Try it.

Find your own phrase. A quote, a word, a sentence that has the power to bring everything back into perspective for you. You will discover that there are so many gaps in the day, empty moments that can be used to refocus yourself on what is really important. The mantra has been a valuable tool for great spiritual leaders for hundreds of years. Successful people remind themselves of their goal in every waking moment of every hour of every day. Whether you seek to be a successful football player or successful in the spiritual life, the same principle applies. The mantra is a tool that will help you to stay focused—to keep your heart and mind fixed on your goal in every moment of every day.

ↄ ↄ ↄ

Sometimes life shakes us up a little. We become disoriented, overwhelmed, consumed by the day-to-day happenings of our lives. -

Britain's Royal Navy has a practice known as the "all-still." When something goes wrong on a ship, particularly a submarine, the captain announces an all-still. For three minutes no one is allowed to move or speak. Our lives are an expression of what is within us. Life is an overflow of the heart. If within you are confused, frustrated, and exhausted, your actions will tell the same story.

Three minutes of silence and stillness can have an exponential effect in the middle of a turbulent situation. In my own life I have found that between meetings, phone calls, or in the middle of a group project, an all-still can make all the difference. It is an opportunity to catch my breath and put things in perspective.

∾ ∾ ∾

Prayer contributes to the health and well-being of the whole person. Studies in the latter part of the twentieth century reveal that people who pray recover faster from serious illnesses and are less likely to suffer from depression or mental illness. We are human beings—a delicate composition of body and soul, linked carefully by the will and the intellect. Maximum health and well-being can be reached only when we attend to each of the elements of our being. Ignoring the spiritual component of our being necessarily reduces our health, effectiveness, well-being, and efficiency.

Carl Jung, one of this century's most distinguished psychiatrists, in his book *Modern Man in Search of a Soul,* wrote, "During the past thirty years, people from all civilized countries of the earth have consulted me. I have treated many hundreds of patients. Among all my patients in the second half of life—that is to say, over thirty-five—there has not been one whose problem in the last resort was not that of finding a religious outlook on life. It is safe to say that every one of them fell ill because he had lost that which the living religions of every age have given to their followers, and none of them has been really healed who did not regain his religious outlook."

Is it merely a coincidence that, in this age marked by its rejection of religion and spirituality, the incidence of depression and mental illness has escalated so dramatically?

Unfortunately, we live in an age when matters of the spirit are neglected and, in some ways, looked down upon. Faith is a liberating force. Religion is a liberating force. Spirituality is a liberating force. It is natural for human beings to pray: we are naturally spiritual beings. We live in a material world, but we are not solely material.

∽ ∽ ∽

If you read every book ever written on baseball, would that make you the greatest baseball player ever? You learn to ride a bicycle only by riding a bicycle, to play football by playing football, to cook by cooking. You become a great baseball player only by playing baseball. Prayer is a lot like love. We are born with a natural ability and capacity to love. This ability to love develops when we exercise it. We learn to love by loving. The only way to learn to pray is to pray. Books, teachers, guides, mentors, role models, and coaches all help to perfect our abilities, but there is no substitute for the actual practice—whether it is baseball, cooking, football, love, or prayer.

As I write these words about prayer, the words of Henry David Thoreau echo in my mind: "I went to the woods because I wanted to live deliberately. . . . I wanted to live deep and suck out all the marrow of life . . . to put to rout all that was not life . . . and not, when I came to die, discover that I had not lived. . . ."

I go to the woods of prayer each day because I want to live life deliberately. I pray because I want to live life deeply and suck out all the marrow of life! I go to prayer to put to rout all that is not life, to separate those things that are important from those that are of little or no consequence. I go to the woods of prayer, because I do not want to come to die and discover that I have not lived.

Go to the woods of prayer. Go to the classroom of silence.

From these places you will emerge capable of living life to the fullest—attuned and empowered to live life deliberately.

～ ～ ～

In December 1993, I traveled to Ireland for the first time. For almost a month I gave talks across the country to small groups and large groups. It was my first international speaking trip and my first Christmas away from home. I was twenty years old and had never seen a white Christmas. I spent that Christmas in Ireland with a man who has since become one of my dearest friends. We sat by the fire and told stories, and the stories ignited a fire within us. We both have a passion for stories and storytelling. This is one of the stories he told me that Christmas:

There was once a troubadour. We are told he was a startlingly handsome man, with beautiful olive skin and raven black hair, with eyes as green as river reeds, with long thick lashes. He was very handsome in every way, full of the tone and sinew of youth. His family, rich and respected, dressed him in the finest threads and velvets, and his popularity among the ladies was unmatched. He had everything, didn't have to work for a living, and had a host of comrades who loved and adored him.

He went as a brave soldier to war with the blessings of the whole town. When in battle, he was laughing with his friends as he engaged the enemy, looking on it as a sort of game. In fact, he was so self-confident in the middle of danger that he was knocked from his horse and while unconscious was dragged by his foot, which was caught in the stirrup. When he came to, it was night. He was near a small pool of water in a clearing, the horse was grazing, and his foot was still caught. He was on his back and looking up into the sky. It was one of those very black nights, with no moon but a few very bright stars. Everywhere there was silence. He gazed up at one of the stars, and his whole life and its meaning passed before him for assessment.

He fell unconscious again, and the fever raged in his body for weeks. Eventually he returned to his family, and they kept vigil by his bedside, as they felt each hour might be his last. Many visitors came to see him—priests, bishops, the town mayor, even a cardinal.

At last, one morning, those river reed–green eyes opened up to the sound of a bird on the window singing. All he wanted to do was hold the bird closer and listen to its song. Weak as he was, he got out of bed and tried to catch the bird, but it fled from him, off the windowsill and onto the roof opposite his room. At that moment he remembered the midnight sky, and the last thing he remembered was looking up at that bright star while his life flashed before him.

This young man was so loved and revered by his family and all the townspeople that shortly afterward they gave him a great party to celebrate his return to health. From far and wide, all the family's friends traveled to join the celebration, but he was changed. All the things he used to do with his friends he found he could no longer enjoy, and all the dazzling clothes his parents put on him he had no interest in. All he could think about was that night sky and the bright star. And when they would catch him in this reverie and ask him what he was so preoccupied with, and he would tell them, they'd shove another brew in front of him and say, "You'll get over it."

Every day he could not wait to get out of the city into the countryside, into the fields of flowers. One day he lay on the ground and put his fingers and toes into the moist earth of the meadow, and he stayed there with his face in the ground the whole afternoon. Another day he found a stone that was marbled in glittering dust, and he stared at it all day. This was a very different person from the happy-go-lucky warrior who had set out for battle a short while before.

He spent all his days in the countryside, and his parents knew they were losing him, that wonderful son on whom they depended to carry on the family, to take over the family businesses, and perhaps one day to become governor of the province. He smiled at them and he loved them, but little by little they were losing him. Then one day he realized how much he loved God. The God who did not say anything in the dark midnight sky but was there, the God who was in the bird that sang a song to his awakening, and in the moist and good earth that allowed him just to lie there, and in the poppies that dazzled his eyes with blazing scarlet colors and the humming of bees and the iridescence of butterfly wings. He realized that this God he loved was the unseen gift all around him. His parents thought he had gone off the deep end and threw endless parties to try to get him to snap out of it. They even sent him to talk to the priests, who only shook their heads.

Finally, one day at a great party, when he was dressed in the most dazzling clothes his parents could procure for him, he stripped down naked in front of all the assembly, minister, priests, family, women, friends, goats and sheep, the sky, the earth, the village. Not that he was an exhibitionist; no, it was a sign that he - didn't belong to this life anymore, and he ran from the city with a song in his heart to find some cloth of the field to cover his body. There was a song in his heart and a gentle spirit that was born of the fever. Later he would find an old place and begin to build it up with stones, through freezing winter rains. His worship to the glory of God was the kingdom of the earth.

The greatest contribution that the midnight sky made to him was not the image for which he had lived so long, but the true beauty within man and woman. The fever burned away the image so that he could see what he had never seen before. He turned the page and changed. His parents could no longer see in him the camaraderie they lacked in themselves. The women could no longer see in him the need for a lover that they lacked in their own lives. He changed, and they couldn't see in him anymore what they were themselves. They would have to grow to find in him what was in themselves all along.

What was now looking out from those green eyes was not the image, but the magnificent light he had become. He would walk in the fields, and the birds and the animals would go to him. Once a great mountain lion came and lay at his feet.

Why did he call these things brothers and sisters? Because they were. A wild animal will not lie down beside a person devoted to the image, because the image is the stagnation of regressive energy, copulation, pain, fear, doubt, and power. But a lion will lie down peacefully at the feet of a great light and find a oneness with it, because the light that it sees and senses is the life force of its very being.

This man lived the rest of his life being a glory of God, a glory to the God who had emerged in him. He sang of the glory of life and tried to educate people, not in doctrine, but in the simplicity of knowledge. He lived no hypocrisies but was devoted only to God. He became hated and despised, because he tried to shine in the darkness while other people guarded the light switch.

This is a true story. The dashing young man was Francis of Assisi.

∽ ∽ ∽

There is no greater force to live by than faith. Prayer gives us vision, courage, strength, and endurance. Prayer dissolves our prejudices, banishes our narrow-mindedness, and melts away our judgmental tendencies by expanding our hearts, minds, and spirits.

We pray to God on our knees—but we also pray in peace, joy, love, and laughter.

Life is a prayer.

Perhaps now would be a good time to take a couple of minutes to pray. This is the rest of the prayer Francis wrote in the twelfth century. Born in Assisi in Italy, he was the founder of the Franciscan Order of Friars. He had a profound love of nature and approached all living beings, creatures, and entities as brothers and sisters. His prayer is as profound and powerful today as it has ever been.

> *Lord, make me an instrument of your peace.*
> *Where there is hatred, let me sow love.*
> *Where there is injury, let me sow pardon;*
> *where there is doubt, let me sow faith;*
> *where there is despair, let me sow hope;*
> *where there is darkness, let me sow light;*
> *and where there is sadness, let me sow joy.*

> *Divine Master, grant that I may not so much seek*
> *to be consoled as to console;*
> *to be understood as to understand;*
> *to be loved as to love;*
> *for it is in giving that we receive,*
> *it is in pardoning that we are pardoned,*
> *and it is in dying that we are born to eternal life.*

THE SEVENTH DAY

Wouldn't it be nice to have one day a week just to rest, reflect, and be renewed? Would you be happier, healthier, maybe even a better person? What is stopping you? I believe that honoring the seventh day makes sense even for an atheist.

The rhythm of life is founded on ancient tradition, eternal mysteries, modern knowledge, and common sense.

The seventh day has its roots in the Judeo-Christian scriptures and tradition. As discussed in part 4, in the book of Genesis we read, "On the seventh day God rested from all the work that He had done." Why did God rest on the seventh day? Was God tired? Of course not. God did not need to rest, but He foresaw our "need" for rest. In foreseeing our need for rest, God established the seventh day as a holy day to be set aside for rest and renewal.

God did not create the Sabbath for His sake. God created the Sabbath for our sake. The Sabbath doesn't help God, it helps us.

By instituting the seventh day as a day of rest and renewal, by setting this time aside, God provided another instrument to restore and maintain rhythm in our lives—the rhythm of life that gives birth to peace, harmony, effective living, and optimum health and well-being.

THE THIRD INSTRUMENT

The first and second instruments help us to establish the rhythm of life day by day. The third instrument—the seventh day—helps us to anchor our weeks in the rhythm of life. Here, we will discuss the seventh day as a time of rest and renewal, and as an instrument in creating and maintaining a rhythm in our lives that enables us to achieve and maintain our maximum capacity in every area of our lives.

The seventh day is an ancient tradition founded and based on our most human needs. It is a Jewish tradition and a Christian tradition. Other religious traditions also honor one day of the week as a day of worship and rest. In this age that has not been kind to tradition, I believe there is a great need to embrace this wonderful, life-giving tradition of the seventh day.

The tradition of the Sabbath emerged from our legitimate need as human beings for rest. The seventh day tradition upholds, protects, and ensures our legitimate need for rest and relaxation, for a change of pace, for time with family and friends, for time to turn toward the transcendental, and for time to renew our connection with God. It is a tradition as relevant today as it was five thousand years ago.

The modern conception of life respects only action. To be spending your time in a worthwhile manner, you must be doing or achieving something. The crudest and most basic measure of this attitude is moneymaking. This mind-set affects even the way we spend our recreation time. People are so caught up in this obsession with action and activity, they feel they must be doing something constantly. Prayer is an inner activity. When you pray you take on the appearance of doing nothing. And because the fruits, benefits, and rewards of prayer are internal, you appear to be achieving nothing. Nothing could be further from the truth.

Not every person with their eyes closed is asleep, and not every person with their eyes open can see.

Our political, social, and cultural movements do not uphold the journey from point A to point B. The philosophical foundation of the lifestyles celebrated by the modern media screams out, "Life is about what you have and what you do." Pleasure, possessions, and power are the three pillars of this philosophy. The emphasis is on *having* and *doing* rather than on *becoming*. The truth is, what you become is infinitely more important than what you do or what you have.

The third instrument invites us to set aside one day each week to relax and refocus, to remind ourselves of the priorities of our lives. One day a week to turn our backs to the wind, to dust the dirt from our feet and our souls, to drift and dream, and to open ourselves to peace, tranquillity, leisure, and simple appreciation of life. Be creative. There are thousands of ways to spend the seventh day. Broaden your horizons.

Read one of those books you have been meaning to read for years.

Spend time with your family.

Take an afternoon nap.

Paint a picture.

Read poetry.

Write a poem.

Make some memories.

Speak your love.

Play catch with your son.

Get a little exercise.

Spend time with your friends.

Eat a bowl of chocolate ice cream.

Go to church.

Visit someone who is lonely.

Start a journal.

Find the time.

Just sit and listen to music . . . if you can play, play.

Get a massage.

Give a massage.

Go fishing.

Plant a garden.

Spend time with children. Dostoyevsky, the famed Russian novelist, wrote, "The soul is healed by being with children."

Lie on a beach and soak up the sun and watch the clouds.

Seek out a forgotten friend.

Talk by the fire.

Run.

Speak your love again.

Watch a movie together.

Sleep under the stars.

Laugh a little.

Laugh a little more.

Go to a play.

Apologize for always being so busy.

Visit a museum or an art gallery.

Listen.

Go back and read the novels you studied in your last year of high school.

Dance slowly, arm in arm.

Swim.

Get to bed early.

Visit with solitude.

Befriend silence.

Ponder the thoughts of poets, philosophers, sages, seers, and
saints.

Go for a picnic.

Get a group of friends together for a game of touch football.

Take up one of your grandmother's hobbies.

Keep a promise.

Walk in the park.

Gather up all of those photos you have lying around and put
together an album.

Watch a sunset.

Listen to the rain.

Write a love letter.

Bake some cookies.

Call your mother . . .

✧   ✧   ✧

These types of activities renew us, refresh us, bring rhythm to our
lives, lead us toward maximum health, liberate our hearts and
minds, and remind us of who we are and what is really important.

Fill the seventh day with enriching experiences that bring new
meaning and depth to your life. Step back and get a good look at
life, and then immerse yourself more fully in it.

A good starting point would be to try to do at least one activity
in each of the four areas of legitimate need—physical, emotional,
intellectual, and spiritual—on the seventh day.

✧   ✧   ✧

Everything happens according to the seasons. Nature is based on
certain cycles. These cycles are the untapped power of our lives. If

a farmer plants the seed in the winter, will he have a crop in the spring? No, he will have wasted his time, effort, energy, and seed. It is knowledge of the cycles, seasons, and rhythms of nature that makes a farmer successful.

Today, it is common knowledge and practice that a rested field yields a plentiful crop. I wonder, the first time a farmer decided to let a field rest for a year, did his neighbors and friends say, "Oh, - that's a clever idea"? Absolutely not. They laughed at him, made fun of him, talked about him behind his back, and thought he was crazy. The next year, when he brought in his crop from that field, he had the last laugh. The following year, when there were three or four fields resting, he smiled to himself with a gentle sense of quiet satisfaction. Ten years later, when every farmer in the district was using the resting field method, he had become a legend.

The cycles of nature hold the untapped power of our lives, too. As you begin to discover those cycles and live by them, your friends will think you are crazy for leaving the party early, or for passing up "an irresistible opportunity" at work, or for changing the way you spend your Sunday. But over the weeks, months, and years ahead, as you bring the harvest of your life to be weighed, they will soon see that your way is better. They will turn to it. They too will begin to seek the rhythm of life.

∽ ∽ ∽

The question becomes: Are you prepared to give your health and happiness priority over your bank balance and your toy collection? The rhythm of life should be a priority in our lives. The seventh day as a day of rest is a very powerful tool in creating and maintaining the rhythm of life. Acknowledge the wisdom behind the Sabbath tradition. Use this day. Accept this gift. Allow this day of rest to regulate your week, to provide a macrorhythm for your life.

Do you ever feel that you just need a day off? A day to relax, to be with family and friends, to do nothing at all, a day to take it easy?

Embrace the seventh day. Allow yourself to be renewed and re-freshed. For thousands of years, wise men and women of every culture have been tapping the power of the Sabbath, in one form or another, to maintain rhythm in their lives. From this rest and reflection of the seventh day, we emerge with a keen sense of what our priorities are and return to our work and to the world rooted once again in our life principles.

∽ ∽ ∽

There once lived a man whose name was Jude. He was an apostle of Jesus Christ and was renowned throughout the region as a wise and deeply spiritual man. People traveled great distances, venturing across foreign lands, to seek his advice and healing.

One day Jude was relaxing outside his hut when a hunter came by. The hunter was surprised to see Jude relaxing and rebuffed him for loafing. It was not the hunter's idea of what a holy man should be doing.

Jude recognized these thoughts running through the hunter's mind and also noticed that the man carried a bow for hunting. "What is your occupation, sir?" Jude asked.

"I am a hunter," the man replied.

"Very good," Jude said. "Bend your bow and shoot an arrow." The man did so. "Bend it again and shoot another arrow," said Jude.

The hunter did so, again and again. Finally he complained, "Father, if I keep my bow always stretched, it will break."

"Very good, my child," Jude replied. "So it is with me and all people. If we push ourselves beyond measure, we will break. It is good and right from time to time to relax and re-create ourselves."

If you don't break from the tensions of daily living, they will break you.

∽ ∽ ∽

What is music made of? Yes, rhythm, of course. What else? Yes, notes. When you write music, do you write only notes? No. In music the rests are as important as the notes. Great musicians know the power of rest. If you listen to a great public speaker, you will discover that the way that person pauses is as powerful as the words he or she speaks. It is true also in life. The rests are as important as the activity. The silence is as important as the noise. The rest makes the activity more powerful and efficient. The silence makes the noise more meaningful.

Walt Whitman once wrote, "I loaf and invite my soul." Loafing opens the heart and mind to allow peace and tranquillity to flow in. We all need a time to relax and listen to the voice within, the voice that reveals the truth that makes us free.

Leisure increases the richness of life. The wise make time to loaf. In this modern age obsessed with noise and movement, we seem incapable of relaxing. Take it easy.

Let us conclude our discussion with a reflection from Leonardo da Vinci. Born in Italy in 1452, Leonardo was a painter, sculptor, architect, musician, engineer, mathematician, and scientist. Leonardo da Vinci was unquestionably one of the greatest intellects in human history.

> Every now and then go away,
> have a little relaxation,
> for when you come back to your work
> your judgment will be surer;
> since to remain constantly at work
> will cause you to lose power of judgment . . .
>
> Go some distance away
> because the work appears smaller and
> more of it can be taken in at a glance,
> and a lack of harmony or proportion
> is more readily seen.

The Art of Slowing Down

There is an art to slowing down. In our busy world it is not easy to master this art, but it is necessary. Our lives have a habit of gathering a momentum of their own, plunging forward, with or without our consent. Learn to slow down and access life. Take your foot off the accelerator and look about and within.

Slow down. Breathe deeply. Reflect deeply. Pray deeply. Live deeply. Otherwise you will spend your life feeling like a bulldozer chasing butterflies or a sparrow in a hurricane.

PART SIX

THE WAY
OF EXCELLENCE

A Childhood Lesson

⌖

I don't know where it came from, or why I developed it, but for as long as I can remember it has been a part of me. I have always been fascinated with famous and successful people.

When I was a child, I often dreamed of being a sports champion. So I looked to my sporting heroes—soccer champion Pele, golfing great Greg Norman, and cricket legend Don Bradman—and I said to myself, "I hope that happens to me one day."

As I grew older, my fascination with famous people expanded to include men and women from all walks of life—movie stars, entrepreneurs, politicians, religious leaders, musicians, and artists. I began to read about them and watch movies and documentaries about their lives and work. I studied their lives with an insatiable curiosity.

Looking back now, I realize I was searching for clues. I wanted to know the secrets of their success. What makes a champion a champion?

Over time, I began to see how their success was achieved. Whether it was to make $100 million, to become a world-class football player, to raise a wonderful family, to become a great political leader, to be an inspirational artist or author, or to live a life of heroic holiness—I discovered that for the most part all of these people possessed a basic set of qualities. Their success wasn't just good luck. I began to see a pattern emerge. Regardless of their field, each of them applied a set of principles to their individual situation, which produced phenomenal results.

There is a pattern. It is what leaders, legends, heroes, great achievers, champions, and saints do to excel in their given field. This is the way of excellence, from start to finish. Let me tell you about how I believe they achieve it.

The first thing they do is work out where they are—point A—and who they are—self-knowledge. They take a good, long, hard look at themselves. They establish their needs, talents, and desires. They define and list their strengths and weaknesses. They define who they are and where they are. They write it down.

The very next thing they do is work out where they want to go—point B. They call that the dream, their goal or ambition. They define it precisely, and they write it down. They dream without limits.

Now that they know where they are and who they are—point A—and where they want to go—point B—they establish which path will take them there the quickest. They have a vision. They pull together a plan. It may be an imperfect plan, but it is a plan nonetheless.

Those who fail to plan can plan to fail.

The next thing they do is begin to work the plan. They walk the path. They move in the direction of their dreams. And as they walk that path, they allow all of their actions to be guided by a life principle that summarizes in one sentence their purpose and ambition.

Every morning when they wake up, the first thing they do is remind themselves of their goal. Every night before they go to bed, the last thing they do is remind themselves of their goal. They remind themselves of that goal in every waking moment, of every hour, of every single day. They never let that goal out of their sight. They harness the power of common thought.

They do not let anything get between them and their goal. They are dedicated to their path and plan. They walk the path with unrelenting energy. They begin to use all their time, effort, and energy in pursuit of their goal.

If something does come between them and their goal, they consider it an obstacle, and they find a way to go over it, under it, around it, or through it. Guardians of the threshold try to hold them back, delay them, discourage them, and persuade them to walk other paths. But they resist distraction. They believe in their path and plan.

They realize they cannot do it alone. They take time to love and be loved. They cherish people—realizing that nothing worthwhile can be achieved without the love and help of others.

They are infectious. Everything they do and say communicates the passion and vision of their dream. They master communication. Who they are, what they do, and how they do it conveys a powerful message.

They experience difficulties and heartache, but they push on, always keeping sight of their goal. They meet and become intimate with real pain and deep suffering, but they resist the temptation to become bitter and jaded. They fall, but they get back up. They fall again, but they get back up again. They fall over and over, but every time they do they get back up. They persevere, and they persevere, and they persevere. They never give up.

In time they reach their goal. They grasp their dream. They achieve their ambition. It is not luck. It is not freak chance. Success, achievement, excellence, and greatness are not accidents. They are not just gifts from God for a favored few. They are the fruit of discipline. They are the result of a well-implemented plan.

∾ ∾ ∾

When we witness success and achievement in other people's lives, the temptation is to belittle it. We may say to ourselves, "Well, to be a Major League Baseball player is not the most noble goal," or, "To be rich and famous, that's not the most noble goal." The question becomes: Do we even have a goal? Do we even have a point B in our lives? Or are we just wandering around in circles at point A, enslaving ourselves to all types of self-destructive behavior and saying to ourselves, "I hope that happens to me one day," or, "I would give my whole life to be able to do that"?

Take, for example, Itzhak Perlman, whom we discussed earlier. Do you think he ever said to himself, "What is the least I can do and still become the finest violinist in the world?"

Hearing Itzhak Perlman play the violin is more than a musical experience—it is a shattering eclipse—a symphony of sensory and spiritual delight. Itzhak Perlman does something much more than play the violin brilliantly. How do you suppose he came to be so gifted?

Every morning Itzhak Perlman wakes up at five-fifteen. He showers, has a light breakfast, and begins his morning practice session, which lasts for four and a half hours. He has lunch, reads for a while, exercises, and then begins his afternoon practice session, which lasts for four and a half hours. In the evening, he has dinner and relaxes with his family. This is Itzhak Perlman's schedule every single day of the year, except for concert days.

On the day of a concert, he wakes up at five-fifteen, showers, has breakfast, and begins his morning practice session, which lasts for four and a half hours. He has lunch, reads for a while, exercises, and takes a nap for ninety minutes. When he wakes, he gets dressed and goes to the concert venue. There they perform a sound check and have a brief rehearsal. Forty-five minutes before the concert, Mr. Perlman is found alone in his dressing room. Two security guards are placed outside the locked door with explicit instructions to let no one in under any circumstances.

What do you think he does?

He prays. Itzhak Perlman prays. How do you think Itzhak chooses to pray at this time? Do you think he says, "God, will you please let me play the violin brilliantly tonight?" This could be, but it is not the type of petition that leaves Itzhak wondering if God will answer his prayer. When Itzhak Perlman says to God, "Will you please let me play the violin brilliantly tonight?" he does not doubt for one single moment that God will answer his prayer.

Why? Because Itzhak Perlman plays the violin brilliantly for nine hours a day, every single day, day in and day out, in an empty room, for nobody but his God. Itzhak Perlman upholds his part of the deal. Passion. Dedication. Belief. So when Itzhak Perlman says, "God, will you please let me play the violin brilliantly tonight?" he knows with absolute certitude that God will answer his prayer.

Is that the end of Perlman's prayer?

Absolutely not. So how does he spend the other forty-four minutes of prayer? Itzhak Perlman then visualizes what he wants to take place at the concert that night—how he wants to harness his brilliant performance. Do you think he merely tells himself, "I'll go out to the middle of the stage, play the violin, the people will all stand up and clap, and then we will all go home"? Absolutely not.

He visualizes exactly what he wants to achieve; he visualizes much more, because Itzhak Perlman doesn't just play the violin brilliantly. He reaches into the very depths of people. He grasps ahold of their souls and lifts them up as high as he can. Itzhak Perlman makes people cry, and they don't know why they are crying. He makes people feel and hear things they have never felt or heard before—things that cannot be put into words but must be witnessed and experienced to be understood and believed. He shares his excitement and passion for life through his music, filling his audience with an inexpressible joy. He energizes people. He inspires people. He moves people. He motivates people. He touches people. He changes people. In his own way, he makes a difference in people's lives. And having raised up their souls, he sends them home, knowing that he has instilled in them an excitement and passion for life that is almost uncontainable.

Moments of genius. The inexpressible expressed.

That is what he visualizes in his prayer. You would be mistaken to think that Itzhak Perlman aspires just to play the violin.

Later that night, Itzhak Perlman lies in bed at his hotel, and just before he goes to sleep, a gentle smile comes across his face. He is filled with the quiet satisfaction of knowing that all around that city there are men and women tossing and turning in their beds because they cannot get to sleep. They cannot sleep because their lives have been changed.

Itzhak Perlman has found a way to touch other people's lives, to raise others up, to share his passion for life. He knows that there is no greater satisfaction and fulfillment than to make a difference in another person's life—and that is what it is all about.

Sit in a dark room, turn up the volume, and listen to the theme from the movie *Schindler's List.* It is the first song on the sound track, and you will know that it is not by chance that Itzhak Perlman has achieved excellence, success, and greatness.

What Is Success to You?

If you ask most people what they want from life, as I have taken to doing in recent years, you will discover that they want to achieve success. Some people want to be successful in the workplace and others on the sporting field. Some want to be successful parents and others want to be successful at living their beliefs or the practice of their spirituality. But if you ask all these people to define success, you will end up with as many different answers as there are people.

The Oxford Dictionary defines success as "the accomplishment of an aim; favorable outcome; or, the attainment of wealth, fame, or position."

If this is what success is, please, please tell me there is more to life than success. Or tell me that success is something else, something more.

"There is only one success—to be able to spend your life in your own way," was Christopher Morley's observation. Mark Twain counseled, "The secret of success is to make your vocation your vacation." Ralph Waldo Emerson's definition of success is perhaps the most famed. He wrote, "To laugh often and much; to win the respect of intelligent people and the affection of children; to earn the appreciation of honest critics and endure the betrayal of false friends; to appreciate beauty, to find the best in others; to leave the world a bit better, whether by a healthy child, a garden patch, or a redeemed social condition; to know even one life has breathed easier because you have lived. This is to have succeeded."

I suppose each of us must ultimately define success for him- or herself.

The rhythm of life is a foundation for success. Once we lay this foundation in our lives, everything we turn our hands to will be successful, because we will know what to turn our hands to. But more important, we will find a happiness that is rare, true, and lasting.

As a child, I discovered that the key to success in any field is not a secret. There are no secrets to success. Gimmicks and quick fixes do not lead a person to success. Neither do fast-talking, empty philosophies. Success in any field—business, sport, politics, music, art, or spirituality—depends upon a deep and profound understanding of who you are and what your needs, talents, and desires are.

The key to success is character. The key to your success is your character. And while the foundation of character is self-discipline, the essence of character is personality. Your unique personality holds the secrets to your success.

I believe the greatest success is to be constantly growing, changing, developing, and evolving into the better person I know I can be. In any activity that assists you in this "becoming," you will find success. Why? In the long run you won't be successful at something you don't enjoy doing. Enjoyment is an indispensable ingredient for success. We are successful at the things we enjoy, the endeavors we love, the labors we are excited and passionate about. It is easy to be passionate about the things that challenge us to become the better person we know we can be.

Before too long we become bored, dissatisfied, and discontent with any activity that cannot be employed as a tool in the process of growth and development.

∽ ∽ ∽

Success is the intimate and harmonious relationship among need, desire, and talent. When these three are understood and pursued in balance, the result is extraordinary.

Mozart had a great talent, but he also had a burning desire to make music and a great need, as do we all, to touch other people's lives. The delicate blend of these three—need, desire, and talent—produced a result that leaves us awestruck, even today, more than two hundred years after his death.

Do you remember in school when you would write an essay? You would begin by writing a rough draft, and then you would write a more polished version of your piece. Perhaps you would even write a third, fourth, or fifth draft before writing a final draft to hand in to your teacher.

Mozart never made copies of his music. Mozart never wrote a rough draft. No copies. No drafts. No practices. No corrections. Just a final manuscript. Just the brilliance you hear in his music on paper the first time he wrote it down. That, my friends, is extraordinary. It is greatness. It is a phenomenal blend of need, desire, and talent. It is an unfathomable mixture of genius, legend, heroism, passion, and prophecy. It is nothing less than the Divine shining through a human being.

He lived only thirty-six years. In that brief lifetime, Mozart composed six first-rate operas, twenty-one piano concertos, twenty-four string quartets, seventeen masses, assorted chamber music, and other solo concertos. And, of course, forty-one symphonies.

Chance? Luck? I don't think so. Passion. Discipline. Perseverance. Commitment.

∾ ∾ ∾

Creating the rhythm is about setting the stage for your needs, desires, and talents to emerge, to be understood, and to be fulfilled. The rhythm of life allows us to know, understand, and pursue each of these—need, desire, and talent. The result is success, yes—but an elevated success of which most people of the world do not know—the kind of success that brings with it fulfillment, satisfaction, happiness, health, a deep and abiding peace, and the unalterable reward of becoming "the-best-version-of-yourself."

We desire success, fulfillment, happiness, and to become better people, but we torment ourselves. We do this by failing to find the appropriate relationship among need, desire, and talent. We rush off in pursuit of "success!" Many men and women find some type of "success"—they make extraordinary amounts of money or rise to unimaginable levels of fame, but they do not find happiness or fulfillment in that success. Why not?

These people don't understand their needs, they have little understanding of their talents, nor do they seek out their truest and deepest desires. The result is discord, unhappiness, and dissatisfaction. The great juxtaposition of their so-called success and their personal dissatisfaction is confusing, even horrifying.

Success is to become who you truly are.

A poet must write poetry, an artist must paint, a musician must make music, a lover must love, an athlete must run. When a poet writes poetry, she subconsciously but delicately creates the link among her need, her desire, and her talent. The result, or by-product, of this great mixture of need, desire, and talent is peace, joy, and a deep sense of satisfaction and fulfillment. For the poet not to write poetry would be insanity. For the poet not to write poetry would quite literally produce insanity.

We become mad by attempting to be other than who we truly are.

We cannot be happy trying to be someone else, however good or great that person may be. We will never find happiness and fulfillment following someone else's dream, however great or noble their dream may be.

True success lies in seeking to discover who you truly are individually and uniquely; finding your own special gift, talent, or ability; and developing that gift for the benefit of all. Such success enriches the individual in every way. This type of success enriches society.

Success is not just an achievement, it is a contribution.

WHY ARE THEY SUCCESSFUL AT EVERYTHING?

Have you ever noticed that successful people seem to be able to do everything well? This is not because of some freak chance, but because of the foundation upon which they build their lives. The foundation of their lives is a strong commitment to personal development—to struggling to become the better person they know they can be in every area of their lives—which in turn transforms their family, relationships, community, country, and world. Truly successful people have character. Part of that character is an unwavering commitment to excellence. They know the art of discipline. Successful people just have better habits than the rest. You are your habits.

Successful people are in the habit of being disciplined. Undisciplined people are in the habit of being unsuccessful.

Some people wake up each morning and just stagger through the day. Some people wake up to be successful.

Whether it is success in the business world, success in the spiritual life, or success on the sporting field, the principles are the same. The application of these principles to any person's life necessarily breeds character and, in turn—success, fulfillment, and happiness.

Don't be a *do* person, be a *be* person. You are not a human doing, you are a human being.

∽ ∽ ∽

You may decide to reject the vision of life I am laying before you in this book. That's okay. But regardless of what you choose to seek from life, which rainbow you choose to chase, there will be difficult times that will put you to the test, and you will need courage and perseverance to achieve your goals and dreams.

What is it that sets men and women of great achievement apart from the rest of humanity? What do Mahatma Gandhi, Martin Luther King Jr., John F. Kennedy, Warren Buffett, Albert Einstein, John Quincy Adams, Ronald Reagan, Charlie Chaplin, Michael Jordan, Leonardo da Vinci, Beethoven, Mother Teresa, and Billy Graham all have in common? What empowers them to touch and affect so many people's lives? What allows them to grasp success and reach levels of achievement that for most people are simply unfathomable?

Passion. They are passionate about what they do. Belief. They believe in what they do. Commitment. They are committed to what they do. Courage. In the face of situations where other people would lose heart, they take heart. Perseverance. Through the discouragement of failure, rejection, and criticism, they persevere and keep at it, always staying focused on their goal and dream.

Passion, belief, commitment, courage, and perseverance.

And so it will be with your life. There will be tough times— there are for everyone. There will be times of fear and trembling. There will be times of discouragement and disillusionment. Have courage, smile, keep your chin up, laugh often, be kind to yourself, stay focused, be gracious and appreciative, think happy thoughts, and carry on regardless.

1. THE KNOWLEDGE PRINCIPLE

Ralph Waldo Emerson once wrote, "What lies behind us and what lies before us are small matters compared with what lies within us." Shakespeare counseled, "To thine own self be true." Socrates advised, "Know thyself."

Lasting success, fulfillment, and happiness depend on self-knowledge. There is no greater practical wisdom than knowledge of self. The knowledge principle is, simply, "Know yourself."

In our earlier discussions, we have asked ourselves these questions: What are my dreams? What are my legitimate needs? What are my desires? What are my talents? What is the relationship among my needs, desires, and talents? Who am I? Am I evolving into a better person each day? What are my addictions? Which path should I take? What star am I following?

All of these questions were designed to challenge us to seek to know ourselves a little more. From this knowledge of ourselves, we are able to create and maintain a lifestyle that intimately links our dreams, hopes, needs, desires, and talents—while at the same time leading us to change, grow, develop, and become the-best-version-of-ourselves.

Wise people know themselves and live from that knowledge. If I know that to be healthy and happy I need seven hours of sleep each night, and I sleep for only five, I am a fool. I am worse than the ignorant person who cannot make the connection between his lack of sleep and his poor health and unhappiness. I possess the knowledge but do not use it.

There is a Japanese proverb that speaks of the three most valuable possessions in this life. The third is the sword, because it empowers you to defend yourself and those you love from intruders and tyrants. The second is the gem, because it empowers you to buy and trade for the satisfaction of your temporal needs. But the Japanese believe the most valuable possession is the mirror, because it empowers you to know yourself.

Great men and women know themselves. They know their strengths, their weaknesses, their faults and failings, their flaws and defects, their talents and abilities, their needs and desires, their hopes and dreams, their potential and purpose. From these pieces of knowledge they weave a life of beauty and splendor. "Know yourself" is a character principle of legends, heroes, champions, leaders, and saints.

Fear holds us back. We refuse to look in the mirror, not always physically, but emotionally, intellectually, and spiritually. I have heard it said that an alcoholic cannot look him- or herself in the eyes when looking in the mirror. We are scared of what we will find. So we think and talk only of our good qualities and achievements, but in doing so, we shun some of life's most rewarding and fulfilling lessons. If only we would take a good look at each of the major areas of our being each day, we would discover our dreams, hopes, needs, desires, talents, and potential. If only we knew what we needed, we would be very wise indeed. But so often we refuse to look at anything but our strengths and desires. Weakness and need are much more valuable companions and teachers.

Each day during your sacred hour, take the time to make a daily personal assessment. Ask yourself the difficult questions. Try to discover what makes you feel good about yourself and what makes you happy—not momentary pleasures, but the true pleasures of life, which taste better and better as each day passes.

The things of this world compete for our allegiance. To be true to yourself, you must form an allegiance with the things of this world only inasmuch as they lead you toward your completion, fulfillment, and perfection—point B—to become the-best-version-of-yourself.

To know one's self is a constant and continual process. Observe yourself. Be aware. Watch yourself in the moments of the day. Listen to yourself. Notice how you act or react in certain situations.

The fullness of life comes from knowing yourself—needs, desires, talents, strengths, weaknesses, limitations, and potential—and living from the wisdom of this knowledge.

∽ ∽ ∽

Perhaps you are familiar with Leonardo da Vinci's famous painting *The Last Supper*. Leonardo was living in Milan at the time he painted it, and when he committed himself to that particular composition, he decided he wanted to approach it in a unique way. He wanted to find thirteen men to pose, one for each of the disciples and one as Jesus. He wanted each of his models to look exactly as he envisioned Jesus and each of the disciples to have looked. And so his search for these men began.

One day while he was sitting in church, the voices of the choir were so angelic that he turned around and looked up into the choir loft. As he did, his gaze fell upon one young man in the choir. He perfectly matched how Leonardo had visualized Jesus to look. After church Leonardo approached the young man, explained his project, and inquired as to whether he would be interested in posing for the painting. The young man agreed, and the following week he spent four days posing for Leonardo in his studio in Milan.

Leonardo's search continued, and he quickly found someone to pose as Peter, Simon, and Matthew. Within eleven months he had found and painted all the persons in the scene except for Judas.

Leonardo could not find his Judas. He looked everywhere. He would walk through the streets of Milan, some days for endless hours, searching the nameless faces in the crowds for a man who embodied how he envisioned Judas to have looked. Eleven years passed in his search for Judas when he finally realized he had been looking for his Judas in the wrong places.

Leonardo thought, If I am to find a man who has the qualities and appearance of Judas, I must look where such men are gathered. With that in mind, Leonardo went to the prisons in and around Milan, searching for a man with pain and anger in his eyes, with harsh impatience on his face, with the scars of pride and bitterness on his cheeks, and with the marks of brokenness in his features—a man who looked to him like Judas.

After many days and many prisons, he came across that man. He explained to the man what he was doing and asked him if he would be willing to pose for the painting. The prisoner agreed, and Leonardo made arrangements for him to be brought to his studio in Milan under guard.

The following week he was brought to the studio, and Leonardo began the final stage of his work. As he painted, Leonardo noticed that the prisoner was growing more restless and distressed, even by the hour. Leonardo observed that the man would look at him, and then at the painting, and every time he seemed to be filled with a certain remorseful sadness.

By the middle of the second day, Leonardo was so disturbed by what he was witnessing in his model that he stopped work and said to him, "Is there something wrong? Do you not like my work?" The prisoner said nothing, and Leonardo inquired once more, saying, "You seem very upset, and if I am causing you pain in any way, perhaps we should stop." The man looked at the master painter and then at the painting one more time. As his gaze fell away from the painting, he lowered his head, lifted his hands to his face, and began to weep inconsolably.

After several minutes, Leonardo was finally able to settle him down. "What is it?" he asked.

The prisoner looked expectantly into the artist's eyes and said, "Do you not recognize me, master?"

In confusion, Leonardo replied, "No, have we met before?"

"Oh yes," the prisoner explained. "Eleven years ago I posed for you, for this same painting, as the person of Jesus."

‹∞ ‹∞ ‹∞

In each of us there is a Judas and a Jesus. Our lives here on earth are an incomplete work unless we can discover the Judas and the Jesus within us. We must come to know our strengths and our weaknesses. It is often very easy to find the Jesus within us. Too often we shrink from the task of examining our faults. Yet it is only by knowing the flaws and defects of our character that we can begin to work to overcome them.

Our weaknesses are the keys to our richer, more abundant future. Our strengths are already bearing the fruit they can. Our weaknesses are the unfarmed lands of our character. Pull the weeds from that land, till the soil, plant some seeds, and we will yield a great harvest.

Most people don't want to know about their weaknesses. This is a classic sign of mediocrity. While the rest of us are standing around arguing for our weaknesses, trying to convince people that our lack of character is our character, the heroes, leaders, legends, champions, and saints who fill the history books went looking for their weaknesses. They didn't hide their weaknesses, and they - didn't hide from them. They woke early each morning and went out to face them, because they knew their weaknesses were the keys to their richer, more abundant future.

If you want your future to be bigger than your past, start to transform your weaknesses into strengths.

Are you prepared to face the Judas in you?

‹∞ ‹∞ ‹∞

When God was creating the universe, some of the angels were discussing where each of them felt God should hide the truth. One angel said, "I think God should hide the truth at the very summit of the highest mountain." The next proclaimed, "I think God should hide the truth at the very depths of the ocean." Another said, "No, I think God should hide the truth on the farthest star."

God overheard the angels and spoke up, saying, "I will hide the truth in none of these places. I will hide the truth in the very depths of every man and every woman's heart. This way, those who search humbly and sincerely will find it very easily, and those who do not will have to search the whole universe before they do."

> Know thyself; know your strengths and weaknesses; your relation to the universe; your potentialities; your spiritual heritage; your aims and purposes; take stock of thyself.
>
> —SOCRATES

2. THE DREAM PRINCIPLE

⌒━✦━⌒

Intention /ality.

Life, in a sense, is a long succession of choices and decisions. How do you make your decisions? On what do you base your decisions? Do you have a process that you trust and use faithfully?

In a similar sense, life is made up of hopes and dreams. You dream the dreams and you make the decisions. From an infinite number of possibilities you must decide how to spend your life. The form your life takes depends on the decisions you make.

What is different about the way legends, heroes, champions, leaders, and saints make decisions? What is their decision-making process?

They allow themselves to dream. They imagine perfect circumstances. They place no limitations upon their decision-making process. They ask: What would be best? What is the will of God? If I could do anything, what would I do?

Most people base their decisions on the limited resources available to them at the present moment. For example, Ralph is a senior in high school and wants to go to college. The first question he asks himself is, "What colleges can I afford?" After gathering that data, he then makes a decision based on the options he perceives to be available to him.

Legends, heroes, champions, leaders, and saints ask themselves, "Which college would be most suited to my needs? Which college will most help me grow and become the-best-version-of-myself? Which college will most assist me in the pursuit of my dreams?" And before they make decisions, they employ the dream principle—they dream without limit. They remove themselves from space and time. They remove all limitation from the initial stage of their decision process. If they discover that the best college for them is Yale, and that Yale costs $20,000 a year more than they can afford, they don't throw out the best option, they find a way to get the money. If they have only a 3.4 grade-point average and to get into Yale they need a 3.7, they don't abandon the best option and their dream. They find a way. They go to another college for a year and increase their grade-point average.

The great people of history remove all limitation from their dreams, and once they establish their dream, they seek it with unrelenting energy.

Do not dream like a bank manager. A bank manager tells you only what you can afford based on your realized potential. The greater part of all of us is our unrealized potential. It is true—physically, emotionally, intellectually, and spiritually. Do not let the guardians of the threshold prevent you from moving on and grasping your dreams. Do not let the emotional, intellectual, and spiritual bank managers discourage you from becoming the better person you know you can be.

Try also not to allow your dreams and decisions to be formed, affected, or guided by fear, anger, hatred, greed, or lust. It takes courage to dream, because most of us have an awful fear of failure. Our fear of failure confines us to the dim gray twilight of life. We allow phrases like "What if I fail?" and "I can't do it" to infect our inner dialogue.

The human spirit thrives on victory, growth, change, and development—and all of these involve making the impossible possible. Eleanor Roosevelt wrote, "You must do things you cannot do. It strengthens character, builds courage and strength, confidence and belief."

Columbus, Einstein, Edison, Rachmaninoff, Henry Ford, the

Wright Brothers—the dreamers of the dreams—made the unknown known, the impossible possible.

Dream without limits.

ဏ ဏ ဏ

On my desk at home where I write, I have a photograph of myself when I was seven years old. It is always amusing to watch how different people react to the photo once they discover it is not my little brother or nephew, but me. Some perhaps think me vain and egotistical. Some wonder, and others ask, "Why?"

My seventh year was very special. It was the year that set the stage for the rest of my life. It was the year that I learned life's first lesson. It was the year I learned to love life. If you have heard me speak, you have perhaps heard me tell this story. If you have read some of my other writings, you have perhaps read it in one form or another. I beg your indulgence as I tell it once more.

First grade was the best and the worst two years of my life. I - didn't seem to have any friends, and those I thought were my friends seemed always to be making fun of me. One day, one of the cool kids called me "ugly," and that seemed to stick as a nickname. Apart from all this, I had one other problem that was seriously troubling me.

Week after week in first grade, I remember coming to the school gate on Friday afternoons and finding three or four of my brothers standing around waiting for my mother. They were always very happy and excited, because once again the school week was over and the weekend had begun. But week after week on Friday afternoon, I found myself coming to the school gate sad.

I can still recall one Friday afternoon in particular. The school bell rang, and everyone rushed out of class and ran toward the gates. I gathered my things together slowly, packed my school bag, tidied my desk, and then dragged my bag slowly toward the school gate, where I found four of my brothers. Once again they were very happy and excited because the weekend had come around. That Friday afternoon I was particularly sad.

I remember my mother coming to pick us up. We all walked down the street to where she had parked the car, and as we got close she took our bags from us and put them in the back. One by one we got into the car, and as I climbed in I burst into tears. I had been holding the tears back all afternoon, and I couldn't hold them back any longer. My brothers looked at me, wondering what had happened, and when my mother saw me crying, she said, "What's wrong?"

In first grade on Friday afternoons, we had our spelling test. Between sobs I explained to my mother that I had failed my spelling test again. I always failed. I couldn't spell. That day my mother took me home and held me in her arms and said, "Everything is going to be all right. We will practice your spelling and you will get better."

Then my mother said to me, "How many did you get in your spelling test today?"

I said, "Six out of twenty."

My mum said, "That's fine. If you get seven next week, on Friday afternoon I will take you straight from school and buy you a big bar of chocolate."

The next Friday I got seven, and I got my bar of chocolate. In the following weeks—eight, nine, ten . . . and more chocolate. Twelve, fourteen, sixteen, and still more chocolate. Eighteen, nineteen, twenty . . . and even more chocolate. Until finally I had developed a love for chocolate . . . but I could spell.

I could spell. I had made the impossible possible. I had climbed my Mount Everest, I had walked on the moon, I had won my Olympic gold medal.

For me, at the age of seven, I believed my chances of learning to spell were less than most people's chances of climbing Mount Everest or walking on the moon. It just seemed impossible. It was too big, and I was too small. But on that day when I first scored twenty out of twenty on my spelling test, I realized I had achieved the impossible. I wasn't aware of it at the time, but my life changed forever that day, and as the days and weeks passed, I developed a deep belief that I was capable of anything. I had achieved the impossible, and impossible had been deleted from my vocabulary.

I began to dream without limits.

The following year I repeated first grade, made wonderful friends, continued to do well in spelling, and began to really enjoy life. The journey continues. That photo sits on my desk to remind me of first grade, to remind me that I am capable of even the things that seem impossible.

It is through the mastery of small disciplines that we become capable of greater things and, indeed, anything.

3. The Vision Principle

The vision principle cannot be put in words any better than my golf coach used to say it: "If you can't see the shot, you can't hit the shot."

If there is something you wish to do or become in your lifetime, create a plan for the accomplishment of that dream. Do not wait around foolishly believing that one day by some cosmic wave of events everything will be perfect and your aspirations will achieve themselves. They won't.

God has endowed us all in so many different ways. Engage your talents and abilities.

Goals and plans bring out the most in the human spirit.

Leaders, legends, heroes, champions, and saints are in the habit of constantly planning and setting goals. They never entertain the illusion that there will be no problems. When problems and challenges emerge, they assess them and define them clearly and precisely. Then they create a plan to overcome or alleviate the problems, thus creating confidence and reducing fear.

If you have a problem, face it. If you don't, you empower the problem and paralyze yourself with fear.

Our essential purpose—to become the-best-version-of-ourselves—provides an overall vision, but each area of our lives needs a specific vision.

Have a vision.

4. The Life Principle

As a teenager, and since, observing the lives of legends, heroes, champions, leaders, and saints, I discovered that just about every single one of them has, or had, what I call a life principle. A life principle is one sentence, phrase, or idea that sums up the focus of a person's life.

In the early 1980s, there was a popular film titled *Wall Street*. It was the story of Gordon Gecko, the biggest trader on Wall Street. The movie reveals a trail of greed, lust, lying, cheating, using, and insider trading. Gecko's life principle was "Greed is good."

In the earlier part of this century, a young woman from a very wealthy family left home to join a convent to live a life of poverty, chastity, and obedience. But before too long, she began to hear a voice within her calling her to something more. Within, she felt an unquenchable concern for the poor and suffering of the world. It began simply as a desire. A healthy desire. A noble desire. A desire to help the poor. This young woman felt a need to serve her neighbor. She had a talent simply to love and uphold the dignity of the poor.

In 1997 Mother Teresa died, leaving behind a legacy of love and service in almost every country around the world. She is an icon of compassion in our age. Mother Teresa's life principle was "To live a life of service to God and neighbor by caring for the poorest of the poor."

Mother Teresa's life principle constantly challenged her to be a better person. Her life principle led her to fulfill her legitimate needs. She discovered a rhythm to life, lived in accord with that rhythm, and developed into an extraordinary human being.

Did Gordon Gecko's life principle lead him to be a better person?

The people of ages to come may find it difficult to believe that one such as Mother Teresa ever walked the earth in flesh and blood. She was a hero, a teacher, a warrior, a prophet, a saint, a champion, a queen—and a tremendous success in her field. Mother Teresa is a legend. Everything she did helped her to become the-best-version-of-herself.

The lives of successful people have direction. They do not react to the day-to-day happenings; rather, each of their lives is a conscious action, moving toward a specifically defined goal, directed by a carefully considered philosophy, which is summarized by a single principle—a life principle.

Their life principle brings them into focus, keeps them focused, and protects them from becoming distracted.

Every day, hundreds of options exist for us to expend our time, effort, and energy. Dozens of opportunities emerge in the day-to-day happenings of our lives that distract us from what is really important. Successful people do not allow these distractions to take a grip on their lives. In each moment of decision throughout the day, they carefully consider the opportunity before them in relation to their life principle. They constantly ask themselves, "Will this help me achieve my goal?" "Will this help me along the path toward point B?" They use their life principle as their guide or navigator. It becomes the guiding principle of their lives and the anchor of their dreams.

The whole world will get out of the way for someone who knows what he wants and where he is going.

∽ ∽ ∽

As I explained earlier, until I was nineteen, my goal and ambition was simply to excel in the business world, to make a lot of money, and to enjoy the things of this world. But at nineteen, God touched my life in a special way, opening my eyes. It was at that time that I began to really reflect on life and the world in which we live. It was at that time that I first began to really pray and meditate.

Today, my life principle is this: "Who you become is infinitely more important than what you do or what you have." This idea brings me to focus on change, growth, and development. It challenges me to dedicate my efforts and energies to those activities that will help me to become the-best-version-of-myself. When an opportunity emerges in my life, I can weigh its worth simply by this one idea, this life principle, by asking myself these questions: "Will this opportunity help me to change, develop, and grow?" "Will I *become* a better person through the pursuit of this opportunity?" "Will this opportunity help me to fulfill my legitimate needs?" "If I accept this opportunity, will I be following my star?"

Without the direction and guidance that a life principle brings to our lives, we are like ships headed for shipwreck. Without a foundational principle, we find ourselves in the dark and confusing abyss of deciding based upon "what we feel like" at any given moment. Our feelings are transitory and always changing. If we make our decisions based upon our ever-changing feelings, our lives will have no theme, no rhythm, no continuity, and no consistency. We will lose the thread of our lives, we will lose our own personal story, and we will become insane. Quite literally.

We should develop the habit of viewing our current life questions in relation to a life principle.

Our life principle becomes the tool for bringing focus to our day. It is practical, it is effective, and the more we stay focused on this principle, the more we are able to attend to our legitimate physical, emotional, intellectual, and spiritual needs. The more we attend to these legitimate needs, the more we are energized. This energy maximizes our capacity in each area of our lives. By planning our days according to our legitimate needs, with the guidance and direction of this life principle, we know we are doing as much as we can without sacrificing the rhythm—and there is a certain peace and liberation that comes from that knowing.

All of these work together to create and form the rhythm of life. The rhythm annihilates restlessness by giving birth to balance, harmony, and peace. It is about knowing our limits and never exceeding them—for our own good. It begins by having a goal, a focus, a foundation, a life principle.

Take a blank sheet of regular letter-size paper and ask someone to hold it for you, horizontally, by the long ends. Now, try to punch a hole in it. You can't do it, can you?

Okay! Now this time, take the same piece of paper and ask the other person to hold it exactly the same way, but instead of trying to punch a hole through it with your fist, poke a hole through the sheet of paper with your index finger. What happens? Your finger goes straight through, yes? *Focus.* Focus achieves results in our lives. That is why we need a life principle. It brings focus to our lives.

Crystallize your purpose. Work out what your life principle is going to be. Write it down in your own words. Adopt someone - else's if it seems appropriate. Use mine if it works for you. But write it down, stick it on the wall next to your bed, write it in your planner, put it on the dash of your car, tape it to your wardrobe door, put it on your desk, your screen saver, wherever necessary. Put a copy of your life principle everywhere, until it becomes such a constant and habitual part of your daily thought patterns and processes that you no longer need the visual stimulation.

Remind yourself of your goal in every waking moment of every hour of every day—that's what successful people do. They dream the dream, define the dream, continually visualize the dream—and they achieve the dream.

Then live it. Allow your life principle to become the foundation of all activity in your life. Let it become your guide and adviser in times of decision, let it become your comforter and assurance in times of fear and doubt. Allow it to affect every decision and action of your day. Allow it to become your life principle—the foundation of all you are, all you do, all you have, and of all you are becoming.

Once you have decided upon your life principle you can test it by asking these questions: "Does my life principle build me up and make me more fully and perfectly myself?" "Does my life principle enrich, ennoble, and empower me?" "Will it help me to become the better person I know I can be?"

Who you become is infinitely more important than what you do or what you have.

5. THE THOUGHT PRINCIPLE

In my late teenage years, as I began to reflect on some of the ideas I am now sharing with you, I searched for practical ways to center my lifestyle on my life principle. This question became my touchstone: "What will it take today for me to become the better person I know I can be?"

The first thing I did was write this question down on a blank piece of paper and stick it on the wall next to my bed. I did this because I wanted that question to be the first thing I saw each day. I wanted it to be the first thing I saw each day because I wanted it to become the theme of my day.

Have you ever woken up with a song in your head? What happens? Even though you don't like the song, you can't get it out of your head. You find yourself humming the song all day. You hate the song, yet you discover you know all the words to the song.

There is something very powerful about these first moments of the day. I don't know exactly why, but I know they are powerful. The wise thing to do would be to harness the power of that moment. That is why I stuck that question next to my bed.

Then I wrote it down again—"What will it take today for me to become the better person I know I can be?"—and I stuck it on the mirror in my bathroom. I wrote it down again and stuck it on my closet door, on my desk, on my planner, on the dash of my car, on my fridge . . . I put it everywhere. Why? I wanted to be reminded of my goal in every waking moment of every hour of every day. Why? That is how the legends, heroes, champions, leaders, and saints achieved all they did.

I don't have those pieces of paper everywhere anymore, I just automatically think of that question—"What will it take today for me to become the better person I know I can be?"—3,972 times every day. It has become a habit.

Human thought is creative. What you think, becomes. What you allow to occupy your mind forms the reality of your life and affects the whole world for generations to come. Thought determines action. Before too long, you will be living out what has already happened in your mind. Good or bad, everything happens in your mind before it happens in reality. If you can control what happens in your mind, you can control every action of your life.

A basketball player steps up to the free-throw line. The scores are tied, there is one second left on the clock, it is 3–3 in the series, the NBA championship is at stake, and he has one shot. If he imagines himself missing the shot, what will he do? Of course, he will miss the shot. Thought determines action. If he imagines himself making the shot fifteen times and missing it nineteen times, what will he do? He will miss. The actions of our lives are determined by our last, most dominant thought.

Your future is forged and your actions determined by your most dominant thoughts.

Jack Nicklaus didn't think only occasionally about being a great golfer—it was his most dominant thought for years. Cal Ripken Jr. doesn't think occasionally about being a great baseball player—it is his most dominant thought. Shakespeare didn't think occasionally about being a great writer—it was his most dominant thought. Michelangelo didn't think occasionally about being a great painter—it was his most dominant thought. Francis of Assisi didn't think occasionally about the wonder of God and His creation—it was his most dominant thought.

What is your most dominant thought? The answer to that question will tell you a lot about who you are and what you are doing with your life. The thought principle is "Thought determines action."

> It's a funny thing about life;
> if you refuse to accept anything but the best,
> you very often get it.

> —SOMERSET MAUGHAM

6. The Dedication Principle

❦

Have you ever given your best, your all, to anything? What do you think would happen if you did?

Love doesn't count the cost. Tiger Woods loves golf. Michael Jordan loves basketball. Mahatma Gandhi loved the people of India. Beethoven loved music. Michelangelo loved to paint. The legends, heroes, leaders, champions, and saints who fill our history books loved what they did. People of this caliber dedicate their whole being to their pursuits.

What are you willing to dedicate yourself to completely? What are you willing to throw your whole energy into? What are you willing to pursue wholeheartedly?

Dedicate yourself to becoming the-best-version-of-yourself. In everything you do, remember your essential purpose. View everything in relation to becoming your best self. Everything makes sense against the backdrop of the purpose of our lives. Everything finds meaning in relation to our essential purpose.

Love yourself by becoming the-best-version-of-yourself.

Dedicate yourself to choosing the-best-version-of-yourself in every choice you make. I've never known anyone more in love with life than those who are dedicated to being all they can be.

This is the dedication principle: "In order to love what you do, you must do what you love."

7. The Belief Principle

We live by faith. Whether we are able to recognize it or not, this is a universal truth. Some people say that they don't believe in anything, but they believe in their belief that they don't believe in anything.

Without faith we would be driven to the depths of despair.

In many ways, our faith is so habitual that we are unaware of it. Every day you get into your car and drive down the street. You have faith that the other cars will stay on their side of the road. It isn't an act of faith that you remind yourself of every time you get into your car. But without that faith you would be driven mad by the anxiety that the other cars were going to breach their boundary and come crashing into you.

∽ ∽ ∽

Beyond our belief in ideas and other people is our belief in ourselves. Some of us believe that we are worthy of love, and others believe that they are not. In both cases, our beliefs limit or create our experience of life. Some people believe that they are worthy of other people's time and attention, and others do not. Both believe. They just have different beliefs. And in both cases, the belief determines the reality.

You are here for some reason. You have been born to live one life. Out of the infinite possible lives you could construct out of the opportunities that will present themselves to you, you must choose your one life.

You have been created for some specific work. Nobody else has been entrusted with your role in human history. If you do not play your part, you part will go unplayed.

Foster the belief that you were born for a reason . . . and with every passing day you will begin to see the reason unfolding before your eyes.

God and the universe are conspiring to bring you in touch with all the circumstances necessary to discover and celebrate your genius. All you have to do is prepare yourself and cooperate by choosing the-best-version-of-yourself in the moments of each day.

This was Albert Einstein's reflection: "There are two ways to live life. One is as though nothing is a miracle. The other is as though everything is a miracle."

The choice is yours.

This is the belief principle: "You were created for a purpose, and everything happens for a reason."

> Be not afraid of life.
> Believe that life is worth living,
> and your belief will help create the fact.
>
> WILLIAM JAMES

8. The People Principle

I believe one of the greatest problems in relationships today is caused by a simple modern fallacy. In our age, understanding is posed as the foundation of relationship. It is not. The foundation of relationship is acceptance.

It is a great wisdom to accept people where they are on the journey. Acceptance is the welcoming open arms of relationship.

The people principle is, "People deserve to be cherished."

In order to cherish people, we must look beyond our personal preferences, prejudices, and judgmental inclinations to discover and reverence the wonder and marvel of the individual.

It is helpful to remember that we are all at different points along the path. Our ability to love and cherish people increases infinitely as we learn to accept people for who they are and where they are on their own journey. Some people are at places we ourselves have been before, others are in places we have not yet been. It is a journey—trust that the same God who is moving you toward your purpose and dreams is moving them toward theirs. Even when you cannot understand people, accept them, cherish them.

Along the way, you will meet many people. Some of them you will help, assist, advise. Others will help, assist, and advise you. It has been my experience that when you think you are there to help someone else, chances are they are really there to help you. Our students make the best teachers.

Without the help of others, you will never make the journey. It is simply part of the divine plan that we make this journey to-gether.

It is a funny thing I have observed about life—mistakes are almost always and inevitably one's own responsibility, but one's successes, triumphs, and worthwhile achievements are rarely ac-complished without the help of others.

The greatest barrier to loving people, to cherishing people, and to accepting people is our inability to see ourselves in them. Take a closer look. We are one. To see ourselves in others and others in ourselves—that is wisdom.

My father always told me that the key to success in business is personal relationships. My mother always told me that the key to a rich and rewarding personal life is personal relationships. I have discovered that the key to an abundant spiritual life is personal re-lationship.

Life is relationship.

How are you relating? How are your relationships?

People are a gift. Each person who crosses through your life is a chance to love, a chance to really live. Cherish people.

9. The Communication Principle

⌥——

The communication principle is, "Be clear, concise, open, and honest."

Communication is an art. I have seen some great communicators at work. These are some of the lessons I have learned:

Let others talk.

Avoid arguments.

Don't complain.

Give honest and sincere compliments.

Be more ready to compliment than to criticize.

Invite input.

Make a point to remember people's names; it is music to their ears.

Never be afraid to seek advice.

Never criticize someone in front of other people.

Be aware of other people's desires.

Find joy and pleasure through taking an interest in people.

Talk about yourself only if asked.

Smile—it is contagious and opens people's hearts.

Learn to listen.

Remember people's birthdays and anniversaries—it shows you care.

Encourage people to share about themselves.

Engage people where they are—talk in relation to their interests.

Help other people to discover their uniqueness, to feel special and important, without patronizing them.

Respect other people's opinions.

Admit when you are wrong.

Be kind and friendly to every person you meet.

Ask questions people respond to positively.

Encourage other people in their dreams—particularly children.

Try to see it from the other person's point of view.

Hold up ideals.

Challenge people gently.

Talk about your own failures.

Appeal to higher motives.

Always look for yourself in others and others in yourself—it affirms the oneness of the human family.

Affirm the highest values of the human spirit.

Never pass up an opportunity to speak a kind word of appreciation. There are 6 billion people on the planet, and 5.9 billon of them go to bed every night starving for one honest word of appreciation.

10. The Final Principle

It is a long journey. Some make it, and others fall by the wayside. We all love the beauty of the diamond, but we forget the time and pressure it took to make it. Along the way we become discouraged. It seems too hard. It isn't. It seems impossible. It isn't.

There will be setbacks and failures. Winners are inspired by failure. Losers are afraid of and discouraged by failure. In the wake of failure, winners want to do more, to be more, to do a better job next time. When faced with failure, losers become overwhelmed by the fear of greater failure. They allow that fear to smother them and in the process achieve what they wanted to avoid—a greater failure. The greatest failure is to not try.

There are always plenty of reasons to give up. Think of reasons not to give up, to stay strong, to stay focused, and to persevere.

Once you set yourself at something, keep your eye on your goal and employ the final principle: "Never give up!"

If there ever was a tale of American leadership and perseverance, it is that of Abraham Lincoln. Lincoln was born into poverty in 1809.

Throughout his life he continually faced setbacks and defeats. He twice failed in business, lost eight elections, and suffered a nervous breakdown.

Defeat and failure were often beckoning him, inviting him to quit, but he refused that invitation, and his story is one of extraordinary perseverance. This is a sketch of his life:

In 1816, Lincoln's family was forced out of their home, and he had to go to work to support them.

In 1818, his mother died.

In 1831, he failed in business.

In 1832, he ran for the Illinois House of Representatives and lost.

In 1832, he lost his job. Later that same year, he decided he wanted to go to law school, but his application was rejected.

In 1833, Lincoln borrowed some money from a friend to begin a business, but by the end of the year he was bankrupt. He spent the next seventeen years paying off that debt.

In 1834, he ran for state legislature again and lost.

In 1835, Lincoln was engaged to be married, but his fiancée died and it broke his heart. In 1836, Lincoln suffered a total nervous breakdown and was confined to his bed for six months.

In 1838, he sought to become Speaker of the state legislature and was defeated.

In 1840, he sought to become elector and was defeated.

In 1843, he ran for Congress and lost.

In 1846, he ran for Congress again; this time he won and finally made his way to Washington.

In 1848, Lincoln ran for reelection to Congress and lost.

In 1849, he sought the job of land officer but was rejected.

In 1854, he ran for Senate of the United States and lost.

In 1856, he sought the vice presidential nomination at his - party's national convention. He got fewer than one hundred votes and lost.

In 1858, he ran for the United States Senate again and lost again.

Then, in 1860, Lincoln decided to run for president. . . .

I mean, based on what?

His track record?

He won and went on to become one of the greatest presidents in the history of the United States and one of the finest models of leadership in modern times. In a speech, Lincoln said, "The path was worn and slippery. My foot slipped from under me, knocking the other out of the way, but I recovered and said to myself, 'It's a slip and not a fall.' "

> I've missed more than nine thousand shots in my career, I've lost more than three hundred games, and twenty-six times I've been trusted to take the game-winning shot and missed. Throughout my life and career I've failed, and failed, and failed again. And - that's why I succeed.
>
> —MICHAEL JORDAN

THE TEN PRINCIPLES OF
EXCELLENCE

Ten principles. Do Michael Jordan, Jack Nicklaus, and Cal Ripken Jr. employ these principles? Yes, absolutely. Did Shakespeare, Beethoven, and Michelangelo employ these principles? Yes, without a doubt. Did Francis of Assisi and Mother Teresa employ these principles? Yes, unquestionably. Did their success manifest in different ways? Certainly. Were their achievements each unique and different? They were. But the principles that we find at the core of their success are the same.

PART SEVEN

❧❧❧

LIVING THE LIFE
YOU WERE BORN
TO LIVE

Enjoy the Journey

One of our greatest failings as human beings is our inability to be present in our own lives. It may sound absurd, but it is true. Let me explain. How often do you find yourself in the company of a person, even in the middle of a conversation with a person, yet are thinking about other people and places? Often, we are distracted by the past and the future. Those distractions rob us of our lives. The past is history. The future is a mirage. The past was the present. The future will be the present. The only reality is now.

The other way this failing manifests itself is in our tendency to put off important matters. We tell ourselves, "When I get that promotion, I will spend more time with my wife and children," or, "I will exercise next week, when I have this project out of the way." Each activity has its own priority and place in our lives, whether it is work, prayer, leisure, exercise, or friendship. The rhythm of life helps us to give each activity its own place—every day—and immerses us in the abundant life.

Over and over I have watched interviewers ask famous and successful people, "What would you change if you could do it all again?" So many of them reply by saying they would enjoy their rise to fame and success a little more if they had another chance. But you never hear them say, "I would work harder and spend less time with my family and friends." Just last year I saw an interview with Billy Graham. The interview concentrated mostly on the works and achievements of his life, but toward the end the interviewer asked, "What would you do differently if you had to do it again?"

The change that came over Billy Graham's features I have never seen before. The interviewer had asked one of those questions that I suppose all interviewers dream of asking. A question that invites the host and his audience into the deepest recesses of the guest's heart. It was as though a veil had been torn away. The expression on Graham's face was one of knowing, and it lingered there for a long moment. He paused, not to think how to answer, but to pull himself together. It was obvious he had asked himself the same question before. He looked down, swallowed, then looked back up again and said, "I would spend more time with my family."

        ৎৎ ৎৎ ৎৎ

Life is a journey. Enjoy the journey. Whether you are setting out to become a legend, a hero, a champion, a star, a leader, or a saint—enjoy the journey. If you do not enjoy life, you will be no good to anybody. The destination, the victory, the achievement—these last only a moment, and then they fade like the morning dew from the grass into little more than pleasant memories.

Success is not a destination—it is a journey.

Another of my favorite songwriters, James Taylor, once wrote, "The secret of life is enjoying the passing of time." The joy is not in the destination; the joy is in the journey. If you cannot find peace in the journey, you will not find peace in the destination. Our passion, enthusiasm, and excitement should be for the journey. Don't put off important things using a destination, or an achievement, as an excuse. Take it easy. Slow and steady. Let things have their place.

Be present in your own life. It is an amazing and rare gift. When you meet a person who has this gift, there is no mistaking it. People who are present to their own lives have this striking ability to focus on who and what is before them. They give the people and the matters at hand their complete and undivided attention. When you stand before such a person in conversation, he is able to make you feel as if no one else exists. It is just you and him. The noise around you, the people around you, even in rush hour on Madison Avenue, do not take even a breath of his attention from you and the conversation. For those few moments, it is as if nothing else exists. For those few moments, you are his life. To give his attention to anything else would be to miss something of his own life. Often we do.

Robert Hastings sums it up perfectly in his story "The Station." Let me share it with you:

Tucked away in our subconscious is an idyllic vision. We see ourselves on a long trip that spans the continent. We are traveling by train. Out the windows we drink in the passing scenes of cars on nearby highways, or children waving at a crossing, or cattle grazing on a distant hillside, or smoke pouring from a power plant, or row upon row of corn and wheat, of flatlands and valleys, or mountains and rolling hillsides, or city skylines and village halls.

But uppermost in our minds is the final destination. On a certain day at a certain hour we will pull into the station. Bands will be playing and flags waving. Once we get there so many wonderful dreams will come true and the pieces of our lives will fit together like a completed jigsaw puzzle. How restlessly we pace the aisles, damning the minutes for loitering—waiting, waiting, waiting for the station.

"When we reach the station, that will be it!" we cry. "When I am 18." "When I buy my new 450SL Mercedes-Benz!" "When I put the last kid through college." "When I get a promotion." "When I reach the age of retirement, I shall live happily ever after!"

Sooner or later we must realize there is no station, no

one place to arrive at once and for all. The true joy of life is the trip. The station is only an illusion. It constantly outdistances us.

"Relish the moment" is a good motto. Especially when coupled with Psalm 118:24: "This is the day which the Lord has made; let us rejoice and be glad in it." It isn't the burdens of today that drive men mad. It is the regrets over yesterday and the fear of tomorrow. Regret and fear are twin thieves who rob us of today.

So stop pacing the aisles and counting the miles. Instead, climb more mountains, eat more ice cream, go barefoot more often, swim more rivers, watch more sunsets, laugh more, and cry less. Life must be lived as we go along. The station will come soon enough.

Be the Difference That
Makes the Difference

◦━━◦

What do all great men and women in history have in common? What raises a person beyond success, achievement, and excellence to the realm of greatness? Greatness is attained beyond the pursuit of our own fulfillment. True greatness is achieved by making a difference in other people's lives. What moves a person from success to significance? Making a difference in the lives of other people.

History is full of examples of great men and women, but we must be careful not to confuse greatness with fame or fortune. Fame and fortune are external qualities of a person's life. Greatness is an internal quality of a person's character, which emerges in his or her actions.

Some examples that readily come to mind are people like Gandhi, Helen Keller, Martin Luther King, Mother Teresa, and Jesus. But most of the people who have developed and mastered this greatness of which we speak are not public figures or celebrities. They are mothers and fathers, teachers and doctors, preachers, rabbis, ministers, priests . . . They are people from all walks of life who turn their talents, efforts, and energies toward the uplifting of other people. They make a difference in other people's lives. When you meet such a person, you see a certain calm in her eyes and she seems to be unusually happy. She is quietly confident and occupied with a serene satisfaction.

There is no greater satisfaction than laying your head on the pillow at night and knowing you have touched another person's life, made his burden lighter, taught her some infinite wisdom, made him laugh, allowed her to cry on your shoulder, lent him an understanding ear . . . made a difference.

∾ ∾ ∾

One of my favorite childhood movies was *Willy Wonka and the Chocolate Factory.* It is the story of Mr. Wonka, the most successful and famous candy maker in the world, and his search to find someone to continue his work when he is gone. Wonka places five golden tickets randomly inside candy bars and announces a contest. Each person who finds a golden ticket will win a one-day tour of the Wonka Chocolate Factory—which no one has been inside for twenty years—and a lifetime supply of chocolate.

Charlie, the child of a single mother in England, dreams, wishes, prays, and hopes that he will find one of the five golden tickets. But his family is desperately poor, and he has no money to buy chocolate bars. One day on his way home from school, Charlie finds some money in the street, buys two Wonka bars, and finds the fifth and final golden ticket.

The next day, Charlie and four other children from around the world, each with a companion of his or her choice, enter into the mysterious and magical world of the Wonka Chocolate Factory. Charlie asks his grandpa Joe to go with him, and they set off on an adventure to live out Charlie's wildest dream.

The other four golden ticket winners are fatally flawed with large doses of selfishness, and one by one they find themselves leaving the tour of the factory prematurely. But Charlie is gentle, kind, and thoughtful.

Wonka takes them from one wonderful exhibition to another, showing them all the wonders of his candy-making genius and imagination. Before long it is just Charlie, Grandpa Joe, and

Wonka left on the tour—but as they come out of the Wonka-Vision Studio, Mr. Wonka's tone and mood change dramatically. He bids Charlie and his grandfather farewell and asks them to show themselves out. And with that, Wonka disappears into his office.

Standing at the office door, Charlie looks at Grandpa Joe. Dumbfounded, he says, "What happened? Did we do something wrong?"

"I don't know, but I'm gonna find out," Grandpa Joe replies as he storms into Wonka's office.

Mr. Wonka's office is just as magical as any other room in the factory. Everything is in halves—half a desk, half a clock, half a picture, half a statue, half a mirror . . . Grandpa Joe says to Wonka, who is sitting at his desk, writing a letter, "What about the chocolate? The lifetime supply of chocolate for Charlie!"

"He doesn't get any," Wonka replies spitefully.

Mr. Wonka appears to become quite angry and begins to explain why it is that Charlie gets no chocolate. He goes to the filing cabinet and takes out half a photocopy of the contract Charlie and the other children had signed at the beginning of the tour and half a magnifying glass. Wonka yells at Grandpa Joe, explaining that because they drank fizzy lifting drinks they had violated the contract and that Charlie was no longer eligible for the lifetime supply of chocolate. "You're a crook, a cheat, a swindler," accuses Grandpa Joe as he turns to leave.

This is where the plot thickens. In Charlie's pocket is one Everlasting Gobstopper, which Wonka had given him during the tour. It is the very Gobstopper that Wonka's rival, Mr. Slugworth, had asked Charlie to get for him in exchange for more money than he could earn in ten lifetimes.

As they leave the office, Grandpa Joe says to Charlie, "If Slugworth wants an Everlasting Gobstopper, that's just what he'll get."

With that, Charlie stops, takes Grandpa Joe's hand off his arm, turns around, and walks back into the office, where Wonka is still sitting at his desk, writing. From his pocket, Charlie takes the Everlasting Gobstopper and says, "Mr. Wonka!" as he places it on the desk. Without another word, he turns around and begins to walk slowly from the office.

Wonka doesn't look up, and he doesn't look at the Everlasting Gobstopper. He doesn't have to. He knows without looking. He just reaches across the desk and grasps the Gobstopper and whispers gently, "And so shines a good deed in a weary world."

With great excitement, Wonka swings around, calls Charlie back, and explains that it was a test to see if he would betray his promise never to show the Everlasting Gobstopper to anyone— and that Charlie has passed, and won, and that now he is going to give Charlie the chocolate factory.

I cannot describe to you the joy I felt as a child each time Charlie took the Everlasting Gobstopper from his pocket and placed it on the desk. I feel the same joy even today when I watch the movie. It is intense. It's exhilarating. His innocence, I suppose, his honesty, his sincerity and integrity—all symbols of hope for a weary world.

"And so shines a good deed in a weary world." This is what our world needs. It is what we need. It is what makes the world a joy to live in. It is what fills us with a tangible sense of our own worth and wealth.

Our every action is an opportunity to carry the torch of hope to an often weary world. Each day is filled with endless possibilities to make a difference. It doesn't take much, for it really is a weary world for so many people. It is a world full of people desperately hungry for sincerity, honesty, and goodness. Most of them are men and women just like you and me. They don't have the power to change the world single-handedly, so they think change must be someone else's responsibility. The truth is, no one has the power to change the world single-handedly, but each of us has the power to make a difference.

Ideas change the world. Good ideas change it for the better. Bad ideas change it for the worse. Men and women share their ideas through their words and actions. What ideas are you sharing with the world?

Charlie shared the idea that honesty, integrity, and goodness are more important to a person's happiness than money. As a child, I watched that movie and I wanted to be like Charlie. In my childhood, I didn't understand it as I do now. That didn't matter. I knew that his deed was good and true, and I wanted to be like Charlie, and that was enough. Through his action, Charlie shared his idea—and ideas are contagious.

Ideas change the world of today and form the world of tomorrow.

ھ ھ ھ

Make a difference. It is not that hard. Make a habit of making another person's day. Every day.

Have you ever received an unexpected letter? I love to receive letters, and I am fortunate to receive many, every day, from people all around the world. They come from family and close friends and also from people I have never met. It's a wonderful feeling to receive an unexpected letter—the excitement teetering on impatience as you open the envelope. Yet for most people it is a rare joy.

Do you remember the last time you received an unexpected letter? It was a wonderful experience, wasn't it? Do you remember the feeling? Did it make your day?

Write one. Write an unexpected letter today. Write a letter to an old friend whom you haven't seen in years or to someone you love whom you haven't written to in a while. It isn't that hard; it - doesn't take that much. Write a short note on a small piece of paper, put it in an envelope, address the envelope, and take it down to your post office. It will cost you the price of a postage stamp and five minutes of your time to make someone's day.

Or when was the last time you bought someone a box of chocolates or a bunch of flowers? Not because it's someone's birthday or anniversary or for any reason other than to brighten up his or her day. When was the last time you baked someone some chocolate-chip cookies?

When was the last time you sat down the people you love and told them of your love for them? It's best to express it in your actions, but it doesn't hurt to say it. Perhaps you are married. When was the last time you told your spouse how much he or she means to you? When was the last time you sat your husband or wife down and said, "You know, for me, you are sun, rain, fire, ice, New York, L.A., and every town along the way"? It doesn't take that much, but it makes a difference.

Whisper, "I love you," in your sleeping child's ear.

These things may seem simple and external, but they reflect a much deeper quality in a person. Spiritually, we strive to be patient because God is patient, we seek to be kind because God is kind, we try to be humble and gentle because they are the ways of God, we seek to love and be loved because God is love.

Yet above everything else, beyond everything else, before everything else, after everything else, and during everything else—God is a giver. God always gives. He never takes. He only gives. Always giving. Giving is God's life and existence. For God, giving is the perpetual motion of His being. That is why to give a box of chocolates or a bunch of flowers, or to take time to write a letter, is an act of greatness. It is an act of greatness because it is an act that emerges from the heart and mind of God. If all our actions could be performed with this disposition, we would be living life to the fullest.

I promise you with absolute certitude that there is no faster, surer way to share in the life, the power, and the infinite joy of God than to give.

Give of your time, give of your talents, and give of your resources to make a difference in other people's lives. It is the way of greatness. This is the way of God. It is the way of legends, heroes, stars, champions, leaders, and saints. I hope and pray that it becomes your way, and mine.

As a child, my father used to tell me, "Whatever you give to another will return to you ten times." Life has taught me that, like so many things my father said to me, it is a wise and true statement. Another saying I recall from my childhood is "You get what you give." When you refuse to give, holding on tightly to everything you have, you live in the realm of lack and limitation. When you give, you perform a significant and vital attitude change. By giving, you express abundance—and what you express in thought, word, and action will become the reality of your life. Here, veiled mysteriously by the act of giving, we discover the abundant life.

When you give to assist in someone else's need, you learn very quickly that the satisfaction of giving is greater than the satisfaction of having.

As time goes by, you realize that many of the things you once thought you needed, you don't really need. With this realization of your own abundance, you are able to give more. Have you noticed that although God is always giving, He is never without? God is not lack or limitation—God is abundance. For God, giving is like breathing—let it become so for you and for me, and our lives will be full of excitement, passion, satisfaction, contentment, and fulfillment.

Otherwise we will become like the monkey who realized one day that his master had left the lid off the peanut jar. The monkey waited for his master to leave the house for his afternoon walk. When the master left, the monkey jumped onto the table where the jar was, only to realize that the jar was only half-full and too tall for him to reach the peanuts. The monkey knocked over the jar, but none of the peanuts fell out. So he reached into the jar and grabbed a large handful of peanuts, and his eyes lit up. But as he went to take his hand out of the jar, he realized his hand wouldn't fit through the mouth of the jar while it was full of peanuts. The monkey looked at the peanuts and pulled harder and harder, to no avail. He could see the peanuts, hold the peanuts, but he couldn't enjoy them. Torture.

When the master returned, the monkey was still on the table, clenching the handful of peanuts, refusing to let go. Foolish monkey.

Finding our place in the world, finding our place in our local community, and making a difference in our own way all give meaning, purpose, and a deep, deep sense of fulfillment to our lives. We must not only find it for ourselves, but help every individual to find the same.

∽ ∽ ∽

The enemies of making a difference are doubt, fear, discouragement, and selfishness. Some people never try to make a difference because they doubt they can. Some people fear to try in case they fail. Some people start to make a difference but compare the good they are doing with all the evil they can imagine in the world and become disabled by discouragement. Some people are so absorbed in themselves that they never think of anyone's needs but their own.

On the other hand, some people trust that they were put here on this earth to make a difference in some way, large or small. Those same people know the fear of failure as much as anyone, but they face that fear, immerse themselves in that emotion, and move forward bravely. They fight off discouragement by keeping things in perspective. When things get tough, they take life just one day at a time. When things get really tough, they take life one hour at a time. And when things get unbearably difficult—they take heart, hold firm, and take life moment by moment. One by one. Little by little. They are not strangers to doubt, fear, discouragement, or selfish desires, but they find a focus in their lives and commit to that focus.

By now you are aware of my great love for stories. Parables, fables, and stories are the most effective and powerful way to convey any idea or message. Here is a story that I would like you to recall when doubt, fear, discouragement, and selfish desires attempt to steal you away from your life's work of making a difference.

∽ ∽ ∽

Once upon a time, there was a young boy who lived just near a beach. Every afternoon the boy would walk along the beach.

One day as he was walking, he noticed that as the tide had gone out it had left many starfish stranded on the beach. He realized that if the starfish were left there, they would die before the water returned. So as he walked along the beach, one by one he picked up the starfish and threw them back into the water. He couldn't pick them all up because there were too many, but the ones he could pick up he did.

From that day on, the boy would spend his afternoons walking along the beach throwing the starfish back into the water. Then one day as the boy was walking, an old man came walking in the other direction. The old man saw what the young boy was doing and cried out, "What are you doing, boy? You'll never make a difference. Why don't you just enjoy your walk?" The boy ignored the old man and continued to pick up the starfish, one by one, and to throw them back into the water. But as the old man got closer, he came right up to the boy and said, "What are you doing? What are you doing, boy? You'll never make a difference. Why don't you just enjoy your walk?"

The boy just stood there and said nothing. Then the old man grabbed the young boy by the arm, turned him around, and made him face down the beach. As the young boy and the old man looked down the beach, they could see that there were many, many starfish. The old man said, "Look, boy, there's hundreds of them, there's thousands of them. Look how many you have missed. You'll never make a difference. Forget about them. Just enjoy your walk."

Just then, the young boy bent down and reached into the sand one more time and picked up one more starfish. And standing up, he threw the starfish as far as he could into the ocean. Then, looking deep into the old man's eyes, he said, "I made a difference for that one."

FOUR SIMPLE STEPS

There are four simple steps that will empower you to make a difference in other people's lives and lead you along the path of greatness.

STEP ONE

When you wake up tomorrow morning, remind yourself of your goal, your point B, your essential purpose—to become the-best-version-of-yourself.

STEP TWO

The next step is to ask yourself, "Whose day can I make today?"

STEP THREE

Now ask yourself, "How can I make that person's day?"

STEP FOUR

When you have made these first three steps, shower and have breakfast, but then, just before racing into the day, take a few minutes to plan, reflect, and pray. Find a quiet place, and in that silence visualize how you would like your day to unfold. Make plans to fulfill your legitimate needs physically, emotionally, intellectually, and spiritually. Take a moment to become aware of, and to appreciate, all you have and all you are, and then you will be ready for the day.

If you faithfully commit yourself to this simple four-step plan of action for the next ten days, your life will begin to be filled with the fruits of the rhythm of life—peace, joy, an increased ability to love, an increased ability to be loved, a rare happiness and satisfaction, a profound sense of fulfillment, and the love, excitement, and passion for life that are the essence of God, the essence of the human being, and the intended essence of the human experience.

You will then find yourself on the verge of greatness. You will have discovered the power of making a difference, and life will issue you the challenge to continually and consistently engage that power in your daily life.

After a while, you learn that it's better to write an unexpected letter than to sit around waiting for the postman to deliver one. Sooner or later, you discover that it is better to help someone plant a garden than to wait for someone to bring you flowers. Let it be sooner for you.

The temptation is to say, "I am just one person; what can one person do?" Look at what other men and women have done in just one lifetime: Billy Graham, Mother Teresa, Beethoven, Michelangelo, Frank Lloyd Wright, Albert Einstein, Michael Jordan, Steven Spielberg, Bill Gates, Abraham Lincoln. They too could have used the same excuse, "I am only one person." They didn't. Rather, they dedicated themselves to the passionate pursuit of their dreams. Theodore Roosevelt offers us a starting point: "Do what you can, with what you have, where you are." Francis of Assisi offered this advice to his brothers: "First do what is necessary, then what is possible, and before long you will be doing the impossible."

The good we do is never lost; it never dies. In other people, in other places, in other times—the good we do lives on forever.

Be the difference that makes the difference!

Leaders, Critics, Dreamers, and the Future

꧁══✦══꧂

We are living during a very interesting period of history, a time of transition. Transition periods are the most important, yet you rarely read about them in history books, because it's difficult to judge exactly when they begin and when they end. They lie subtly sandwiched between other periods in history. We are living in such a transition period now, but to understand this time in which we live, and particularly this transition, we must first try to understand what is on either side of this transition.

The reality is that our civilization is in decline. There are five signs that emerge in a declining civilization. These signs can be found in the decline of almost every civilization in recorded history. They take different forms depending on the culture of the people of the time and the technological advancement of the age, but ultimately the same devastating result is achieved.

These are the five signs of a declining civilization: a dramatic increase in sexual promiscuity; the political undermining and disintegration of family values; the cultural destruction of the family unit; the killing of the innocent; and a radical increase in nonwarfare violence. These signs have played a major role in the decline and collapse of every civilization in recorded history. So much so that once these signs have emerged to some level of general occurrence and acceptance, no civilization has been able to prolong its existence for longer than one hundred years.

In our own culture, these signs gained initial prominence during and after World War I. They were compounded and spread even more widely by the effects and consequences of World War II, and by the end of the 1960s, they were rampant. At the turn of the millennium, they have all but been generally accepted as valid views and forms of behavior. Therefore, using a date even as late as the 1960s as the landmark for the general emergence of these signs, our civilization is left with only sixty years. This is not a prediction, it is not a prophecy, it is a reality set in the past. It is a lesson we have continually failed to learn from history. And sixty years is a short time for one person, never mind a civilization.

When current generations ignore the past, they destine themselves to relive the mistakes and miseries of every age.

We live in a critical time in history. The future of humanity and the world is in danger unless radical change is adopted. This change must focus primarily not on the external realities of the world, but on the interior mysteries of our being. God is not going to destroy humanity, nor is God going to bring the world to an end. But, collectively and progressively, we have involved ourselves in a complex process of self-destruction and so have endangered the world and all creation. This process of self-destruction gathers its force and momentum in the ideology that anything and everything can be exploited and consumed for profit and our own satisfaction. The result is disorder. The disorder begins with misplaced priorities in our hearts and leads to disorder socially, politically, culturally, economically, environmentally, and spiritually. This produces chaos and destruction—gradual at first, but escalating.

What does all this mean? Is the world going to end? No. Is humanity going to be wiped out completely? No. We are passing from one time to another. One civilization is dying, and another will emerge. We are in a transition.

To understand this a little more, we should turn to our history books to learn another lesson. There is, I believe, a remarkable parallel between the time in which we live and the later years of the

Roman Empire. The Roman Empire was great. It was mighty. It was powerful. And the people of that time believed that the Roman Empire would continue ruling and conquering and enjoying the fruits of ruling and conquering forever. There came a time, however, when some of the people began to realize that the Roman Empire, even as great and as powerful as it was, would not last forever. The sages and the seers of that era perceived that the empire was in decline and that before too long it would give way to something new.

A very similar progression now waits on the doorstep of human history. The "modern Western empire" has reached that point. It has achieved its pinnacle. It may linger there at the top momentarily, but not for long. Today's climate makes Nero's Rome look like the Mad Hatter's tea party. The people of our age, just like the people of the Roman Empire, believe that the modern Western empire will continue ruling and conquering forever, and that forever we will go on enjoying the fruits of our ruling and conquering. Like most things, it cannot last forever and soon will begin to fall away, making way for something new.

History also teaches us that the Roman Empire gave way to a wonderful period in history—the Middle Ages. Culturally, socially, politically, economically, and spiritually, the Middle Ages were a vibrant and vital time of growth, discovery, and progress. I am not suggesting that we go back to the Middle Ages. I am suggesting that on the other side of this current transition is potentially a time unmatched by any other in history.

There is one question that the people of any age are always asking, whether consciously or subconsciously: "What will the future hold?"

The twentieth century has been marked by tremendous advancement in the material and scientific realms. Six hundred years passed between the invention of the plow and the invention of the automobile. It took only sixty years from the invention of the automobile to the space age. This single fact alone helps us to understand the confusion that has also marked the twentieth century. This rapid change has challenged people to reassess their view of reality. The results have not always been positive or progressive. Perhaps because of this rapid change alone, and the associated confusion, we now find ourselves preparing to be catapulted into a new period in history.

The twenty-first century will be marked not by rapid increases in technology, but by dramatic and radical increases in people's awareness of the transcendental, a growing understanding of the vital role spirituality plays in our existence, and the importance of tending to all of humanity's legitimate needs.

To whom, then, does the future belong? If we look closely at other transition periods in history, two groups of people emerge very strongly. The first are what we know as critics—people who criticize. Critics exist in any period, of course, but in a time of transition they multiply faster than ever. What do they criticize? They criticize the old, they criticize the new, they criticize the change, they criticize the change for being too fast, and they criticize the change for being too slow. They criticize everything and anything. A critic is never hard to find. The questions we should consider are, "When did a group of critics ever usher in a new movement in history?" Never. "When will a group of critics ever usher in a new movement in history?" Never.

So to whom does the future belong?

The second group of people that a transition raises is leaders. They are men and women of vision, courage, persistence, confidence, generosity, conscience, integrity, creativity, enthusiasm, character, and virtue. They have the extraordinary ability to ignore the chaos, confusion, troubles, and difficulties that surround them and to remain focused on the task at hand. They have the awe-inspiring and profound ability to pierce through time into the future and envision how they wish, think, or believe, the future should be. Then they return to the here and now and work tirelessly to make their vision a reality. They are able to share their vision and muster support from others for that vision. They are extraordinary communicators both in word and deed, and their mere presence energizes and inspires people. Against all odds, doubts, and criticisms they are able to trust, follow, nurture, and share the goodness within them.

The future belongs to people such as these. They are leaders. You rarely hear them criticizing anything or anyone, because they are too busy getting the job done, ushering in a new movement in history.

They say the darkest hour is right before the dawn. But the darkest hour gives birth to the greatest children of light. From the dark hours of history are born legends, heroes, champions, prophets, sages, leaders, stars, great teachers, and saints.

The future will be what we make of it. Leadership is not an elite class. It is a role each of us is born into. It is a position of influence. Granted, some people exert more influence than others, but all of us exert some, and by our influence, people's lives are touched. People hear what you say, and they listen, and they are affected. People watch how you live, and they learn, and they are influenced.

Be a leader. Do not be afraid. Do not internalize the proclamations and criticisms of the "timid souls" and self-appointed kings of nonexistent kingdoms. When you speak to yourself, let your interior dialogue be confident, optimistic, and visionary. Dare to live the life most people only fantasize about! Do not be a destroyer of dreams, be a dreamer of dreams. Along the way, think often of Albert Einstein's words: "Great spirits have always encountered violent opposition from mediocre minds."

Life is not a popularity contest.

Those who wish to be free from criticism inevitably end up doing nothing worthwhile. I am often criticized. It is not something I will ever become accustomed to, and it drains tremendous energy from me if I am not careful. In the face of criticism, I like to spend my sacred hour carefully reflecting on the following two quotes.

I do the very best I know how—the best I can;
and I mean to keep doing so until the end. If
the end brings me out all right, what is said
against me won't amount to anything. If the
end brings me out wrong, ten angels swearing
I was right would make no difference.

—Abraham Lincoln

ဢ ဢ ဢ

It is not the critic that counts; nor the man
who points out how the strong man stumbled; nor where the doer of deeds could have
done them better. The credit belongs to the
man who is actually in the arena; whose face
is marred by dust and sweat and blood; who
strives valiantly; who errs, and comes short
again and again, because there is no effort
without error and shortcomings, who does
actually try to do the deed; who knows the
great enthusiasm, the great devotion, and
spends himself in a worthy cause; . . . who,
at worst, if he fails, at least fails while daring
greatly. . . .

Far better it is to dare mighty things, to
win glorious triumphs even though check-
ered by failure, than to rank among those
timid souls who neither enjoy nor suffer
much, because they live in the gray twilight
that knows neither victory nor defeat.

—Theodore Roosevelt

ဢ ဢ ဢ

Any society or community at any time in history needs leadership. Our age is no different and perhaps more in need than any other age. The need is for authentic leadership—in our families, in our communities, in the business world, on the sporting field, in the areas of the arts and culture, in politics, and in our churches.

One thing is certain. In a land where there are no musicians; in a land where there are no storytellers, teachers, and poets; in a land where there are no men and women of vision and leadership; in a land where there are no legends, saints, and champions; in a land where there are no dreamers—the people of that land will most certainly perish. But you and I, we are the music makers; we are the storytellers, teachers, and poets; we are the men and women of vision and leadership; we are the legends, the saints, and the champions; and we are the dreamers of the dreams.

How Do You
Perceive the World?

How do you see the world? What is your perception of the world? The great danger is for us to fall into the trap of believing that the whole world is like the city we live in. The temptation is to fall into the subconscious lethargy of thinking that the whole world is like the street we live on.

Most people think they have got a pretty good grip on reality, a fairly broad view, but sometimes our view of reality can become distorted. How do you perceive the world?

You see . . . if we reduced the world's population to one hundred people, proportionally . . .

Fifty-seven of those one hundred people would be from Asia. Twenty-one would be from Europe, fourteen from North and South America, and eight from Africa.

Fifty-one would be women, and forty-nine would be men.

Sixty-eight of those one hundred people would not be able to read and write.

Six of those one hundred people would own and control more than 50 percent of the world's wealth. All of those six people would be U.S. citizens. Three of those six people would live on the north shore of Long Island . . . on the same street.

Thirty would be Christian, seventy would be non-Christian.

One of those one hundred people would be just about to die,

one would have been just born, and only one of those one hundred people would have been to college.

How do you perceive the world? Maybe in your world everyone goes to college, but on planet Earth only one out of every one hundred people goes to college.

Fifty percent of American children live separated from their biological fathers.

One-third of the world is dying from lack of bread. One-third of the world is dying from lack of justice. And one-third of the world is dying from overeating.

What is your view of the world? How do you perceive the world?

This is the way I see it. Life comes down to two simple realities. People were made to be loved, and things were made to be used. Your problems, my problems, and indeed all the world's problems come from our misunderstanding of these two simple principles. You see . . . we love things and we use people.

It would not be too much to dedicate one's whole life to the reversal of these simple realities.

Love is our greatest desire—to love and be loved. We know how to love, because we know how we wish to be loved. It is the central precept and principle of every major religion. It is the answer to every question. It is the solution to every problem.

The answer is never to love less. The answer is always to love more.

The question is, "What do we love?"

You can choose not to love the right things, but you cannot choose not to love. We all love—we cannot help but love, for that is what we were created for. Love is what gives meaning to our lives. Love is the direction of our lives. What you love and what captivates your imagination determines how you live your life. Love is our greatest desire, our greatest need, our greatest talent, and our greatest yearning. Love is our identity. Until we love, we never truly know who we are. Love is natural, original, and spontaneous. Love is power.

If you could only love enough, you could be the most powerful person in the world.

We hold back that infinite power to love because when it is released—although it achieves all the good in the world—it also makes us vulnerable and ushers in the possibility of suffering. We waste opportunities to love.

To love deeply, you must let go of those illusions of perfection, that pretense of being completely in control, and open yourself to that mysterious gift, pleasure, power, and grace we call love. That surrender and openness creates a radical vulnerability. Love is to step beyond the comfort zone.

My mother has always enjoyed her garden, but she particularly loves growing orchids. Mum has grown them in our backyard ever since I was a child. When my brothers and I were younger, we used to play a lot of soccer and cricket in the backyard. One of us was always crawling toward the kitchen to confess the accidental assassination of one of Mum's orchids.

I overheard a conversation one night between my mother and father. My mother was venting that we were killing all her orchids. My father listened, and a little time passed before he said calmly, "Well, one day they won't be here to play in the yard and break the orchids. When that day comes we will wish they were, so let's move the plants."

The people you love will not always be near you. Love them. Seize the opportunity.

The most wonderful thing about love is that it is highly contagious. Love demands a response. Love determines the response. Love begets love. Here's a simple example. If you're walking down the street and you smile at someone coming in the opposite direction, what happens? Usually he smiles back. But in the event he does not smile back, and the next day you see him again and smile again, then what happens? Eventually he smiles back. Love demands a response. Your love sets off a reaction, a ripple effect. Love begets love.

Teilhard de Chardin wrote, "The day will come when, after harnessing space, the winds, the tides and gravitation, we shall harness for God the energies of love. And, on that day, for the second time in the history of the world, man will have discovered fire."

If you have bought into the modern definition of success—"getting what you want out of life"—you have probably alienated yourself from the most important reality and truth of life. Love is a free gift.

We sacrifice love for so-called progress. We sacrifice love for so-called success. We sacrifice love for so-called more important things—no such things exist.

Tell me what you love and I will tell you who you are. What you fall in love with determines everything.

Our desire to love and be loved never rests. Though we may sleep, our desire to love never does. It is as constant as our very breathing—and as necessary. Our true identity is deeply intertwined with this desire and ability to love.

We cannot live without love. Without love there is no joy, excitement, passion, or satisfaction in life. You cannot live without love for yourself. You cannot live without love for your God. You cannot live without love for your neighbor. You can try, but you will end up bitter and miserable. And that bitterness and misery will kill you in the end. You will appear to be alive, but in truth you will be dying. You cannot live without love.

Love or perish; there is no other choice.

CAN YOU HEAR THE MUSIC?

For me, one of the greatest joys in this world is music. Can you imagine a world without music? What a weary, weary world it would be without music. Music is expressive of every human feeling and emotion, but it most aptly expresses joy and love. What holds music together? Rhythm.

What holds our lives together? Rhythm. Is your world a world without music? Is your life a song without rhythm?

Rests and pauses are as important in great music as the notes themselves. Rests and pauses are as important in great lives as activity.

It is natural for us to want a better world for our children to grow up in. We must recognize that achieving great change for the common good takes a long time. Those working for good are not in a hurry. They are patient, and because they are patient, they are wise. They do all they can to bring on this good without losing the rhythm of life themselves. They never sacrifice the rhythm.

You must find the rhythm, your rhythm. The rhythm that connects you with the rest of creation in harmony and peace. The rhythm that most effectively allows the grace of God to work within your life. The rhythm that allows you to find that sacred balance that gives you strength, courage, and confidence to be yourself. The rhythm that leads you along the path of growth and perfection. The rhythm of life that unveils and fulfills your legitimate needs.

The rhythm of life is a powerful thing.

∾ ∾ ∾

In the beginning of part 5, I suggested that any adequate solutions to the problems and challenges that face us in the world today must be both accessible and applicable to everyone, everywhere, regardless of age, color, creed, or culture—and their practicality must impact and be deeply intertwined with people's day-to-day living. I believe the rhythm of life offers such a solution.

Let me issue one warning. The rhythm of life may be the solution to many of the world's problems, but in this day and age—in a world obsessed with speed, noise, greed, lust, and activity—the rhythm of life is a radical, countercultural, revolutionary act.

∾ ∾ ∾

If you decide to walk the path I have described in this book, not everyone will understand. Some of your family and friends will ridicule you, they will accuse you of being a dreamer, and they will tell you that you are crazy.

The people who cannot hear the music think that the people who are dancing are crazy.

Don't let that bother you. And even if it does bother you, don't let it discourage or distract you from walking the path. If they understood the path, they would be on it. Some of them are bitter because once in their youth they tried to walk this path and gave up, and now in their old age they believe it is too late for them to seek that path again. This path is not for everyone. Everyone can choose and walk this path, but very few actually have the strength, courage, discipline, and perseverance to do what it takes to walk it.

That is what sets them apart. That is what makes them legends, heroes, champions, leaders, and saints.

᠆ᵔ᳁ ᠆ᵔ᳁ ᠆ᵔ᳁

Rhythm or no rhythm, life isn't always easy. Sometimes I find myself deliriously happy. I have had many mountaintop experiences, but life isn't always lived on the mountaintops of the world. Sometimes we find ourselves in the valleys of fear and doubt or in the abyss of suffering and loneliness. At those times it is easy to become discouraged, to abandon the way, to let the critics get you down. At those times, travel in your mind to a small orphanage in Calcutta, and on a wall there you will find these words:

People are unreasonable, illogical, and self-centered.
LOVE THEM ANYWAY.

If you do good, people will accuse you of
selfish, ulterior motives.
DO GOOD ANYWAY.

If you are successful, you win false friends and true enemies.
SUCCEED ANYWAY.

The good you do will be forgotten tomorrow.
DO GOOD ANYWAY.

Honesty and frankness make you vulnerable.
BE HONEST AND FRANK ANYWAY.

Big people with even bigger ideas will be shot down
by small people with even smaller minds.
THINK BIG ANYWAY.

People favor underdogs, but follow only top dogs.
BE THE UNDERDOG ANYWAY.

What you spent years building may be
destroyed overnight.
BUILD ANYWAY.

People really need help
but may attack you if you help them.
HELP THEM ANYWAY.

Give the world the best you have
and you'll get kicked in the teeth.
GIVE THE WORLD THE BEST YOU'VE
GOT ANYWAY.

The Measure of Your Life
Will Be the Measure
of Your Courage

❦

Everything in life requires courage. Whether it is playing football or coaching football; crossing the room to ask a girl out on a date or rekindling a love that has grown cold; starting a new business, battling a potentially fatal disease, getting married, struggling to overcome an addiction, or coming humbly before your God in prayer—life takes courage.

Courage is essential to the human experience. Courage animates us, brings us to life, and makes everything else possible. Yet courage is the rarest quality in a human person.

The most dominant emotion today in our modern society is fear. We are afraid. Afraid of losing the things we have worked hard to buy, afraid of rejection and failure, afraid of certain parts of town, afraid of certain types of people, afraid of criticism, afraid of suffering and heartache, afraid of change, afraid to tell people how we really feel . . . We are afraid of so many things. We are even afraid to be ourselves.

Some of these fears we are consciously aware of, while others exist subconsciously. But these fears can play a very large role in directing the actions and activities of our lives. Fear has a tendency to imprison us. Fear stops more people from doing something with their lives than lack of ability, contacts, resources, or any other single variable. Fear paralyzes the human spirit.

Courage is not the absence of fear, but the acquired ability to move beyond fear. Each day we must pass through the jungles of doubt and cross the valley of fear. For it is only then that we can live in the high places—on the peaks of courage.

Take a moment to wander through the pages of history— your family's history, your nation's history, human history—and extract from those pages the men and women you most admire. What would they be without courage? Nothing worthwhile in history has been achieved without courage. Courage is the father of every great moment and movement in history.

I have felt the chilling winds of fear and self-doubt rush against my skin. I have discovered that courage is learning to recognize and master that single moment. That moment is a prelude—a prelude to courage or a prelude to fear. So much can be accomplished in one moment of courage. And so much can be lost to one moment of fear.

No one is born with courage. It is an acquired virtue. You learn to ride a bicycle by riding a bicycle. You learn to dance by dancing. You learn to play football by playing football. Courage is acquired by practicing courage. And like most qualities of character, when practiced our courage becomes stronger and more readily accessible with every passing day.

∽ ∽ ∽

Have you ever been awakened in the morning by the alarm clock in the middle of a wonderful dream? What happens? You try to go back to sleep. Maybe you can and maybe you can't get back to sleep, but what doesn't happen? The dream doesn't return. Life is that dream.

If you knew you were going to die one year from today, what would you do with the next year of your life? Do those things. Go home tonight and make a list. Then set about making those things happen. Revisit that list every day, check on your progress, and renew your resolution. Use the words in this book each day to inspire you to make them happen. Because life is short and you are dead an awful long time. Live life passionately. Laugh often, love always, cultivate soul, don't be afraid to dream the big dreams, and embrace your God.

Our world is changing so quickly. It can be a little frightening at times. It is easy to become so busy worrying about the future that we forget to live our dreams. There is something wonderful about a dream. It is not the achievement of the dream that matters most, but rather the pursuit of those dreams that are born from deep within us. The pursuit of the dream is life; it does something mysterious to us, fills us with hope, passion, and enthusiasm, and expands our capacities as a human person in every way.

So what are we waiting for? We get only one shot at life. Isn't it time for a little soul-searching? Visit a quiet church in the middle of the day. Take a walk in the park. Turn off the television and talk to your children. Open the paper and look for the job you've always wanted. Keep a promise. Tell your mum you love her. Restore an old Ford. Make friends with your neighbors. Say yes instead of maybe. Watch a sunset. Write your spouse a love letter. Fly a kite. Say sorry. Ask that girl out on a date. Try a food you've never tasted before. Make peace with God.

Do not waste your life, because life is there—all you have to do is reach out and embrace it. Anything is possible. Whatever your dream is, make it happen. Have courage. Start today. You will be amazed what life will give you in return for a little bit of courage.

Courage is a choice.

Be certain of one thing: The measure of your life will be the measure of your courage.

LET YOUR LIGHT SHINE!

In the process of writing this book, I have returned to Austria on a couple of occasions. I have returned to Gaming and to the former monastery where I discovered life anew. Now I have shared with you, as I promised myself I would, what I discovered in the mountains a couple of hours outside of Vienna—the rhythm of life.

What is contained in these pages has the power to change your life. I know, because these ideas have changed my life and continue to enrich my life every day.

I know a woman who has carried her passport around with her for thirty-four years. She has never used it, but she never goes anywhere without it tucked safely away inside her handbag.

Thirty-four years ago she had an opportunity to take a trip, but for many reasons at the last minute she decided not to. She never will take that trip, and she will always regret not having taken it when she had the chance.

You are holding a passport in your hands right now, with valid visas to higher levels of consciousness and more abundant living. I know it is a valid passport—I have used it myself. But it is not enough just to have a passport. You must make the journey. Be confident. Do not be afraid. Have courage. Take it one step at a time. Make the journey.

A life well invested has few regrets. A life lived richly has few apologies to make. Find the rhythm of life.

If you have come this far, you have obviously found some value in the ideas that fill these pages. Don't set this book down now on a shelf to gather dust. Start again. Keep it near to you. When you come to the end for a second time, start again. Read five pages a day perpetually. Make it a lifelong companion. It is the only way for the ideas to take root in our practical, everyday lives.

I have tried to fill these pages with ideas that we can read over and over again, each time revealing a new layer of meaning. They are ideas that resonate deeper within us each time we read them— and even deeper again when we take the time to reflect on them slowly and quietly.

As the ideas in this book begin to change your life—as you begin to experience the power of the rhythm of life—share this book. Give a copy to a friend as a gift. Suggest it to your family. Help others discover the rhythm of life.

∽ ∽ ∽

Rarely does a day go by when I don't think of my high school motto: *"Luceat lux vestra."* It is Latin, taken from the fifth chapter of Matthew's gospel, and means "Let your light shine."

The legends, heroes, leaders, champions, and saints we have spoken of throughout this book, and who fill the pages of our history books, are just symbols of the goodness and greatness within us all.

Do not let your life be like a shooting star that lights up the sky for only a brief moment.

Let your life be like the sun, which always burns brightly in the heavens, bringing light and warmth to all those on earth.

Live the life you were born to live!

Let *your* light shine!

Whether you received *The Rhythm of Life* as a gift, borrowed it from a friend, or purchased it yourself, we're glad you read it. We think you will agree that Matthew Kelly is a most refreshing voice, and we hope you will share this book and his thoughts with your family and friends.

∽ ∽ ∽

If you would like to learn more about Matthew Kelly and his work, please visit:

www.MatthewKelly.com

or write to:

info@MatthewKelly.org

ACKNOWLEDGMENTS

Books have a life of their own. They do of course start as an - author's dream, but by the time they reach the shelf in a bookstore so many people have made unimaginable contributions in order to transform the author's dream into a reality.

I would like to thank . . .

Meghan McLaughlin, Tom Dierker, and Mimi Citerella for helping me to refine the original manuscript . . .

Joe Durepos for convincing me that it was time to share this work with a larger audience . . .

Caroline Sutton for opening my mind to new possibilities and helping me sculpt this new edition into so much more than I previously envisioned . . .

The Simon & Schuster team . . . Chris Lloreda, Trish Todd, Lisa Sciambra, Marcia Burch, Sona Vogel, Jan Pisciotta, Thea Tullman, Debbie Model, Mark Gompertz, Mike Rotondo, and Christina Duffy . . . for their energy and enthusiasm . . . and for thinking outside of the box on this one . . .

My staff at The Matthew Kelly Foundation, who work tirelessly in their effort to further my quest to share this message, which is transforming so many people's lives.

The people who have bought multiple copies and passed them on as gifts to people who were outside my circle . . . Thanks for inviting me into your circle of influence . . .

I am more grateful to each of you than you will ever know. Your name and photo are not on the cover, but in a very real way this is your book.

Most of all I hope that working on this book has filled you with a deep sense of satisfaction . . . and that whenever you see someone reading a copy . . . or pass through a bookstore and see a copy on the shelf . . . you will feel a warm glow within you . . .

ABOUT THE AUTHOR

Matthew Kelly has dedicated his life to helping people and organizations become the-best-version-of-themselves. Born in Sydney, Australia, he began speaking and writing in his late teens while he was attending business school. Since that time, four million people have attended his seminars and presentations in more than fifty countries.

Today Kelly is an internationally acclaimed speaker, author, and business consultant. His books have been published in more than twenty-five languages, have appeared on the *New York Times*, *Wall Street Journal*, and *USA Today* bestseller lists, and have sold more than fifteen million copies.

He is also the founder of the Dynamic Catholic Institute, a Cincinnati-based nonprofit organization whose mission is to reenergize the Catholic Church in America by developing world-class resources that inspire people to rediscover the genius of Catholicism.

Kelly is also president at Floyd Consulting, a Florida-based management consulting firm.

His personal interests include golf, piano, literature, spirituality, and spending time with his wife, Meggie, and their children, Walter, Isabel, Harry, Ralph, and Simon.

2/7/2021

Dreams:

To sit quietly with someone in quiet and
write about it.

To be interested in life, to take chances, risks

Fail.

See Ed Sheeran in concert

smoke pot.

Tan

Hang glide

Play the bass guitar

Perform heroically and have people applaud
me because they are inspired

Perform to 100,000 people

Have more arm and length strength

Build/Design a log cabin

Fish in the boundary waters

Have more time for exercise

Carsrult